The Liberty Leaders

A Family Dinner Table Textbook

by Donald R. Gallerani

The Liberty Leaders

Leaders

A Family Dinner Table Textbook

This book is dedicated
with love to my grandchildren
Jane Evelyn
Alison Christine
Joshua Benjamin
and to my future grandchildren not yet born.

It is devoted to my entire family
and to every American family that cherishes
God's gift of Liberty

Table of Contents

Introduction

"...And let me offer lesson number one about America:
All great change in America begins at the dinner table.
So, tomorrow night in the kitchen
I hope the talking begins.
And children, if your parents haven't been teaching you
what it means to be an American,
let 'em know and nail 'em on it.
That would be a very American thing to do."
President Ronald Reagan's Farewell Address
January 11, 1989

The extraordinary Ronald Reagan was undeniably an American original. His words gave validity to straightforward ideas and common sense, enforced with the blessing of confidence by recognizing the narratives of yesterday. To not take serious that quote from Reagan, we would inflict an incredible disserve to our children and grandchildren.

We are slowly losing our history. Vital American history.
Irrelevant, politically correct issues are clouding truly magnificent American achievements. Textbooks throughout the United States are omitting the pertinent thoughts, words, and deeds from those who came before us with ideas and visions that are the bulwark of liberty, traditional thinking and the inspiration for American greatness. Some curriculums do far worse than diminish the founders, they insult them. Take this article from Megan Rolland at 'The Oklahoman' in October 2010. "Oklahoma City Public Schools purchased Flocabulary, an education tool that uses rap and hip-hop to engage at-risk students, but complaints have caused administrators to take a second look....one of the rap songs, refers to the founding fathers as "Old Dead White Men.""
It is a vile attempt in a school curriculum to treat our founders as petty and irrelevant? The easy way out of this deceit is simple. Teach the truth. Explain it with passion.

If the public school system fails in this category, it is incumbent on the guardian's of our children's minds to unapologetically step up and take over. Without hesitation curiosity opens many doors. Our intellect demands it. Knowledge is indispensable to problem solving as we look into the past to grasp answers to questions our present generation faces today. It is paramount that each generation do this. We study bygone history in order to acquire a richer understanding of what our ancestors faced, and most importantly, to avoid the pitfalls that befell them in their societies and government.

Who were the men and women that possessed the courage to let their voices be heard? Who influenced their lives? What is the high cost to us as a family, a community, and as a nation if we allow their contributions to the cause of freedom to be erased from our memories, swept away like dust? Socrates has told us that, "The only good is knowledge and the only evil is ignorance." Perhaps it is borderline 'evil' to abandon the great wisdom that paved the way for so much we enjoy and sadly take for granted. Names like Cicero, John Locke, and Charles Secondat Baron de Montesquieu would pave the way to enlightening the thinking of Benjamin Franklin, Adam Smith, George Washington, John Adams, Thomas Jefferson, James Madison, and Edmund Burke. Later visionaries like Alexis de Tocqueville, Abraham Lincoln, Milton Friedman, and Ronald Reagan would take their cues from the combined works of their predecessors and the cycle continues, getting stronger with new experiences, provided they are not ignored. Frederick Douglass and Harriet Tubman defied all odds and rose to enduring prominence. These are names of honor.

John Locke's *Two Treatises of Government* provided the testament that men were born free to elect their own leaders and not to be subjects to the whims of monarchs. Adam Smith's *The Wealth of Nations* set forth a criteria for free enterprise that rocked the thinking of 18th century Europe and beyond to our shores. Thomas Paine's *Common Sense* ignited the spirit of the American colonists to revolt against the shackles of the British crown. The Bible with its religious references has no equal and was referred to often throughout history. Collectively, these books and others influenced significantly the minds of our founding fathers to create a pact of self government based on natural law and individual independence. They drew inspiration from their countrymen as well. The silversmith and blacksmith who traded their anvils and bellows that stoked the hot coals of their foundries for muskets, the farmer who had walked behind their plow horses to now march in defiant front lines, along with merchants and common folks who left the comfort of their homes to challenge tyranny. Gifted leaders that would follow would reflect on the accomplishments and the pitfalls of those who came before them, making their own indelible mark on history. Understanding these individuals, despite their human flaws and weaknesses will go a long way to restoring the fundamental core values that distinguished America from the rest of the world bar none. It answers the question, "what it means to be an American." I figured the best way to reopen the discussions as to why the American people are great, why our unique American way of life is significant, and why our founding fathers visions continuously prove themselves insightful, no matter how society evolves, was to put the accomplishments of the liberty leaders I have chosen into a compendium. My research took me down many roads so for the sake of limitation I devoted the names herein to my own inquisitiveness.

Does this book introduce everyone that had a hand in freedom? Hardly.

The purpose of this writing is to expand on the lives of those whose names are mentioned, to provide a more detailed look into their contributions far beyond that of an average textbook paragraph or two. The combined life experiences of these historical figures blended together, created a blueprint for individual freedoms and traditional ideals, the likes the world has never seen before or since. The challenges they faced and overcame must be heralded. Their visions must be shared as an inspiration to our children. The leaders of today and tomorrow must be as dedicated to the preservation of the rights of free people as were the leaders who conceived them. Failure to comply would be cataclysmic to society. Tyranny, as history proves, would fill the void.

I began my intro by quoting Reagan, let me summarize by quoting him again.

"Our Founding Fathers, here in this country, brought about the only true revolution that has ever taken place in man's history. Every other revolution simply exchanged one set of rulers for another set of rulers. But only here did that little band of men so advanced beyond their time that the world has never seen their like since, evolve the idea that you and I have within ourselves the God-given right and the ability to determine our own destiny. But freedom is never more than one generation away from extinction. We didn't pass it on to our children in the bloodstream. The only way they can inherit the freedom we have known is if we fight for it, protect it, defend it and then hand it to them with the well thought lessons of how they in their lifetime must do the same. And if you and I don't do this, then you and I may well spend our sunset years telling our children and our children's children what it once was like in America when men were free..."

Reflecting on his words, I am confident readers will come away with a renewed reverence for moral American ideals with a greater love and respect for the liberty leaders.

So after saying grace, let the dinner table conversation begin.

Marcus Tullius Cicero
Tully

We study the writings of leaders whose voices were respected in their time and in ours, no-matter that they lived thousands of years before, for we learn that human behavior is consistent throughout recorded history.

Cicero (also known by his Anglicized name of Tully) was one of the greatest orators in ancient Rome, renowned as a politician, lawyer, philosopher and writer. He was born in 106 BC to a wealthy family and became well educated in Rome studying public speaking and law. He entered the military for a short while, but soon after became a lawyer defending private citizens. Later, he married Terentia, a woman of wealth and influence and traveled to Athens Greece and Rhodes, to further his academic work studying philosophy. Coming back to Rome, he returned to law making a name for himself with brilliant lectures and later entered politics, becoming a member of Rome's Senatorial Party. Cicero used his unique talents as a lawyer and statesman to try to save his beloved Roman Republic from ruin and political upheaval. Together with his wife they raised a daughter and later a son and soon he rose to the top of Roman hierarchy. Elected as a consul, he exposed a conspiracy of his political rival Catiline to overthrow the government and in so doing ordered the execution of those supporting Catiline. In 58 BC, he was exiled out of Rome when Julius Caesar and other Roman Senators believed the conspirators did not receive full access to the law. Cicero remained in exile in Macedonia, using his time to read and write about philosophy. In 55 BC he begins writing *On The State*, a book inspired by the Greek philosopher Plato, published in 51 BC. In it he notes the world as he sees it with its shrinking moral standards and a corruption of old habits of responsibility in public life.[1] The sequel to *On the State* was *On Law*, an unfinished book which was also inspired by Plato. In *On*

Law he notes that "Law is the highest reason implanted in nature, which commands what ought to be done and forbids the opposite. This reason, when firmly fixed and fully developed in the human mind, is Law. And so...Law is intelligence, whose natural function it is to command right conduct and forbid wrongdoing."[2]

After his return from banishment he saw the beginning of the reign of Julius Caesar in 48 BC and was pardoned by the dictator. In 45 BC, he wrote extensively on works that have been admired for centuries which included his treatises, *On Supreme Good and Evil*; *Conversations at Tusculum*, *The Nature of the Gods*, and others. A year later, he was an eyewitness to the assassination of Caesar at the base of Pompey's statue by conspirators of which he took no part in, but did not condemn either. He wrote following the death of the emperor, *Foretelling the Future*, *Destiny* and *Duties*. In 43 BC Cicero aged sixty-three was put to death on December 7 by order of Mark Anthony, a man loyal to Caesar.

It is fortunate for historians and scholars alike that so many of his letters and orations survived the deterioration of time, many were written to and published by Atticus, his friend of many years. The subjects he embraced were varied, his Greek philosophy brought to the world literature that would otherwise have been unknown. His widely read Latin orations have been studied throughout history. The education of our founding fathers benefited greatly by the ethical philosophical contributions of Cicero.

"He wrote about how a state should be organized,..his big idea, which he tirelessly publicized, was that of a mixed or balanced constitution. He favored not monarchy, nor oligarchy, nor democracy, but a combination of all three. His model was Rome itself, but improved. Its executive had quasi-royal powers. It was restrained partly by the widespread use of vetoes and partly by a Senate, dominated by great political families. Politicians were elected to office by the People."[3]

The many works of Cicero were important influences behind the drafting of America's liberty documents. As an eyewitness and participant to Roman politics and the treachery between powerful factions that emerged, this Roman diplomat saw the crumbling of the Roman Empire through civil wars, and captured in his writings, his thoughts in opposing tyranny, his ideas on natural law, justice, liberty and divided powers of authority that clearly affirmed the basis of our founding documents. John Locke was influenced by his thoughts on 'natural law.' Montesquieu on his coequal branches of government. John Adams first book was his cherished copy of *Cicero*. Thomas Jefferson was second to none in his admiration and study of the Roman orator, he possessed over forty books by Cicero in his personal library. James Madison, having learned to read and write Latin studied and translated Cicero at the University of New Jersey under the tutelage of John Witherspoon. He noted with others that ancient republics fell when conspiracies from within, fed with a desire for absolute power destroyed their government through tyranny. Madison, Adams, Jefferson and the men of their time were required as a prerequisite for entering college, to read, understand and decipher the Greek and Latin prose that Cicero provided.

"True law is right reason in agreement with nature; it is of universal application, unchanging and everlasting; it summons to duty by its commands, and averts from wrong-doing by its prohibitions. ... It is a sin to try to alter this law, nor is it allowable to attempt to repeal any part of it, and it is impossible to abolish it entirely. We cannot be freed from its obligations by senate or people, and we need not look outside ourselves for an expounder or interpreter of it. And there will not be different laws at Rome and at Athens, or different laws now and in the future, but one eternal and unchangeable law will be valid for all nations and all times, and there will be one master and ruler, that is, God, over us all, for he is the author of this law, its promulgator, and its enforcing judge. Whoever is disobedient is fleeing from himself and denying his human nature, and by reason of this very fact he will suffer the worst penalties, even if he escapes what is commonly considered punishment."[4]

"... if Nature is not to be considered the very foundation of Justice, that will be mean the destruction [of the virtues on which human society depends]. For where then will there be a place for generosity, or love of country, or loyalty, or the inclination to be of service to others or to show gratitude for favours received? For these virtues originate in our natural inclination to love our fellow-men, and this is the foundation of Justice...for I think that these ought to be maintained, not through fear, but on account with a close relationship to God. But if the principles of Justice were founded on the decrees of peoples, the edicts of princes, or the decisions of judges, then justice would sanction robbery and adultery and forgery of wills, in case these acts were approved by the votes or decrees of the populace. But if so great a power belongs to the decisions and decrees of fools that the laws of Nature can be changed by their votes, then why do they not ordain that what is bad and baneful shall be considered good and salutary? Or, if a law can make Justice Injustice, can it not also make good out of bad? But in fact we can perceive the difference between good laws and bad by referring them to no other standard than Nature; indeed, it is not merely Justice and injustice which are distinguished by Nature, but also and without exception things which are honourable and dishonourable.[5]

"To be ignorant of things that occurred before you were born is to remain always a child."
Cicero (Orator Chapter 34 Section 120)

"Let the welfare of the people be the ultimate law"
Cicero -On the Laws

"I am not ashamed to confess I am ignorant
of what I do not know"
Cicero -Tusculan Disputations. I. 25. 60

"The highest good is either to live according to nature or to
follow nature and live, so to speak, by her law.
Cicero- Republic and Laws

"A nation can survive its fools, and even the ambitious.
But it cannot survive treason from within.
An enemy at the gates is less formidable, for he is known and
carries his banner openly. But the traitor moves amongst those
within the gate freely, his sly whispers rustling through all the
alleys, heard in the very halls of government itself. For the
traitor appears not a traitor; he speaks in accents familiar to his
victims, and he wears their face and their arguments, he appeals
to the baseness that lies deep in the hearts of all men.
He rots the soul of a nation, he works secretly and unknown in
the night to undermine the pillars of the city, he infects the body
politic so that it can no longer resist.
A murderer is less to fear."
Cicero - speaking to Caesar, Crassus, Pompey and the Roman Senate

"Nothing is more damaging to a state, nothing so contrary to
justice and law, nothing less appropriate to a civilized
community, than to force through a measure by violence where a
country has a settled and established constitution"
Cicero - Republic and Laws

John Locke
"The Philosopher of Freedom"

Out of the Western European 'Dark Ages' sprang the Enlightenment or the Age of Reason. It stimulated the spread of scientific analysis, physics, and reason that challenged long held superstition and religious authoritarianism. In essence, the truth about reality. Political and social issues were shared in writings and John Locke, who was born on August 29, 1632 was considered to be one of the most influential intellects of the Enlightenment, as well as one of the greatest philosophers in Europe at the end of the seventeenth century. His impact on America's founding fathers goes far beyond praiseworthy, Locke was a societal governing trailblazer. Educated at the Westminster School in London, he was later accepted to the Christ Church College at Oxford University. Enamored by philosophy, he was energetic in his pursuits and received his Bachelor Degree followed soon after by earning his Master's Degree in 1658. Oxford provided the surroundings and stimulus for the study of medicine which interested him as well, procuring him a Bachelor of Medicine diploma. In 1666 his knowledge of medicine brought him into the company of Lord Ashley, a central figure in public life and the leader of the Whig party. Locke saved Lord Ashley's life through a successful operation and became attached to his career and household for the next fifteen years.[6]

Locke's 'theory of mind' defined that the human wit and judgement was a blank slate and knowledge is established through the sense of perception and life experience. 'Natural law' as reasoned by Locke, revolved around the concept that the use of reason coupled with the rules of virtuous behavior and knowing the difference between good and evil was naturally inherent. Rather than declaring a list of moral rules or a code of ethics, Locke deferred to the ethics of Jesus Christ, considering his injunctions superb. "The gospel contains so perfect a body of ethics..."[7] It was however, his work on political studies that influenced Voltaire, Rousseau and our own American revolutionaries.

Locke's opinion of government that he set forth in his writings, *Two Treatises of Government* would later influence the Americans focused on liberty, men like Franklin, Adams, Jefferson and Madison as well as inspire Thomas Paine and George Mason. Within the first pages of his book he took the opportunity to dispel the notion that society was not best served by authoritarian and totalitarian ideology, in short, that kings and monarchs possessed God given divine right to rule their subjects with unrestrained absolute power. Locke's work harshly challenged point-by-point the writings of Sir Robert Filmer, author of *Patriarcha: or the Natural Power of Kings* published in 1680. Filmer's view was that regal authority is divinely instituted and has its foundation in the natural authority which Adam had over his children. It is absolute: a subject's rights and liberties are derived from the ruler's "grace and bounty."[8] John Locke vehemently disagreed, acknowledging that all men are born free of all political authority; they are at liberty to choose their governors who, as a consequence, are not absolute and arbitrary but answerable to those who have chosen them.[9] The attack on Filmer's views was only secondary to the more popular political teachings of Thomas Hobbes, author of *Leviathan,* which proclaimed that men were naturally immoral and unable to govern themselves.

The second part of *Two Treatises of Government,* he maintained that the only legitimate form of government is established by the consent of the people steadfast to human rights to life, liberty and property and that rebellion may be necessary when that government fails to defend those virtues. That the state of nature and God created all men equal. There is little doubt that those words were taken seriously by Thomas Jefferson in his draft of the Declaration of Independence. Locke knew that people of different religions must be able to worship as they choose and a government sanctioned religion would be intolerable.

He made a major advance to our understanding of natural law, by emphasizing the nature of man as a maker of things, and a property owning animal. This leads to a more extensive concept of natural rights than the previous discussions of natural law. From the right to self defense comes the right to the rule of law, but from the right to property comes a multitude of like rights, such as the right to privacy "An Englishman's home is his castle." Locke repeated, in ringing words, that a ruler is legitimate so far as he upholds the law.[10] Locke could not conceive of human beings living together without some sort of law and order, and in the state of nature it is the *law of nature* that rules:

"The state of nature has a law of nature to govern it, which obliges everyone; and reason, which is that law, teaches all mankind who will but consult it, that, being all equal and independent, no one ought to harm another in his life, health, liberty, or possessions."[11]

The importance of a person's personal property is acquired by the extent of his labor and the ability to hold onto it is a natural right, that no government can take away. That essential philosophy being the case, a citizen's private property is the mainstay to a nation's financial growth and well being. An individual's physical labor in creating goods is what gives them a certain value.

Ahead of his time in so many ways, he understood that government power must be divided coequally to avoid the peril of leaving power to one person or a group of individuals. His work was considered subversive, labeling him revolutionary. He fled to the Netherlands in 1683, when he was suspected to be part of a scheme to assassinate King Charles II, which would become known as the Rye House Plot. While in exile in Holland, Locke wrote letters on his high regard for good education in children and its' accountability for the good and evil traits in mankind. Children should learn the value of reading *Aesop's Fables* and Bible stories for their moral messages and be an essential part of a parent's guidance in a strong loving family relationship. Locke's writings would go into great depths and scope, outlining the four aims of education; virtue, wisdom, breeding and learning.[12] The letters were published years after he left Holland as *Some Thoughts Concerning Education*, which demonstrated the seriousness of the subject. His educational primer would see many editions and reprintings, greatly influencing children's education for centuries to follow.

He returned to England in 1688. It was at this time the *Two Treatises of Government* was published followed by *The Letter Concerning Toleration*. He died at age seventy-two on October 28, 1704. His work would later be greatly respected and put into action by the founding fathers of the United States. His political philosophy accomplishments were duly noted in the crafting of America's charter of liberty.

"The end of law is not to abolish or restrain, but to preserve and enlarge freedom. For in all the states of created beings capable of law, where there is no law, there is no freedom."
John Locke - Second Treatise on Civil Government 1690

"Every man has a property in his own person.
This nobody has a right to, but himself."
John Locke - Second Treatise on Civil Government 1690

Men being, as has been said, by nature, all free, equal, and independent, no one can be put out of this estate, and subjected to the political power of another, without his own consent."
John Locke -The Second Treatise of Civil Government. 1690

"Wherever law ends, Tyranny begins"
John Locke - Second Treatise on Civil Government Sec 202

"The state of nature has a law of nature to govern it, which obliges everyone in reason which is that law teaches all mankind, who will but consult it, that being all equal and independent, no one ought to harm another in his life, health, liberty or possessions. For men, being all the workmanship of one omnipotent and infinitely wise Maker, all the servants of one's sovereign master, sent into this world by His order, and about His business, they are His property whose workmanship they are made to last during His, not one another's pleasure."
John Locke- Second Treatise of Government Ch I2 Sec 6

"The Bible is one of the greatest blessings
bestowed by God on the children of men.
It has God for its author; salvation for its end, and truth
without any mixture for its matter.
It is all pure."
John Locke- Essay Concerning Human Understanding

"Man being born, as has been proved, with a title to perfect freedom, and an uncontrolled enjoyment of all the rights and privileges of the law of nature, equally with any other man, or number of men in the world, hath by nature a power, not only to preserve his property, that is, his life, liberty and estate, against the injuries and attempts of other men"
*John Locke- Second Treatise of Civil Government,
Chapter VII, section 87-89*

Charles Secondat, Baron de Montesquieu

Praise comes in many forms, paramount is the ability to create a paradigm that stands out for the betterment of humanity. Hailed as one of the most distinguished political philosophers of the 18th century, Charles Louis de Secondat, Baron de Montesquieu, was the first of the great French men to put thought to ink, ink to paper, clenching the principles associated with the Enlightenment. The political designs to govern a civilized society have besieged the thoughts of man since the beginning of time. Montesquieu's suggestions about the separation of powers and the checks and balances on leadership provided the firm footing on which our American Constitution was built.

Charles Secondat was born in 1689 in the southwest city of Bordeaux, France and educated at the Oratorian College of Juilly.[13] He studied science and history and became a lawyer in his district government. After the death of his father in 1713, he was taken in and cared for by his uncle, the Baron de Montesquieu. At twenty-six years of age he married Jeanne de Lartigue. The Baron died a year later, leaving him his fortune, his office in the Bordeaux Parliament and the title of Baron de Montesquieu. At this time five-year-old Louis XV succeeded his great grandfather Louis XIV to the throne in France along with ineffective consuls. This ruling class holding absolute power flirted with tyranny and generated resentment amongst their people. Montesquieu's experience in government and his political observances made an indelible mark in his writings that would follow. He became a member of the French Academies of Science where he traveled throughout the countries of Europe to examine each of their laws, customs and governments. Those travels served him well, and set into motion political theory that would have an impact on the minds of our founding fathers.

In 1721, he achieved literary accolades and celebrity after he published the *Persian Letters*, a book where he satirized French lifestyles. That success was followed by the book that would forever secure his reputation, *The Spirit of the Laws* was a result of his travels throughout the countries of Europe and his extended stay in England to study its government in 1729. This work, written over twenty years, was published in 1748 and achieved a level of epic stature. He believed political liberty was achieved when governed individuals had the peace of mind that tyrannical laws could not be passed arbitrarily.

He asserted, "When the legislative and executive powers are united in the same person, or in the same body of magistrates, there can be no liberty; because apprehensions may arise, lest the same monarch or senate should enact tyrannical laws, to execute them in a tyrannical manner"[14]   He held in high regard England's balance of power between the king, who was the law enforcer, the Parliament, which was the group who made the laws and the English court judges, who interpreted the laws. This was in direct contrast to the French monarch's three Estates structure, which consisted of the aristocracy, the clergy and the people also known as the Estates-General. The idea of coequal branches of government, each with its own unique function, and that oversaw each other, would avoid one branch from achieving too much power. This was the defining feature that so inspired the bulwark of our framers in constructing the U.S. Constitution. Montesquieu believed in a republic, a government ruled by law with the people holding the reins of power and responsibility and that it would be successful and thrive with three ingredients; virtue, education and small geographic borders (James Madison would later disagree with the notion of small borders). Religious toleration was essential to government as well. In *The Spirit of the Laws* he noted a historic truth that, "As virtue is necessary in a republic, and in a monarchy honour, so fear is necessary in a despotic government."[15] Founders like Benjamin Franklin, John Adams, Thomas Jefferson and James Madison held in their personal libraries the works of Montesquieu.   Alexander Hamilton and John Jay along with James Madison cited his work in the *Federalist Papers*. They looked to him for guidance during their struggle for self government. In *Federalist 47*, Madison clarified, "The oracle who is always consulted and cited on this subject is the celebrated Montesquieu. If he be not the author of this invaluable precept in the science of politics, he has the merit at least of displaying and recommending it most effectually to the attention of mankind. Let us endeavor, in the first place, to ascertain his meaning on this point." The Montesquieu principle of separation of powers and the need of checks and balances in the constitution was adopted by Madison in *Federalist No. 51*, entitled, '*The Structure of the Government Must Furnish the Proper Checks and Balances Between the Different Departments*'.[16] This was absolutely essential for the survivability of a republic inspired government. Montesquieu knew from his writings of the ancient Greek and Roman civilization and the founders wisely heeding his advice, feared that too much power in the hands of one person or a select few often times lead to tyranny. If unprincipled men could write the laws and then set judgement, disaster awaited those under their authority. His respect for the law firmly embedded, Montesquieu warned, "...constant experience shows us, that every man invested with power is apt to abuse it, and to carry his authority as far as it will go...To prevent this abuse, it is necessary from the very nature of things, power should be able to check power. A government may be so constituted as no man shall be compelled to do things to which the law does not oblige him, nor forced to abstain from things which the law permits."[17]

Also in his *Spirit of the Laws* he devotes space to embrace economic commerce. "Commercialism can spread to many climes and infect many diverse political cultures, it tends to cure human beings of the prejudices that veil their true worldly needs. In recognizing the common material neediness that constitutes its basic nature, mankind discovers a sense of compassionate "humanity" that blurs previous religious, ethnic, national and party sectarianisms"[18] In short, he defined the blessings of free market principles and favored individual liberty and the blessings of property ownership. His opinion mirrored those of John Locke.

In *Ameritopia*, author Mark R. Levin summed up brilliantly the summation of the contribution of Montesquieu to the American way of government. "Montequieu's dread of despotism, commitment to political liberty, and keen intellect in analyzing both, together with his genius in applying philosophy to the mechanics of politics, were essential guideposts in establishing the Constitution and the American republic."[19]
The eighteenth century French philosopher died at the age of sixty-six on February 10, 1755 and was buried in Paris.

"In republican governments, men are all equal;
equal they are also in despotic governments: in the former,
because they are everything;
in the latter, because they are nothing."
Montesquieu -The Spirit of the Laws; Bk. VI, Ch. 2

"In a true state of nature, indeed, all men are born equal,
but they cannot continue in this equality.
Society makes them lose it, and they recover it only
by the protection of laws."
Montesquieu - The Spirit of the Laws; Bk. VIII, Ch. 3

"Useless laws weaken the necessary laws"
Montesquieu-The Spirit of the Laws; Bk. XXIX, Ch. 16

"Liberty is the right to do what the law permits"
Montesquieu - The Spirit of the Laws; Bk. XI, Ch. 3

The deterioration of a government begins almost always
by the decay of its principles.
Montesquieu - The Spirit of the Laws Book VIII, Chapter 1

"There is no word that has admitted of more various
significations, and has made more different impressions
on human minds, than that of Liberty.
Some have taken it for a facility of deposing a person on whom
they had conferred a tyrannical authority; others for the power
of choosing a person whom they are obliged to obey; others for
the right of bearing arms, and of being thereby enabled to use
violence, others in fine for the privilege of being governed by a
native of their own country or by their own laws.
Some have annexed this name to one form of government,
in exclusion of others:
Those who had a republican taste, applied it to this government;
those who liked a monarchical state, gave it to monarchies.
Thus they all have applied the name of liberty to the government
most conformable to their own customs and inclinations: and as
in a republic people have not so constant and so present a view
of the instruments of the evils they complain of, and likewise as
the laws seem there to speak more, and the executors of the laws
less, it is generally attributed to republics,
and denied to monarchies.
In fine as in democracies the people seem to do very near
whatever they please, liberty has been placed in this sort of
government, and the power of the people has been confounded
with their liberty."
Montesquieu - The Spirit of the Laws Book XI, Chapter 3

Benjamin Franklin

The First American
Citizen of the World
The Father of Electricity

The accomplishments of Benjamin Franklin are both so impressive and monumental it would be impossible to do them justice in this writing. His fame and respect spanned two continents and his story is an American classic. The incredible rise to world wide prominence from less than humble beginnings, showcased to all in his time and ours, the virtue of rugged individualism, hard work, and belief in one's ability, are unquestionably the cornerstone of success and admiration.

Born in Boston on January 17, 1706, the eighth child to Josiah Franklin, a soap and candlestick maker and his second wife, Abiah Folger. At eight years of age he attended grammar school for only two years, went to work in his father's shop until age twelve when he departed to became an apprentice in his brother James' print shop. Throughout this time he became a voracious reader, from the blessings of exposure in his brother's shop to an assortment of available literature. Besides books on arithmetic and geometry, he read the essay from John Locke on Human Understanding. When his brother created the colonies first independent newspaper, *The New-England Courant*, young Benjamin was eager to contribute to the publication, but when his brother harshly refused his submittals, he secretly slipped articles under the door under a pseudonym of "Mrs. Silence Dogood." These articles were accepted, printed and gained high praise from readers. Over time, the stern over domineering hand of his brother took its toll on Benjamin, forcing him to run away from Boston, board a harbor ship and sailed south to settle in Philadelphia where he again found employment in printing.

He was sent to London to buy printers type and supplies on the promise that he would become established as an independent printer by the governor of Pennsylvania. He was misled to the agreement when he learned the promise was not to be kept, forcing him to stay in England, finding employment as a print shop typesetter, and a swimming instructor. Two years later, he returned to Philadelphia where he set up their own print shop with another apprentice. With his business established,, Benjamin and Deborah Read Rogers, a girl he met when he first arrived in Philadelphia, announced their common law marriage on September 1, 1730. They adopted his illegitimate son William, and moved in above the shop. Two more children would follow, a son Francis, who would die as a child of small pox, and a daughter Sally.

As a result of tireless effort, they published many firsts, the *Pennsylvania Gazette* was one of the most successful papers in the city of Philadelphia and the colonies. It had the distinction of printing the very first political cartoon, *"Join or Die,"* a graphic of a snake severed into eight parts each labeled by a colony was created by Franklin himself. The first American novel which was entitled, *Pamela* and the amazingly successful annual, *Poor Richards Almanac*. The almanac, had just about something for everyone within its pages including witticisms of honesty, and hard work, such as "God helps those who help themselves." It was in some instances the only writings found in a colonial home along with the Holy Bible. His keen eye for entrepreneurship had him invest in print shops in other colonial cities and corner the market on paper.

His publications brought him prestige and success that enabled him to retire from business at age forty-two, allowing him to pursue philosophical interests and amusements. As a result, he had a direct hand in improving the city of Philadelphia by creating the first fire department, lending library, police force, hospital, and even street lighting. Benjamin Franklin served as the postmaster general. Retirement allowed him to delve into his scientific interests as well. His discovery of electricity, the invention of the lightning rod, bifocal glasses and the Franklin Stove improved life well beyond the boundaries of his adopted city.

An awareness of civic activities and public positions developed into political affairs. The Pennsylvania Assembly dispatched Ben Franklin to England to represent the colonies in 1757, and his presence was widely admired by London Society. In time, he came to represent not only Pennsylvania, but New Jersey, Georgia, and Massachusetts as well. He urged his wife and family to join him but she refused, feeling uncomfortable in British sophisticated society.

The British monarchy was determined to make the American colonies pay their part for the cost of the French and Indian War. A tax on sugar in 1764 was their first attempt, and Prime Minister George Grenville enforced this tax by demanding that the British navy patrol the American coast and seize any ship that forgot to pay the tax. Since all smuggling cases had to be tried only in British than in colonial courts, and furthermore the decisions were determined not by a jury, but by a lone judge who received a five percent commission on illegal fines and cargoes, it was easy to see the unfairness of the system. This action understandably ruffled the colonialists. The Stamp Act in 1765 was a tax from British Parliament, placed on all paper goods on the American colonists. It was taxation without representation and Franklin strongly opposed it on those grounds. In February 13, 1766 he conveyed his thoughts in person before the Committee of the Whole of the House of Commons when the question was placed before him, "Was it an opinion in America before 1763 that the Parliament had no right to lay taxes and duties there?" he answered, "I never heard any objection to the rights of laying duties to regulate commerce; but a right to lay internal taxes was never supposed to be in Parliament, as we are not represented there."[20] Edmund Burke who was present at this meeting was impressed with Franklin's oratory. Across the Atlantic, multiple colonial mob protests affected commerce with British merchants. Guided by Lord Rockingham and Edmund Burke, pressure was brought to bear on Parliament to act in the colonies favor and the Stamp Act was repealed, however any cause of celebration was short lived, new taxes would soon be imposed and British troops were to be housed in colonial homes to enforce them. In a 1767 letter he scripted to his friend, Lord Kames, "Disputes with America," he foresaw the American Revolution eight years before the resulting violence and bloodshed.[21]

The insight that possessed Franklin in his time is echoed by conservative minds to come centuries later. In a piece he wrote in the *Gentleman's Magazine* under the name of 'Medius' in April 1768, he confronted the attacks on the rich of being hard-hearted by the suffering laboring poor. "I remarked that the condition of the poor in England was by far the best in Europe. Except in England and the American colonies, there was not in any country of the known world, not even in Scotland or Ireland, a provision by law to enforce a support for the poor. This law was not made by the poor. The legislators were men of fortune. By that act they voluntarily subjected their own estates, and the estates of others, to the payment of a tax for the maintenance of the poor. I wish they could be benefited by this generous provision in any degree equal to the good intention with which it was made. But I fear that giving mankind a dependence on any thing for support in age or sickness, besides industry and frugality during youth and health, tends to flatter our national indolence, to encourage idleness and prodigality, and thereby to promote and increase poverty, the very evil it was intended to cure, thus multiplying beggars instead of diminishing them..."[22] A strong argument on the misery that is advanced with the welfare state mentality.

America was growing hungry for independence, and King George would not hear of it. The Boston massacre and the Boston Tea Party were a result of rising tensions. In London January 1774, Franklin was summoned before Privy Council by Solicitor General Wedderburn for his part in handing off letters to the Sons of Liberty that exposed Thomas Hutchinson, the appointed lieutenant governor of Massachusetts of his loyalty to the crown and "urged strict measures against the Americans, including the abridgment of English liberties."[23] The letters were made public and the colonial press destroyed Hutchinson's long career. The king's counsel was furious over the outcome of the Boston Tea Party a month earlier and the Hutchinson affair. Franklin was ordered to stand before them in the crowded Counsel Chambers as many spectators looked on. The abusive language, ridicule and humiliation aimed at him went on for almost an hour. He was stripped of his title of Deputy Postmaster General in North America and retired as a representative agent of Pennsylvania, Massachusetts, New Jersey and Georgia. Leaving as a laughingstock, Franklin went from being a man generous with his praise for Britain and all it offered, into an American revolutionary. As Franklin prepared to leave England he learned that his wife Deborah had died, and returned home a widower.

Franklin arrived back in Philadelphia weeks after the battle of Concord and Lexington marking the beginning of the Revolutionary war. He was named the postmaster general and elected to serve in the Second Continental Congress. In January of 1776 the publication of Thomas Paine's *Common Sense*, the widely read pamphlet supporting independence was heralded by Franklin. *"The cause of America is in a great measure the cause of all mankind."*

In the summer of 1776, a committee of five were assembled with Ben, now seventy, joining John Adams, Thomas Jefferson, Robert Livingston and Roger Sherman to draft the document that would create a nation and challenge governments throughout the world; the Declaration of Independence. The actual draft was penned by Thomas Jefferson at the request of the committee with Franklin substituting Jefferson's words, 'sacred and undeniable' with 'self evident' so as to read "We hold these truths to be self-evident." Franklin believed that it was the natural right of man to quit the state, country or society in which they were born in order to construct one that they believe could thrive.

Months after the adoption of the Declaration of Independence, Franklin was off to France. With the battleground growing, an alliance with France was sought, and Franklin journeyed there as a diplomat, and took along two of his grandsons. The Articles of Confederation were translated and published in France and demonstrated a steadfast resolve that Europe found infectious. It was reasoned that if American triumph over the monarchy could be achieved and liberty established, the wealth of Europe could make its way to our shores.

Franklin wrote, "Tyranny is so generally established in the rest of the world that the prospect of an asylum in America for those who love liberty gave general joy, and our cause was esteem'd the cause of all mankind. Those who are enslaved naturally become base as well as wretched; therefore, we are fighting for the dignity and happiness of human nature. Glorious is it for the Americans to be call'd by Providence to this post of honour. Cursed and detested will everyone be that deserts or betrays it."[24]

In 1778 several weeks of negotiation produced two treaties, one of friendliness and commerce, the other was for mutual defense. At the signing of the treaties, Franklin wore the same jacket that he wore when he was abused by Wedderburn, "to give it a little revenge."[25] His diplomacy was heralded as beneficial to ending the war for independence when it did in 1781 with the British surrender at Yorktown, Virginia. He was able to persuade France to supply soldiers and money for the American cause. His renowned influence as a man of wealth and science gave him the political ability to persuade the French monarch to support rebellion against a neighboring ruler. It was a monumental achievement for America and some say that France's commitment to the colonies caused the dominoes to fall at home, leading to the savage blood-soaked French revolution.

The loose knit Articles of Confederation had to be replaced and a Constitutional Convention in Philadelphia was recommended by Congress. Delegates arrived in May 1787, with General George

Washington chosen as its president. The General Assembly requested and received Ben's assistance to aid in the revisions as the representative to Pennsylvania. All questions of self government were debated with the different republics of ancient history and those existing in eighteenth century Europe were studied and debated as well.

None were found to be acceptable for their political environment.

Months later the U.S. Constitution was adopted on September 17, 1787. Franklin wanted to give a speech before the signing of the final draft, however being too weak to actually give the address himself, he handed it to fellow Pennsylvanian James Wilson to deliver it for him, stating, that though it was not free from imperfections, the wisdom and integrity of the leaders and the people it represents must see to it that it is well administered. In part, his speech outlined the following, "...Sir, I agree to this Constitution with all its faults, if they are such; because I think a general Government necessary for us, and there is no form of Government but what may be a blessing to the people if well administered, and believe farther that this is likely to be well administered for a course of years, and can only end in Despotism, as other forms have done before it, when the people shall become so corrupted as to need despotic Government, being incapable of any other. I doubt too whether any other Convention we can obtain may be able to make a better Constitution. For when you assemble a number of men to have the advantage of their joint wisdom, you inevitably assemble with those men, all their prejudices, their passions, their errors of opinion, their local interests, and their selfish views. From such an Assembly can a perfect production be expected? It therefore astonishes me, Sir, to find this system approaching so near to perfection as it does; and I think it will astonish our enemies, who are waiting with confidence to hear that our councils are confounded like those of the Builders of Babel; and that our States are on the point of separation, only to meet hereafter for the purpose of cutting one another's throats. Thus I consent, Sir, to this Constitution because I expect no better, and because I am not sure, that it is not the best...On the whole, Sir, I can not help expressing a wish that every member of the Convention who may still have objections to it, would with me, on this occasion doubt a little of his own infallibility, and to make manifest our unanimity, put his name to this instrument." As he left the Philadelphia State House (now known as Independence Hall) Franklin was asked by a woman, "Well doctor what have we got, a republic or a monarchy?" to which he famously replied, "a republic if you can keep it."

He passed away on April 17, 1790. Two months previous he served as president of the Pennsylvania Society for Promoting the Abolition of Slavery.

With all the world wide fame and fortune he achieved as a self-made entrepreneur and scientist, his total lifetime experiences had few equals both in his time and now. Where most men would have retired comfortably, Franklin, in his later years, focused his energy to the creation of our nation, arguing for its separation, devoting his wise judgement in the daring Declaration of Independence, and the innovative government limiting United States Constitution. His admiration of Adam Smith's robust free trade and Jefferson's endorsement of "life, liberty, and the pursuit of happiness" as the role of government in the lives of its people puts Benjamin Franklin in a class all its own. Few individuals can come close to his accomplishments in the betterment of his countrymen or for that matter, the world.

"Freedom of speech is a principal pillar of a free government; when this support is taken away, the constitution of a free society is dissolved, and tyranny is erected on its ruins."
Benjamin Franklin- "On Freedom of Speech and the Press"
Pennsylvania Gazette November 17, 1737

"A good example is the best sermon"
Benjamin Franklin, Poor Richards Almanac June 1747

"Your true hero fights to preserve, and not to destroy,
the lives, liberties, and estates of his people.
His neighbors also, and all that are oppressed,
share his cares and his protection."
Benjamin Franklin-Poor Richards Almanac July 1748

"Having been poor is no shame, but being ashamed of it, is."
Benjamin Franklin, Poor Richards Almanac July 1749

"If you'd know the value of money, go and borrow some"
Benjamin Franklin-Poor Richards Almanac April 1754

"Being ignorant is not so much a shame,
as being unwilling to learn."
Benjamin Franklin-Poor Richards Almanac October 1755

"Be civil to all; serviceable to many; familiar with few;
friend to one; enemy to none."
Benjamin Franklin-Poor Richards Almanac April 1756

"I am for doing good to the poor,
but I differ in opinion of the means.
I think the best way of doing good to the poor, is not making
them easy in poverty, but leading or driving them out of it.
In my youth I travelled much, and I observed in different
countries, that the more public provisions were made for the
poor, the less they provided for themselves, and of course
became poorer. And, on the contrary, the less was done for them,
the more they did for themselves, and became richer."
Benjamin Franklin- On the Price of Corn & Management of the Poor
November 29, 1766

"Rebellion against tyrants is obedience to God."
Benjamin Franklin- Motto for the Great Seal

"Those who would give up essential Liberty
to purchase a little temporary Safety, deserve neither..."
Memoirs of the Life & Writings of Benjamin Franklin

"All of us who were engaged in the struggle must have observed
frequent instances of superintending providence in our favor.
To that kind providence we owe this happy opportunity of
consulting in peace on the means of establishing our future
national felicity. And have we now forgotten that powerful
friend? Or do we imagine that we no longer need His assistance?
I have lived, Sir, a long time, and the longer I live,
the more convincing proofs I see of this truth that
God governs in the affairs of men.
And if a sparrow cannot fall to the Ground without His Notice,
is it probable that an Empire can rise without His Aid?"
Benjamin Franklin, The Constitutional Convention

"I believe farther that this new government under the
Constitution is likely to be well administered for a course of
years, and can only end in Despotism, as other forms have done
before it, when the people shall become so corrupted as to need
despotic Government, being incapable of any other"
Benjamin Franklin, The Constitutional Convention

"Our new Constitution is now established, and has an
appearance that promises permanency; but in the world nothing
can be said to be certain except death and taxes."
Benjamin Franklin- Letter to Jean-Baptiste Leroy, November 13, 1789

"Here is my creed, I believe in one God, the creator of the universe. That he governs it by his providence. That he ought to be worshipped. That the most acceptable service we render to him is in doing good to his other children, that the soul of man is immortal, and will be treated with justice in another life respecting its conduct in this."
Benjamin Franklin March 9, 1790

Adam Smith

The Father of Modern Economics

The founding fathers recognized that economic liberty went hand in hand with political freedoms and knew that if a free nation was to endure, it's populace must, as individuals, have the ability to profit from their own labor and to rise and fall on their own choices of trade, commerce and production. Individual success will spawn more success and that will reap positive results for the community and society at large. Adam Smith's life work detailed as much. He was born in Kirkcaldy, Scotland, a small seafaring town across a stretch of the North Sea from Edinburgh in June 1723, and was raised solely by his mother Margaret, as his father, who was also named Adam had died six months before he was born. He was educated at the Kirkcaldy burgh school when he was eight or nine years old. Under his instructor David Miller he was taught to read, spell, write and learn Latin and Greek and was exposed to the use of the theatre to further his education. The young Adam was introduced to the works of Cicero and the popular *Spectator* publication of short stories and essays that held a firm grasp on a righteous code of behavior. His schooling summoned the thoughts to the obligation that each individual had to themselves, to the public good and to the deity, that self-respect and peace of mind are tied together for those living an active social life. At age fourteen he attended Glasgow University where he studied moral philosophy and was exposed to and influenced by the virtues of reason, free speech and liberty. Three years later he went on to Oxford but found that the teachers failed to teach in a meaningful way and the source of his dissatisfaction was the lack of academic competition. His time there was used to explore the realms of financial competition and incentive.

After Oxford, he became a freelance lecturer, a professor, and most importantly a moral philosopher in Edinburgh and a leader in political economics during the opportune time of the Scottish Enlightenment. He met and collaborated with David Hume, another noted Scottish philosopher and economist. The Enlightenment period provided the means to see man and the laws of nature as they truly are, just as the physicist Isaac Newton had formulated laws of gravity surrounding the science of astronomy, it appeared logical that laws of economics existed as well. Adam Smith pursued this avenue of curiosity having witnessed first hand the economic success that centered around the free trade of his home town of Kirkcaldy as compared to other Scottish areas that fell short in that category. His Edinburgh lectures were well received in the years he attended and in 1751 he earned the title of Professor at the University of Glasgow. He published his first book *The Theory of Moral Sentiments* in 1759 which was the summary of his lectures based on his moral philosophy, jurisprudence, ethics and sympathy between the individual and other coexisting members of society. He defied the idea that all moral virtue is based on self interest, but are instead a result of our nature as social beings. On the behest of the British politician Charles Townshend, Smith took a tutoring position for his stepson that enabled him to travel throughout Europe, there he was introduced to many intellectuals including Benjamin Franklin. This was the same Charles Townshend, who as the Chancellor of the Exchequer or Treasurer insisted on the multiple taxes on glass, paint paper and tea on the American colonies to pay the massive debt of the Seven Years War. Taxes that would be known as the Townshend Acts, would ignite violent outbursts from those on the receiving end. All these attributes served him well as he became best known for his ten year masterwork, *An Inquiry into the Nature and Causes of the Wealth of Nations* or better known as *The Wealth of Nations* published in 1776. This book was the culmination of Scottish Enlightenment thinking that set standards in explaining the theory of honorable human behavior and its role in surviving and prospering in society. Of course the London press at the time was preoccupied with the bedlam coming out of the American colonies and the spirited debates from the British Parliament on how best to end the armed rebellion. Smith involved himself with those debates, and the publication of *The Wealth of Nations* was timed to influence members of Parliament to support a peaceful resolution of the conflict as America offered a major point of application for free-market theory.[26] A popular theory by mercantilists of his day was that the wealth of a nation was measured strictly by the money it held within its borders by its banks, and citizens and that trade threatened those holdings by removing that money at times. Smith provided a new approach by outlining that trade provided the engine of economic growth and increased labor from new markets created new opportunities. This allowed for individuals to improve their conditions and make themselves better off. The foundation of human dignity. In the *Wealth of Nations*, Book 1 Chapter 2 he famously wrote; "It is not from the benevolence of the butcher, the brewer, or the baker, that we expect our dinner, but from their regard to their own self interest."[27] The timing in history of his ground breaking treatise coincided with the American Revolution an ocean away and those events helped explain his concerns. He noted the American colonies progress was based on "plenty of good land, and liberty to manage their own affairs in their own way" and that their inclination to follow a republican attitude to government plus their free trade with the West Indies added to their prospering society. He warned the British government too late that the size and distance and expense of overtaxing the citizens and defending the American colonies and their monopoly on their trade practices were not a benefit for their Empire. "It is surely now time that our rulers should either realize this golden dream, in which they have been indulging themselves... If the project cannot be completed, it ought to be given up. If any of the provinces of the British empire cannot be made to contribute towards the support of the whole empire, it is surely time that Great Britain should free herself from the expense of defending those provinces in time of war, and of supporting any part of their civil or military establishments in time of peace, and endeavor to accommodate her future views and designs to the real mediocrity of her circumstances."[28]

Modern day economists look to the works of Adam Smith to demonstrate how an economic system operates as well as the virtues of a free enterprise market system, one that allows all individuals the freedom to pursue their individual monetary interests with limited government interference. In *The Wealth of Nations* he took the opportunity to condemn the attempts of governments, chiefly inspired by 'mercantilism' (the theory that a nations wealth is measured solely by its capital (gold or silver) to reorganize, redirect, and thwart economic activity.[29] Smith pioneered in his detailed writing the positive outcomes of economic freedom which embodied the roles of self interest, the division of labor, and the establishment of free markets. In his observation of pin factory workers he formulated the benefits of the division of labor. He noted that each worker left alone, doing all the work involved with making a pin, maybe one would be produced in a day. However, as revealed in *Book* 1 *Chapter* 1 of *The Wealth of Nations*, he notes that, "one man draws out the wire, another straights it, a third cuts it, a fourth points it, a fifth grinds it at the top for receiving, the head..all performed by distinct hands, though in others the same man will sometimes perform two or three of them. I have seen a small manufactory of this kind where ten men only were employed, and where some of them consequently performed two or three distinct operations...Those ten persons, therefore, could make among them upwards of forty-eight thousand pins in a day."

His expression, 'the invisible hand' was used to describe how individual self interest motivates the most efficient use of resources within an economy. In short, all participants will seek to maximize their self-interests, which produces a cooperative interaction with like minded participants leading to exchange of goods and services in a mutually beneficial manner. It comes as no surprise that President Ronald Reagan greatly respected the works of Smith to reflect his philosophy of Reaganomics.

Reagan learned well the lessons taught two centuries ago by Adam Smith, namely that the wealth of nations is caused by human intellect, wit, discovery and innovation. Ronald Reagan designed his policies on these concepts.[30]

"Concern for our own happiness recommends to us
the virtue of prudence; concern for that of other people,
the virtues of justice and beneficence..."
(from "The Theory of Moral Sentiments" 1759)

"The property which every man has in his own labor,
as it is the original foundation of all other property,
so it is the most sacred and inviolable."
(from "The Wealth of Nations" 1776)

"Every individual necessarily labors to render the annual
revenue of the society as great as he can. He generally, indeed,
neither intends to promote the public interest, nor knows how
much he is promoting it ... He is in this, as in many other cases,
led by an invisible hand to promote an end which was no part of
his intentions. Nor is it always the worse for the society that it
was no part of it. By pursuing his own interest he frequently
promotes that of the society more effectually
than when he really intends to promote it.
I have never known much good done by those who
affected to trade for the public good."
(from "The Wealth of Nations" 1776)

Edmund Burke

The Father of Conservatism

Edmund Burke was born on January 12, 1729 in Dublin, Ireland, raised in the Anglican faith of his father, and held high reverence for his mother's Roman Catholic faith as well. He was educated at a Quaker boarding school, and nearby Trinity College. In 1750, at twenty-one he attended Middle Temple in London to study law. He abandoned law soon after to pursue literary writings. His pursuits resulted in the culmination of holding several titles, among them were author, social and political philosopher and statesman. As an author, his first works were *A Vindication of Natural Society* and *A Philosophical Enquiry into the Origin of Our Ideas of the Sublime and Beautiful* published in 1756 and 1757 respectively. In *A Vindication of Natural Society* he mocked the writings of Henry St. John, Viscount Bolingbroke, a leading political figure who rejected traditional theology. Burke set out to discredit that attack by him and others by explaining that Church and State rested upon the same foundations, so that assaults upon religion might as well bring about the downfall of the state and lead to anarchy.[31]

In 1765 he was appointed to the position of secretary to Charles Wentworth, the Marquis of Rockingham, who was leader of one of the Whig groups in Parliament. Burke became dedicated to unite the Whigs, challenging King George III's power against that of Parliament.[32] The king was seeking to reclaim a more active role for the crown—which had lost some influence in the reigns of George I and George II. Burke's chief comment on this issue was placed in his pamphlet, *"Thoughts on the Cause of the Present Discontents"* (1770). He argued that King George's actions were against not the letter but the spirit of the constitution. The choice of ministers purely on personal grounds was favouritism; public approbation by the people through Parliament should determine their selection.[33]

In England as in America, people had divided into two groups regarding the American war for independence. Those who supported King George III were Tories and those in favor of the war were called Whigs.

As an MP (Member of Parliament) his speech in opposition to American taxation, delivered in Parliament on April 19, 1774, (one year to the day before the Battle of Lexington) was historic. Known as the *Speech on American Taxation,* he vocalized the dangerous course his countrymen were facing concerning the rebellion brewing across the ocean.

"Leave the Americans as they anciently stood, and these distinctions, born of our unhappy contest, will die along with it"[34] "Be content to bind America with laws and trade. Do not burden them by taxes; you were not used to do so from the beginning. Let this be your reason for not taxing....but if intemperately, unwisely, fatally, you sophisticate and poison the very source of government, by urging subtle deductions, and consequences odious to those you govern, from the unlimited and illimitable nature of supreme sovereignty, you will teach them to call that sovereignty itself in question."[35] King George III, unmoved by the simple eloquence of Burke's words found himself, his kingdom and his army and navy thrown into the fire pit of our Revolutionary War. Burke was influenced by Montesquieu and the teachings of Locke.[36] His moral vision recognized the place of natural law in society. He saw natural law as a gift from God that evolved from the life experiences of society and developed into fundamental principles that works favorably for that society.

Natural rights being that all share in equal justice, and the protection of one's labor and property. He concluded that humankind's problems are best solved when those higher principles along with good judgement or prudence are applied. Wild radical abstract theories have no place within an ordered population.

His speech on Reform or Representation in the House of Commons June 1784 outlined this.

"a nation is not an idea only of local extent, and individual momentary aggregation, but it is an idea of continuity, which extends in time as well as in numbers and in space. And this is a choice not of one day, or one set of people, not a tumultuary and giddy choice; it is a deliberate election of ages and of generations; it is a Constitution made by what is ten thousand times better than choice--it is made by the peculiar circumstances, occasions, tempers, dispositions, and moral, civil, and social habitudes of the people, which disclose themselves only in a long space of time. It is a vestment, which accommodates itself to the body. Nor is prescription of government formed upon blind, unmeaning prejudices--for man is a most unwise, and a most wise being. The individual is foolish. The multitude, for the moment, are foolish, when they act without deliberation; but the species is wise, and when time is given to it, as a species it almost always acts right."[37]   It can also be said that Burke held traditions in high regard for they were the good rituals of the past.

He foresaw and supported the Americans in their quest for liberty and freedom from the crown of England. When the peaceful multiple requests from the colonists to acquire a voice in Parliament to suspend arbitrary taxes placed upon them fell upon on deaf ears, they resisted militarily.

After the conflict, while those in America were choosing new leaders in an original representative republic under a Constitution unseen and unheard of before in world history, the French government was being destroyed by a bloody reign of terror and complete anarchy under the likes of Robespierre. In the streets of Paris and surrounding locales, the guillotine saw as many as forty thousand beheadings. It comes as no surprise that in Burke's writing, *Reflections on the Revolution in France*, it laid out his contempt for the uncivilized uprising. In it, he applied all his conservative views. He exposed the sin of the French people to demolish its entire government framework instead of repairing the scant abuses. He chastised them for forsaking their traditions for ideology and for wanting to reinvent their society.

Burke rejected ideology, to him it meant, to take an idealized world view and impose it on others. Conservatism, in Burke's view was not to impose ideology, but instead to refer to sound policies and rights that are tested by time and experience and use them to keep a government from wandering astray from them. Reform over revolution.

His idea of statesmanship was to avoid the tearing down blindly of the existing order and resisting change at all cost: "A disposition to preserve, and an ability to improve, taken together, would be my standard of a statesman."[38]

Burke outlined that the diminishing of morality in France coupled with their receding attention to religion and divine providence was troublesome. In *Reflections* he noted, "You had all these advantages in your ancient states, but you chose to act as if you had never been molded into a civil society and had everything to begin anew. You began ill, because you began by despising everything that belonged to you.....respecting your forefathers, you would have been taught to respect yourselves."[39] The economic conservatism of Burke is revealed in an essay he wrote in 1795 to William Pitt, entitled, *Thoughts and Details on Scarcity.* It responded to England's fiscal hardships resulting in part from the war. Government interference with price and wage must be avoided he argued. "To provide for us in our necessities is not in the power of government. It would be a vain presumption in statesmen to think they can do it."[40] "Labor is a commodity like every other that rises or falls according to the demand"[41]

On other economic matters, Burke found the slave trade was a cancer on a nation. He wrote the *Sketch of the Negro Code* in 1790 that called for the steady elimination of the dreadful practice. He was a strong advocate of private property rights. He recognized that one's own accumulation of property and wealth resulted in maximizing individual productivity which in turn boosted the prosperity of the community. Barry Goldwater's book, *The Conscience of a Conservative* outlined that conservatism is the philosophy of level headed experience. He echoed Burke's thinking as well as did President Ronald Reagan, who like Goldwater, was an admirer of Burke and kept this quote of his at the ready for those who would falsely promote socialism. "Edmund Burke on the threat of socialism: "A perfect equality will indeed be produced -- that is to say equal wretchedness, equal beggary, and on the part of partitioners a woeful, helpless and desperate disappointment. Such is the event of all compulsory equalizations. They pull down what is above; they never raise what is below; they depress high and low together, beneath the level of what was originally the lowest.""[42]

"When bad men combine, the good must associate;
else they will fall one by one,
an unpitied sacrifice in a contemptible struggle"
Edmund Burke- Thoughts on the Cause of the Present Discontents
1770

"When the leaders choose to make themselves bidders
at an auction of popularity, their talents,
in the construction of the state, will be of no service.
They will become flatterers instead of legislators;
the instruments, not the guides, of the people."
Edmund Burke- Reflections on the Revolution in France 1790

"When I see the spirit of liberty in action,
I see a strong principle at work"
Edmund Burke- Reflections on the Revolution in France 1790

"In a democracy, the majority of the citizens is capable of
exercising the most cruel oppressions upon the minority."
Edmund Burke - Reflections on the Revolution in France 1790

"There is but one law for all, namely that law which governs all
law, the law of our Creator, the law of humanity,
justice, equity -- the law of nature and of nations."
Edmund Burke- Speech on the impeachment of Warren Hastings
May 28, 1794

"The true danger is when liberty is nibbled away,
for expedience, and by parts."
Edmund Burke- Letter to the Sheriffs of Bristol April 3, 1777

"The people never give up their liberties
but under some delusion"
Edmund Burke-Speech at the County Meeting of Buckinghamshire
1784

"Whenever a separation is made between liberty and justice,
neither, in my opinion, is safe"
Edmund Burke-Letter to M. de Menonville October 1789

Setauket Presbyterian Church, Setauket, New York

The Role of Clergy in Promoting Liberty

On the road to independence in colonial America, the role of the church and its church goers cannot be ignored. Right from the start "the shining city on a hill" was accredited to John Winthrop, the Puritan minister who along with others seeking religious freedom, came to America in 1630. The Puritans settled in what is now Boston and together with the settlements at Salem and Charlestown created the Massachusetts Bay Colony. Winthrop's wise guidance earned him the title of governor of the new Colony. Religious services were highly regarded as important gatherings and were held in the village meeting halls or in the largest building in town. Churches held many denominations throughout New England. Quakers, Catholics, Jewish, Puritans, Lutherans and in the southern territories Baptists and Anglicans were dominant, but no-matter the denomination, American ministers were delivering the most powerful oratory of at this time. Sermons lasting uninterrupted an hour and more were by far the dominant and most influential communication of the day. The influence of Christianity reformer John Calvin and Calvinism with the Puritan migration to the new world laid the theological foundation of what was to come. The 18th Century saw the arrival of the 'Great Awakening' into the thirteen colonies, starting about 1730, where individual religious participation and spirituality was essential to a fulfilling Christian life. Salvation and deliverance from evil was a principle that originated, not from the authority of the church itself, but directly from Christ's presence into every man, woman and child. Redeemed believers could and should challenge churches who failed to perform in their duties for the changing of the hearts and spiritual liberation of sin. It was an uniquely 'American' religion whose influence became widespread. The message of faith and worship in God played a major role in the

American Revolution by offering the moral endorsement for opposing British oppression, enforcing a conviction to Americans that righteous resistance was justified in the eyes of God. By conveying the Bible scriptures that the Almighty God alone was the Supreme Judge of the World it would place this new nation into God's hands as a land truly blessed.

At the beginning of the war some ministers were persuaded that, with God's help, America might become "the principal Seat of the glorious Kingdom which Christ shall erect upon Earth in the latter Days."[43] The domination of Christianity was the reason the Bible was referred to often by the founding fathers and was the source of verses that promoted the separation from England. "Stand fast therefore in the liberty wherewith Christ hath made us free, and be not entangled again with the yoke of bondage."(*Galatians 5:1*) The stories of Christian persecution and murder under the hands of Roman tyranny were well documented and played well with colonists seeing first hand the oppression of Great Britain rulers as was the biblical story of God's calling to Moses to lead his children out of bondage under the cruel bloody rule of pharaoh.

America is the only nation other than Israel that can trace its origins to a historical sovereign rule of God. The preachers of colonial America were bold courageous patriots who recognized that God had ordained America for the purpose as the 'shining city on the hill' and America would be the means by which the gospel would spread outward to the rest of the world. Proved by the original charters of the colonies that these settlements were established to provide safe havens for the promulgation of the gospel of God. The presidents of the higher establishment of learning which included Yale, Harvard and University of New Jersey (later Princeton) were organized to raise up ministers and missionaries. In its first 150 years since the existence of Harvard you could not teach unless you had become an ordained minister.

Well educated clergymen schooled at such institutions as Harvard, Yale, and Princeton would serve within the ranks chiefly as chaplains and as writers for commanders to deliver orders as well as hold political titles in state and Congressional offices. Preachers like Jonathan Edwards, George Whitefield, Samuel West and others brought overwhelming numbers of people into places of worship. The churches were sacred embassies to heaven.

Jonathan Edwards

"...the Great Awakening had political consequences. This was the first movement that embraced the thirteen colonies that would eventually become the United States. Thanks to it, a sense of commonality began developing among the various colonies. At the same time, new ideas were circulating regarding human rights and the nature of government. Those ideas, joined to the growing sense of commonality among the colonies, would produce momentous events."[44]

In 1734 Jonathan Edwards, a devote Calvinist pastor from Northampton Massachusetts was the leading voice from the religious pulpit in the American colonies and one of the most influential figures during the Great Awakening. His father was a minister and his mother's father was one as well. Exposed to the clergy since birth, and being the only son in a family of eleven children, he was the only one qualified to enter the ministry. He entered college in Connecticut just as he was turning thirteen. In the library of the Connecticut Collegiate School (later to be renamed Yale University) he became familiar with the works of Isaac Newton and John Locke whose philosophies into the natural laws, reasoning and scientific principles were commanding civilized society's acclaim. Locke's views in integrating natural law and the study of government demonstrated a truth in logic that could not be ignored.

Edwards believed in the immorality or 'original sin' of man, the forgiveness of a merciful God and mostly on the need of a personal experience of religious conversion. His popularity would travel outside of Massachusetts into Connecticut and beyond by virtue of his writings and published sermons.

His famous sermon *'Sinners in the Hands of an Angry God'* was delivered with verbal imagery so clear and vibrant, those listening in his congregations, would break into emotional outbursts, changing the direction of their lives to spiritual devotion. Reminding them of the perpetual suffering and torment of hell that awaits "poor, damned hopeless souls" and sinners, he spoke of everlasting redemption "...an extraordinary Opportunity, A Day wherein Christ has flung the Door of Mercy wide open, and stands in the Door calling and crying in a loud Voice to poor sinners; a Day wherein many are flocking to him, and pressing into the Kingdom of God; ...many that are very lately in the same miserable condition that you are in, are in now a happy State, with their hearts filled with Love to Him...and rejoicing in the Hope of the Glory of God."[45] It was a Jonathan Edwards's sermon that first used the terminology, "the Supreme Judge of the World" a phrase that influenced Thomas Jefferson to add it to the Declaration of Independence. He would guide many others with additional works; *The Nature of True Virtue*, and *The End for which God Created the World*. His life works would make him a leader in the American tradition of evangelicalism. Central to Edwards's philosophy was that God, the creator's love was the center of the universe and that a loving God must create in order to share that love with morally responsible beings.[46]

Well known, he preached in the college chapel at Princeton where he was president in January 1758 and died in late March at age fifty-four after contacting small pox from an inoculation. Reverend John Witherspoon was Edwards most renowned successor, becoming the celebrated teacher for James Madison, the New Jersey representative to the Continental Congress and a signer of the Declaration of Independence. Aaron Burr was the grandchild of Edwards and would later become the third Vice President of the United States under Thomas Jefferson.

George Whitefield
The Grand Itinerant

George Whitefield was born on December 16, 1714, in Gloucester, England. An avid reader of plays, he performed on the stage at school and from there learned the technique of projecting his voice, a blessing from God that later was wielded to deliver the messages of God. At college he joined a gathering of Methodists called "The Holy Club" led by John and Charles Wesley. He became a missionary and decided to voyage to America to the new Georgia colony, but before he left England he became an ordained Anglican deacon and preached in churches in London. As his reputation grew so did the worshipers in the crowd. His stay in Georgia lasted only three months and his return to England found many churches unresponsive to his style of preaching. He took his sermon to open fields with no pulpit to stand between him and the assembled folks.

He crossed the Atlantic and ventured to Philadelphia in 1739 at the age of twenty-five. Benjamin Franklin noted in his autobiography that "the Reverend Mr. Whitefield ...was at first permitted to first preach in some of our churches; but the clergy, taking a dislike for him, soon refus'd him their pulpits and he was oblig'd to preach in the fields."[47]

Franklin heard him preach to thousands of listeners in the streets of Philadelphia and analytically calculated that his well trained voice could reach the ears of thirty thousand listeners at a time. Whitefield's prominence reached incredible stature through the power of his voice and the thoughts behind it. He was easily one of the most renowned preachers in all colonial America. Franklin and Whitefield developed a friendship having been involved with printing his sermons and journals. In 1739, noting the results of George Whitefield's ministry through revivals and the resulting Christian influence on Philadelphia city life, Benjamin Franklin later recorded in his autobiography: *"It was wonderful to see the change soon made in the manners of our inhabitants. From being thoughtless or indifferent about religion, it seemed as if all the world were growing religious, so that one could not walk thro' the town in an evening without hearing psalms sung in different families of every street."* He went on to observe that in an often unruly society, reformation in morals was beneficial to all. Always alert and receptive to whatever worked, Franklin promoted revivals.[48]

The churches at the time were unable to hold the number of folks eager to hear Whitefield's sermons, so Franklin had a huge auditorium built solely to meet the demands, later the building would be the first edifice for the University of Pennsylvania.

There is no denying the influence that minister Whitefield wielded on the mindset of the participants in the American Revolution. He was an outspoken mouthpiece behind The Great Awakening, which early in the eighteenth century was the spiritual renewal of faith that brought its followers back to spiritual life through their heartfelt closeness with God. His sermons urged sinners to repent, to follow the teachings of Jesus Christ for salvation and be glorified in God's heaven when their lives were over. His message was aimed at each and every individual, calling them to take personal responsibility for their faith and to pursue a personal relationship with God the creator. In short, religious authority in the Church of England could be confronted when their leaders did not live up to their expectations and new religious orders could be formed. As time passed this great awakening expanded to question the rulings of the King of England and the concept of independence.

In 1764 he told Americans that impending trouble was on the horizon with England. He lamented, "your golden days are at an end, a deep laid plot against your civil and religious liberties.", "My heart bleeds for you America." His political views mirrored that of the Whig Party advocating that the colonialists were rightful to have a voice in Parliament for establishing laws that effect them. He called for the separation of America from the mother country England and like Ben Franklin, went to England and openly opposed the Stamp Act.

Protesters to his sermons would pelt him with rocks, rotten eggs and even dead cats; yet he remained unfazed. In thirty-four years it is estimated that he delivered eighteen thousand sermons, addressing the faithful forty hours a week starting at times at four in the morning ending at ten o'clock in the evening. His words stirred millions of people on both sides of the ocean. He preached to the slave populace and spoke on their behalf. Newspapers referred to him as the "Marvel of the Age."

In his famous sermon, *The Method of Grace*, he started with, "As God can send a nation or people no greater blessing than to give them faithful, sincere, and upright ministers, so the greatest curse that God can possibly send upon a people in this world is to give them over to blind, unregenerate, carnal, lukewarm, and unskilful guides. And yet, in all ages, we find that there have been many wolves in sheep's clothing, many that daubed with untempered mortar, that prophesied smoother things than God did allow..."

He died in 1770 and was laid to rest in the Newburyport Church in Boston. In 1775 colonial soldiers heading off to battle, led by then American patriot Benedict Arnold, assembled at that church. Officers went and uncovered the tomb that held the remains of George Whitefield, they removed from the corpse the clerical collar and wristbands, and cut them into pieces for each of their soldiers to carry into battle for inspiration.

Samuel West

Samuel West was an American patriot pastor at the time of the country's founding. He was born at Yarmouth, Cape Cod on March 3, 1730, worked in the fields as a farmer and attended Harvard College when he was twenty. At Harvard he was acquainted with classmate John Hancock, and knew John Adams there as well, graduating in 1754, he was later ordained in 1761. His devotion to God's law with a deep held respect of lawful authority was in direct opposition to King George III of England's absolute rule over his subjects. The laws of God were legitimate and all men, even kings and monarchs were subject to them. After the Battle of Bunker Hill, he joined the militia members against the crown as a chaplain, preaching to them and raising their spirits. At one point during his service he became greatly respected when he deciphered a discovered letter of treason meant for a British officer, outlining the patriot's ammunition and troop strength. His findings were delivered in person to General Washington's headquarters.

One of his most endearing works was a sermon entitled; *"The Right to Rebel against Governors"* written by West and preached before the Massachusetts Council and House of Representatives on the anniversary of their election in Boston on May 29, 1776. These are excerpts of the sermon.

"The great Creator, having designed the human race for society, has made us dependent on one another for happiness. He has so constituted us that it becomes both our duty and interest to seek the public good; and that we may be the more firmly engaged to promote each others welfare, the Deity has endowed us with tender and social affection, with generous and benevolent principles...The Deity has also invested us with moral powers and faculties, by which we are enabled to discern the difference between right and wrong, truth and falsehood, good and evil;

hence the approbation of mind that arises upon doing a good action, and the remorse of conscience which we experience when we counteract the moral sense and do that which is evil. This proves that, in what is commonly called a state of nature, we are the subjects of the divine law and government; that the Deity is our supreme magistrate, who has written his law in our hearts, and will reward or punish us according as we obey or disobey his commands....the necessity of forming ourselves into politic bodies, and granting to our rulers a power to enact laws for the public safety, and to enforce them by proper penalties, arises from our being in a fallen and degenerate state. The slightest view of the present state and condition of the human race is abundantly sufficient to convince any person of common sense and common honesty that civil government is absolutely necessary for the peace and safety of mankind; and, consequently, that all good magistrates, while they faithfully discharge the trust reposed in them, ought to be religiously and conscientiously obeyed. An enemy to good government is an enemy not only to his country, but to all mankind...The law of nature gives men no right to do anything that is immoral, or contrary to the will of God, and injurious to their fellow-creatures; for a state of nature is properly a state of law and government, even a government founded upon the unchangeable nature of the Deity, and a law resulting from the eternal fitness of things. Sooner shall heaven and earth pass away, and the whole frame of nature be dissolved, than any part even the smallest iota, of this law shall ever be abrogated; it is unchangeable as the Deity himself, being a transcript of his moral perfections. A revelation, pretending to be from God, that contradicts any part of natural law, ought immediately to be rejected as an imposture; for the Deity cannot make a law contrary to the law of nature without acting contrary to himself,--a thing in the strictest sense impossible, for that which implies contradiction is not an object of the divine power. It is our duty to endeavor always to promote the general good; to do to all as we would be willing to be done were we in their circumstances; to do justly, to love mercy, and to walk humbly before God. These are some of the laws of nature which every man in the world is bound to observe, and which whoever violates exposes himself to the resentment of mankind, the lashes of his own conscience, and the judgment of Heaven. This plainly shows that the highest state of liberty subjects us to the law of nature and the government of God. The most perfect freedom consists of obeying the dictates of right reason, and submitting to natural law....The same principles that oblige us to submit to civil government do also equally oblige us to, where we have power and ability, to resist and oppose tyranny; and that where tyranny begins government ends. For, if magistrates have no authority but what they derive from the people; if they are properly of human creation; if the whole end and design of their institution is to promote the general good, and to secure to men their just rights, it will follow, that when they act contrary to the end and design of their creation they cease being magistrates, and the people which gave them their authority have the right to take it from them again....To save our country from the hands of our oppressors ought to be dearer to us even than our own lives, and, next the eternal salvation of our own souls, is the thing of the greatest importance, a duty so sacred that it cannot justly be dispensed with for the sake of our secular concerns. It is necessary that we should thoroughly study the law of nature, the rights of mankind, and the reciprocal duties of governors and governed...To conclude: While we are fighting for liberty, and striving against tyranny, let us remember to fight the good fight of faith, and earnestly seek to be delivered from that bondage of corruption which we are brought into by sin, and that we may be made partakers of the glorious liberty of the sons and children of God: which may the Father of Mercies grant us all, through Jesus Christ. AMEN."[49]

Samuel West was an industrious member of the delegation to construct the Massachusetts Constitution of 1780 along with John Adams and although he was selected as a delegate from Massachusetts in forming the U.S. Constitution, he declined to leave Boston for Philadelphia and was not present. His voice at home however, was strong for the ratification of the new charter of liberty. On December 29, 1799, fifteen days after the passing of the country's first president George Washington, Reverend West as the pastor at the Hollis Street Church in Boston delivered a sermon entitled *Greatness the Result of Goodness* occasioned by the death of Washington.

In old age he continued to preach but as his body and mind were failing him he left the ministry in 1803. He passed away four years later at age seventy-seven.

Jonathan Mayhew

"The Father of Civil and Religious Liberty
in Massachusetts and America"
"Morning Gun of the American Revolution"

Jonathan Mayhew was born in 1720 in Martha's Vineyard, Massachusetts, the son of Experience Mayhew, a minister to the Indian population there. At age twenty he was educated at Harvard, schooled in Puritan literature, graduated four years later and was ordained in 1747 at the West Church in Boston. In 1749 his *Seven Sermons* was published and was highly acclaimed abroad. In 1750 his sermon, *'A Discourse Concerning Unlimited Submission and Non-Resistance to the Higher Powers with some Reflections on the Resistance made to King Charles I'* created a tempest in Boston, having chosen the anniversary of the execution of King Charles I to deliver it. Before the sermon was printed by booksellers, Mayhew was attacked in a Boston newspaper as a "wrangling preacher." For six months, *'Discourse...'* was the topic of public controversy, and according to John Adams, it was "read by everybody, celebrated by friends, and abused by enemies," and continued to be reprinted and circulated in the colonies years preceding the Revolution.[50] He denounced the Church of England whose participants were loyal to the crown. Mayhew was a Pulpit Patriot and according to Robert Treat Paine, the representative from Massachusetts and signer of the Declaration of Independence was called, "The Father of Civil and Religious Liberty in Massachusetts and America."

His famous sermon printed and reprinted twenty six years before the famous signing of our Declaration of Independence centered on the theme that all liberty came from God, and there was righteous justification for people to rebel against those whose reign over the citizenry threatened their 'natural rights' security and property.

George Washington
"Father of the Country"
The American Cincinnatus
First President of the USA

The stature of a man is measured by the gifts of moral leadership he possesses and the respect he is given by the people whose lives are influenced by these qualities. George Washington was not in short supply of either. When the founding fathers designed our three coequal branches of self-government, the role of Executive is required to be able to steer the stormy seas that surge and flow over the ever changing dilemmas that plague human society. It was perhaps, divine intervention that grasped the struggle of this new nation, conceived in liberty, with a faith in God, that provided the country with a torchbearer that would set the role for leaders to come afterwards.

He was born on February 22, 1732 in Westmoreland County in Virginia, the oldest child to Augustine Washington and his second wife Mary Ball Washington, joining two half brothers named Lawrence and Augustine from his father's first marriage to Jane Butler Washington. Later, four siblings would follow, named Samuel, Elizabeth, John Augustine and Charles, but three would die in their youths. Washington's father was a slave-owning tobacco plantation owner, who at the time of his death at age forty nine had amassed ten thousand acres of plantation property, an iron mine and about fifty slaves. The elder Augustine left the bulk of his estate to the two eldest sons. Lawrence received the Mount Vernon property and Augustine got the land in Pope's Creek. George was only eleven at the time his father died and would have to wait till he was twenty-one to inherit two thousand acres in Ferry Farm, three lots in Fredericksburg and ten slaves.

In his father's absence, brother Lawrence, now twenty-five would become his advisor and role model. Lawrence had been schooled in England and was a member of the marines in the King's infantry in the war against Spain, having achieved the title of major.   His prestige earned him the title of adjunct general in charge of the Virginia militia and brought him into the company of the wealthy and influential Fairfax family who lived near the property of Mount Vernon. He married Anne Fairfax, eldest daughter to William Fairfax in 1743. George idolized his brother and was deeply impressed with the stature Lawrence had attained, and wanted for himself to be part of high society. Exposed to luxurious surrounding and extravagant dinner dances held often at the Fairfax Belvoir mansion and estate, the teenage George listened and learned that the social graces required good manners, proper appearance, politeness and respect for all individuals. He tagged along with his brother at every opportunity that availed itself.

He was introduced to guidelines of social etiquette, going so far as to meticulously copy a list of 110 rules of manners and social graces from *"Rules of Civility and Decent Behavior in Company and Conversation."* He studied them well and put them to good use, rules such as "Associate yourself with Men of good Quality if you esteem your own reputation." "In the company of those of Higher Quality than yourself Speak not until you are ask'd a Question." "Contradict not at every turn what others Say."[51]

He quickly learned that to be accepted into upper influential circles he would need to have land, lots of land, as wealth was measured in that commodity. He would also need the resolve to manage it properly, and the stature as a leader to stand out in a crowd, fortunately, he was an imposing figure standing about six foot two inches with reddish hair with a brawny build. Washington said he resembled his father. He was keenly aware that he lacked the sophisticated schooling his two older half brothers were able to obtain in England before their father died, it was a reality that consumed his mind with self doubt when in the company of others. Purpose driven ambition and tempered civility would have to be an acceptable substitute.   George became a land surveyor with the help of the Fairfax family, working with his sister-in-law's brother and his friend, George William Fairfax. He also had a strong admiration for his friend's wife, Sally Fairfax, who was two years older than him and was remarkably popular, charming and well educated. In social settings she could converse with anyone on a wide range of subjects, and he learned much while in her company.

Washington worked for those pioneers looking to settle the large expanses of land along the Potomac River and into the Shenandoah Valley. His entrepreneurship paid well and at age eighteen he was able to purchase for himself over eleven hundred acres. His rugged surveying gave him productive experience in scouting in and around rough territory, exposure to living off the land and contact with the natives. Lessons that would become invaluable later on. When he became aware that Lawrence had developed a steady cough that no treatment at home or under doctor's care in England could cure, the two brothers spent weeks upon the ocean, sailing to the British colony of Barbados in the Caribbean hoping find some relief in the warm tropical weather.

Lawrence's condition worsened, and George contacted smallpox, a disease that oftentimes resulted in painful deaths, however he recovered with the evidence of a few scars on his face. George sailed home to Virginia and Lawrence returned later on, dying shortly afterwards at age thirty-four. The death of his brother and mentor was devastating. Wishing to mirror his integrity, he impressed Governor Robert Dinwiddie enough to bestow on him the rank of a major in charge of a Virginia militia. French occupation into British holdings into and around the Ohio Valley concerned the king of England and a courier was needed to deliver a warning drafted by the Governor Dinwiddie to French military officers at Fort Le Beouf. Washington volunteered heading out in October 1753. He choose an ample frontiersman to guide him through the wilderness, gaining Indian support along the treacherous way and delivered the letter as promised. He was told that the message will be passed to their governor for a response, but the French forts and troops would remain, he returned to Williamsburg. Along the horseback journey homeward, he avoided drowning in an icy river and missed being shot at by a disloyal Indian guide. His mission accomplished after three months, he returned his findings to Dinwiddie, reporting that the French planned to occupy the entire Ohio and could not be removed except by force.[52] Impressed by Washington's disclosure, he was promoted to the rank of lieutenant colonel, and instructed to raise an army and supplies to march two hundred miles and build a fort at the fork in the Ohio River. Lacking formal military schooling, he instructed those under his command with knowledge he learned from books. He was personable yet held a firm hand, going so far as reprimanding harshly those under his command who used unbecoming vulgarity.

Enlisting the help of Indians who traded with the British, they learned that the French had already built an impressive stronghold named Fort Duquesne, strategically located near present day Pittsburgh Pennsylvania and that attack plans were inevitable. Washington's first battle soon ensued, ambushing a French unit, killing their leader and taking captive those still breathing. He ordered the construction of a poorly located fort named Fort Necessity that gave little resistance when they were attacked by combined French and their Indian allies on July 3, 1754. The outcome of the bloodbath forced Washington to surrender and evacuate his remaining troops back to Virginia. This was to be the first battle in what would be called the French and Indian War and an embarrassment to the British. Any hopes that Washington had in having his colonial army integrated into the British ranks were dashed. He sought a position as an officer in King George II regiments but every request was denied. When it was decided that General Edward Braddock would lead two well trained redcoat regiments to capture Fort Duquesne, Washington was brought aboard as an aide to the General with the promise of receiving an officer title after the success of the mission. Washington insisted that scout troops be sent ahead, but the general dismissed his recommendations.

Advice that would prove fatal.

Two months into the march and recovering from severe fever and headaches, Washington met up with Braddock's army a day before they were met by hidden French and Indian snipers that killed General Braddock, his officers and many troops. Amidst the smoke, and crack of gunshot, the shattering of skull and bones and the resulting screams, Washington survived the Battle of the Wilderness, despite having his hat shot off his head and two horses shot dead beneath him. The British abandoned this region and concentrated on the French in the Great Lakes region. Washington now twenty-three was named a colonel-in-chief, not in the British army, but as a leader in the Virginia regiment, ordered to protect settlers from Indian raids. He would expand his desire to achieve notoriety by seeking political office by running for a seat in the House of Burgesses. Consisting of representatives from various Virginia settlements, the House of Burgesses was to help the governor rule and to make laws for Virginia, a step forward to self-government. Washington lost his opportunity, coming in third.

Three years passed, and while in the militia, he ran again and was elected as a representative from Frederick County to the House of Burgesses. At this time the redcoat army attempted again to capture Fort Duquesne and like before young Washington assisted General John Forbes, now in command of a massive six thousand man force. When two separate Virginia militias came upon each other in the back country and opened fire at each other, George realizing the blunder, rode heroically between the lines of fire, swatting away musket fire with a sword, many were killed in the friendly fire. Washington had not a scratch. His bravery duly noted.

The enemy fort was abandoned and aflame and the area now in control by the British in November of 1758. The French were routed from the area and Washington later resigned from the army. All hopes of being a commissioned British officer were left behind. He became aware that British military officers well trained in European traditions had little regard for backwoods style, strategy and tactics. He focused to running the Mount

Vernon estate for Lawrence's widow and turned his affectionate attention to twenty-seven year old Martha Dandridge Custis, a recently widowed, mother of two small children, who was well liked, deeply respected and a tremendously wealthy plantation owner that he met earlier that March.

After a short courtship the two were married on January 6, 1759. Now in a position of elite prosperity, he took serious charge of his now massive land holdings that measured into thousands of acres of tillable land, and the many slaves that came with it. He inherited Mount Vernon after Anne passed away in 1761 and took control of a large tract of land due him from his military service. He was tireless in seeing his properties used for maximum earnings, leaving it only to handle his affairs as a member of Burgesses in Williamsburg. He grew tobacco that was sold to buyers in England, but when the price fell and the cost to harvest it rose, debts mounted. Washington began to bypass the British merchants, opting to grow grains instead. Wheat and alfalfa did not deplete the rich soil like tobacco did and the ability to sell it locally appealed to Washington. He owned a mill to grind the grain and sold the flour.

Washington diligence as a planter over the years paid off, he experimented with crop rotation and fertilizers and different agricultural methods and his debt disappeared, but increase in taxes against the colonials were beginning to try the patience of his fellow citizens. Earlier overseas in London, King George II died in late October 1760 and his grandson George III took over the throne of the English empire. In addition to Great Britain, he inherited the American colonies and the huge war debt inflicted by the cost of the hostilities with France. The king demanded the Americans be taxed to cover the costs for the protection that they received, but offered them no voice in Parliament to air their concerns. His unreasoning stubbornness would be duly noted.

The Stamp Act tax in 1765 was inflicted on the American colonies and soundly rejected by many but perhaps not as audibly than by fellow Virginian and House of Burgesses member Patrick Henry, whose written resolves challenged the King's authority.

When merchant boycotts against English goods took their financial toll, the Stamp Act was dissolved, but new taxes would replace them, and a large British military presence to carry out the demands of the King and Parliament would stoke the embers of revolution. Speaking for two and a half hours, Parliament member, Edmund Burke would later warn his countrymen, "keep the poor giddy, thoughtless people of our country from plunging headlong into this impious war"[53]

Tensions were mounting, the consequences of a stubborn royalty were the Boston Massacre on March 5, 1770, and years later the Boston Tea Party on December 16, 1773 which resulted in the closing of its harbor. News travels quickly throughout major avenues of commerce, bad news travels faster. The House of Burgesses in Virginia was dissolved. In August 1774, the first Continental Congress met secretly in Philadelphia with fifty-five delegates representing the major thirteen colonies to discuss the dwindling of their liberties. George Washington, now forty-two years old, along with Patrick Henry represented Virginia. The purpose of the gathering was to unite behind a common goal of petitioning the King to take serious their taxation concerns. More hostilities arose.

Red coated soldiers were subsequently dispatched to capture weapons caches from the colonialists. The 'minute men' were engaged. Armed bloodshed concluding in the death of both loyalists and patriots in Lexington and Concord dashed all hopes of any calm contentment.

The Second Continental Congress met in Philadelphia on May 10, 1775, mere weeks after the first gunshots were exchanged in Lexington and Concord. George Washington arrived wearing a striking blue military uniform of his own design, a sign of the seriousness of tasks ahead. On June 10, John Adams of Boston advanced the suggestion that a continental army be raised for the defense of American liberty and sent them to rout the imbedded redcoats in Boston. On June 15, Thomas Johnson from Maryland nominated George Washington, seconded by John Adams to be the general of the American army, and it carried an unanimous vote. Accepting the title, Washington addressed the assembly, that he did not consider himself equal to the great responsibility with which he had been honored.[54] He said he would not accept pay as the Commander-in-Chief, but would ask for debt reimbursement after the war. Washington was an excellent choice to lead, being battle tested in wilderness warfare and well versed from years of political legislature matters and as a Virginian it would demonstrate to the British that the armed struggles in New England were not just a local affair but a united American concern.

A courier was dispatched to Mount Vernon with a letter for his wife which read in part, "...You may believe me, my dear Patsy, when I assure you in the most solemn manner, that, so far from seeking this appointment, I have used every endeavor in my power to avoid it, not only from my unwillingness to part with you and the family, but from a consciousness of its being a trust too great for my capacity, and that I should enjoy more real happiness in one month with you at home, than I have the most distant prospect of finding abroad, if my stay were to be seven times seven years..."[55]

The general at forty-three years old was an exceptionally wealthy man and could have easily settled down on his estate, caring for his family, fulfilling the needs of his plantation incomes, indulging in hunting, fishing and card playing as he saw fit. He was ambitious and ever mindful of his reputation and very much aware that his decision made him a marked man, a target for capture and hanging if caught by the enemy, everything he had worked for would be destroyed.

Reviewing his army, he was taken back by all black troop units and other units with black and white soldiers fighting side by side. He believed southern units would not serve alongside their black comrades in arms but he needed the manpower and wanted to avoid them fighting for the British so he encouraged black enlistment. Washington's most trusted valet was a black slave under his employ at Mount Vernon named Billy Lee. Lee attended to the general's needs and rode with him throughout the Revolutionary War. This rag tag volunteer militia would be enlisted till the end of 1776, Washington stipulated, "Discipline is the soul of an army. It makes small numbers formidable; procures success to the weak and esteem to all." With his troops assembled, General Washington left Philadelphia for Boston to assist with the militia there. He directed Colonel Henry Knox into northern New York where they successfully captured cannon and munitions from Fort Ticonderoga, and transported it with difficulty into Boston. The men under his command were able to position the cannons strategically above the British army location. General Howe, the British commander, felt retreat by ship far outweighed a massacre of his infantry. A small victory but considerable struggles lay ahead.

The rebellion for American liberty would be a righteous calling for many, in every town, village and settlement, Thomas Paine's pamphlet, *'Common Sense'* published in early 1776 settled the debate for independence from the crown in London. The influence of his composition was staggering. It cemented in the minds of thousands the rightful cause of independence from Great Britain. Heading to New York in April 1776 to protect that city was necessary, as it was the heart of communications between New England and the colonies to the South. It would prove to be unsuccessful, the patriot army possessed no ships and the British navy was the finest in the world. During this occupation the Declaration of Independence by Jefferson was drafted and published. Months would pass when in the Battle of Long Island campaign, Washington had his line of infantry divided by overwhelming numbers of British soldiers. Many men were lost, still more captured, life saving retreat was the only option. The American rebels fled by the darkness of night from the Brooklyn Heights section of Long Island back to Manhattan, where a God sent heavy fog in the early morning masked their escape to regroup. The city on the Hudson was lost, Washington and his remaining troops had eluded the British army.

Pleas to the Continental Congress for additional men, money and supplies yielded poor results. Washington was aware that his volunteers were rowdy, drunk and disorderly, and serious action would have to be taken. Along with the stress he faced in standing against the best trained, best equipped army in the world, he faced the disturbing realization that his volunteers required strict and severe discipline to focus their attention on the monumental tasks ahead. The agonizing defeat in New York had many in the ranks questioning his competence to lead. Betrayal from fellow officers, desertions and failure to reenlist when their service time was fulfilled tormented the rebel commander. Congress would grant permission for the general to simply take what he needed from local residents. Washington refused. He felt it would betray the trust they were granted and in their eyes, damage their cause. The enemy did not follow that noble lead.

German Hessian troops, hired by England were in place to destroy the uprising, however their barbaric tactics of these outsiders disgusted citizens who witnessed the stealing of their belongings to satisfy their selfishness. The quill pen of Thomas Paine again stirred the emotions of American townspeople to enthusiastically embrace the struggle for freedom with the new writing called 'American Crisis'. It began with this sentence.

"These are the times that try men's souls: The summer soldier and the sunshine patriot will, in this crisis, shrink from the service of his country; but he that stands by it now, deserves the love and thanks of man and woman."

Washington had it read aloud to his assembly, in late December of 1776 to booster morale, he knew that most of his troops service terms were up in about a week. Three days later, under impossible weather conditions of freezing temperatures, snow and wind, he boldly led his men by crossing them in small boats across the Delaware River on Christmas night to take the Hessian troops unaware the next morning. The cold and discomfort during their march intensified tenfold through wet clothing. Blood from some barefooted soldiers stained the snow. The late dawn attack caught the sleeping enemy by surprise. Their commander, Colonel Johann Rall, who arrogantly referred to his rag wearing adversaries as 'country clowns' was killed in the skirmish, leaving his surviving troops to surrender. Washington's strategy paid off, with the added blessing for him that Rall had ignored a note passed to him while he played cards the night before informing him of the gathering of patriots. The unread note, written in English, was found in his boot. Colonel Rall could not read a word of English. At long last a victory was secured in Trenton; Princeton would follow. Washington was able to keep his ranks largely intact by paying his troops from money secured by Robert Morris, the representative from Pennsylvania who was vital in financing the war effort from his own pocket and from money borrowed.

Benjamin Franklin voyaged overseas to France to enlist their government as an ally against their old enemy and the French would oblige.

At Valley Forge, located twenty-two miles north of Philadelphia, Washington's resolve would be further tested with unbearably cold winter conditions inflicting an awful toll on the men. A Prussian drillmaster, Baron Von Steuben was sent to Valley Forge to transform the rag tag group into an efficient well disciplined fighting force. Washington had devised activities to raise depressed spirits-religious devotions, construction of comfortable quarters, amateur theatricals, dances and vigorous sports, one of which was rounders, a direct ancestor of baseball.[56]

The tenacity that Washington demonstrated in battle caught the attention of the enemy and with the citizens of London. The mounting price of the American revolution was grating on their patience. The cost of wasted lives even more so. Washington was not a military strategist, he simply would not give up.

Battles would be lost and won along the way. The distinguished blue suited general, always on horseback, out in front of his troops would be shot at and missed numerous times, would face starvation within his ranks, and a traitorous betrayal by his friend and fellow officer Benedict Arnold. He avoided sickness that ran rampant in the ranks, having built an immunity to the smallpox he suffered years earlier, and yet, through it all, he persisted in inspiring loyalty for the cause of independence.

Another heavy blow came when Charleston, South Carolina under the command of Benjamin Lincoln fell to the British troops led by Henry Clinton in 1780. Washington was unable to assist the southern ranks having been snowed in that winter by blizzards in Morristown, New Jersey. With military assistance from the French, the battle of Yorktown, Virginia took place on October 19, 1781, resulting finally in the defeat of the British army. An embarrassed British General Charles Cornwallis, too humiliated to surrender in person, gave his sword instead to a fellow general to hand over as a sign of surrender. Washington refused it and directed it be given to his General Benjamin Lincoln for acceptance. The last major battle was over. Two years would pass until peace negotiations sent the redcoats back to England with the signing of the Treaty of Paris in November 1783.

Colonial soldiers who were promised back pay wanted to march on Congress as a mob. Washington refused their offer to lead them and instead called for them to disperse. He was well aware of the weakness of Congress under the Articles of Confederation and knew a stronger union was necessary. He retired once again to Mount Vernon to attend to his responsibilities as a gentleman farmer and as an eighteenth century model of the Roman General Cincinnatus, but years later he would reemerge into public service. A Constitutional Convention was called to replace the old and ineffective Articles of Confederation. It would be held in Philadelphia on May 17 to September 17, 1787. Debate on all major issue were discussed, studied, written, and revised over and over. The publication of *The Federalist* was written by Alexander Hamilton, James Madison and John Jay under the alias name of 'Publius,' *The Federalist* was a collection of essays written in favor of the new constitution.

The colonists held George Washington in such high regard and admiration that his presence was requested to add integrity to the proceedings. "The pressure of the public voice is so loud," he wrote to Lafayette, (his French advisor during the war) that he could not resist.[57]

He left his plantation again and after several days on the road, he arrived and entered the red brick Pennsylvania State House, now Independence Hall. Aided by his charisma and patriotic loyalty, he was elected president of the proceedings. Great minds like James Madison, Benjamin Franklin, Alexander Hamilton and delegates from the thirteen colonies would be assembled to voice concerns and hammer out a new government, a republic, unknown in the world at its time, a three branch coequal government that the American people would decide its course. Delegate James Madison proposed the Virginia Plan which would become the foundation for the United States Constitution.

After the Constitution was adopted by the states, the Executive branch needed a leader and electors chose George Washington as the first President of the United States. Amidst bells ringing and cheers from the crowd, he placed his left hand on an opened Bible, and repeated the oath of office from Robert Livingston, on the balcony at Federal Hall in New York City on April 30, 1789, completing the oath of office by adding on his own, the now traditional words, "So help me God." He then leaned forward to kiss the Bible.[58]

"It is done!" Livingston called out, then turning to face the crowds below he proclaimed, "Long live George Washington, President of the United States."

Different titles as to what to call the new leader, names like "His Most Benign Highness" or "His Highness the President of the United States" were discussed in the House and Senate chambers. Some wanted to make him a monarch or king. James Madison remembered Washington's annoyance at the efforts "to bedizen him with a superb but spurious title." It was, indeed, Washington's friend Madison who led the continued resistance in the House.[59]

Washington settled on simply, "Mr. President."

As the forerunner for things to come, Washington knew the nation and the world would be watching with anxious eyes to see how the leader of this experimental republic would perform and he set standards accordingly. Ever mindful of his public image, he was reserved, and aristocratic with social skills honed to the pinnacle of morality and honor since he was a teenager, he set the pace for future administrations by astute decision making based on the careful opinions of those he trusted, he gave his title a broad leeway in his appointments and made himself available to the people. He accepted no salary for his position.

He selected his advisors, known as his cabinet, to help him conduct the business of running the government. John Adams was elected Vice President. The president appointed John Jay, one of the authors of the *Federalist Papers* to Chief Justice of the Supreme Court, Thomas Jefferson would handle foreign affairs as Secretary of State, Henry Knox, his war companion was named Secretary of War, Alexander Hamilton, who was a trusted aide to then General Washington was made Secretary of the Treasury, and Edmund Randolph was named Attorney General. Hamilton demonstrated a clever approach in settling the country's money problems and overbearing debt. He prompted Congress to pass three taxes; one on foreign goods entering our ports, a tonnage tariff that taxed the foreign ship itself and a tax on distilled liquor. The money raised would pay the overdue soldiers for their service, as well as the states for their expenses. Hamilton also help create the Bank of the United States and a year later the United States Mint to print American currency. Before this decision, money was state issued and sometimes not accepted in another state, a federal currency would eliminate this crippling drawback and promote interstate trade. The opinions of Jefferson and Hamilton were to become historic in their disagreements. Hamilton believed the powers of the central government should not be limited to the powers delegated to it by the Constitution but should allow itself any additional authority whenever needed. Jefferson feared that the government could grow too strong, dismissing states rights and stood on the premise that no authorization of powers be granted that are not outlined in the Constitution. Hamilton allies became known as Federalists, Jefferson's were called Democratic-Republicans. It was the rise of the two party system in politics and an arrangement that President Washington abhorred. The feuding between the two political factions in the newspapers became so heated that President Washington wanted to retire when his first term of office was over. It was his ability to quell their arguments and heal their clashes that persuaded him to stay on. He was elected to a second term of office and inaugurated on March 4, 1793. During this time he issued a proclamation declaring neutrality in a new war between France and England and was present for the cornerstone placement for the new capitol building to be built in Federal City (now known as Washington D.C.).

The Whiskey Rebellion was an internal uprising that grabbed the president's attention. Farmers had distilled corn into whiskey and the tax on this byproduct was scorned by many. Resentment turned to anger and anger to violent uprisings. When armed mobs attacked government agents in Pittsburgh and vowed to form an army against Philadelphia, Washington called forth the militia to handle the unrest. Fortunately, the size of the federal militia dispersed any notion of armed conflict and the matter was settled without incident.

President Washington would spend forty-five years in public service ending with two terms as Chief Executive, which would set a precedence for future administrations (except for Franklin D. Roosevelt who sought and won a third term in 1940) before retiring for good at Mount Vernon. These actions compared him with the noble Roman aristocrat Cincinnatus who was named dictator of Rome in 458 BC after his country's army was captured by enemies of the empire. Cincinnatus assembled and led his army into battle, defeated their foes and spared their lives if they agreed to surrender. They capitulated and bloodshed was spared. The mission complete, Cincinnatus gave up the crown and went back to his farm.

The first president delivered his now famous Washington farewell speech. It was a lengthy article, well over six thousand words to the people of the United States, never spoken, but published on September 19, 1796. Covering a broad range of topics and opinions, based on his lifetime experiences, it offered to the nation a guidebook in handling future events. It touched on preserving the union and protecting the law of the land, the Constitution, with warnings that the cost of liberty is high and eternal vigilance is a necessity to preserve it.

Regarding the Constitution he outlined, "Respect for its authority, compliance with its laws, acquiescence in its measures, are duties enjoined by the fundamental maxims of true liberty. The basis of our political systems is the right of the people to make and to alter their constitutions of government. But the Constitution which at any time exists, till changed by an explicit and authentic act of the whole people, is sacredly obligatory upon all. The very idea of the power and the right of the people to establish government presupposes the duty of every individual to obey the established government." He wrote on the virtues of righteousness and religion, "These great pillars of human happiness, these firmest props of the duties of men and citizens," he spotlighted, were religion and morality. "Of all the dispositions and habits which lead to political prosperity, Religion and morality are indispensable supports."

He warned of "the baneful effects of the Spirit of Party" "...domination of one faction over another, ... is itself a frightful despotism...The disorders and miseries which result gradually incline the minds of men to seek security and repose in the absolute power of an individual; and sooner or later the chief of some prevailing faction...turns this disposition to the purposes of his own elevation, on the ruins of public liberty."

In regards to America's role outside its borders. The United States should "observe good faith and justice towards all Nations" and he warned his countrymen, most likely with the bloody French Revolution in mind, "The great rule of conduct for us in regard to foreign nations is in extending our commercial relations, to have with them as little political connection as possible. So far as we have already formed engagements, let them be fulfilled with perfect good faith. Here let us stop. Europe has a set of primary interests which to us have none..."

Washington recommended to strive to defy external threats, and defend a neutral position. He concluded the address, "I anticipate with pleasing expectation...the benign influence of good laws under a free government, the ever-favorite object of my heart, and the happy reward, as I trust, of our mutual cares, labors, and dangers."

George Washington left public service in March 1797 and returned again to his cherished Mount Vernon to oversee his plantation and related business ventures. Inspecting his property on Thursday, December 12, 1799, in a snowy and at times rainy morning, he returned home in wet clothing. The next morning he suffered with a severe sore throat that failed to improve throughout the day. He awoke well before dawn on Saturday feeling ill, Martha summoned doctor James Craik, who drew blood, ordered inhalation of vinegar and hot water followed by a gargle of vinegar and sage tea. The doctor sent for two consultants, Dr. Gustavus Brown and Dr. Elisha Dick. Convinced his demise was close, he murmured to Dr. Craik, "Doctor, I die hard, but I am not afraid to go."[60] The man who jilted death on countless occasions, lost the battle and died at 10:30 p.m. on December 14, 1799, with his wife Martha at his bedside. He was sixty-seven years old. He was laid to rest at Mount Vernon three days after his passing. News of his passing only reached the ears of Philadelphia's citizens on the evening of his burial. President Adams was jolted by the news, he delivered a message to the Senate stating in part the nation had lost, "her most esteemed, beloved, and admired citizen...I feel myself alone, bereaved of my last brother."[61]

The door of the Presidential mansion, Washington's pew at Christ Church, Congress Hall, and the ships in Boston Harbor were draped sorrowfully in black bunting.

Bells tolled throughout America. Following a solemn march of infantry complete with muffled drums and a white riderless horse with reversed boots in the stirrups, Henry Lee, a respected cavalry officer during the Revolutionary War and a Virginia representative to Congress eulogized his war colleague and president to a joint meeting of both Houses on the day after Christmas.

"First in war, first in peace and first in the hearts of his countrymen, he was second to none in the humble and endearing scenes of private life. Pious, just, humane, temperate and sincere—uniform, dignified and commanding—his example was as edifying to all around him as were the effects of that example lasting...Correct throughout, vice shuddered in his presence and virtue always felt his fostering hand. The purity of his private character gave effulgence to his public virtues....Such was the man for whom our nation mourns...."

In his will he requested his long time companion and valet, Billy Lee to be freed immediately, and his estate slaves to be given their freedom after his wife's death, they were to be taught to read and write and to be brought up in a useful occupation.[62] Martha, however freed them a year later.

Many accolades and monuments to honor George Washington would follow. Commemorative coins bearing his image would be purchased by many. The federal city being built along the Potomac would bear his name, as well as a future state, towns and multiple school buildings. Oil paintings of his face and in his military dress uniform would be reproduced by the millions. His likeness would be cast in bronze in locations throughout the country, and on Mount Rushmore in South Dakota his face, sculptured into the solid granite is seventy times larger than life. His distinguished profile on our coinage and his portrait on our paper currency are well known world wide. The quiet man who left the comforts of his farm to endure unimaginable hardships to lead his country to independence declined the role of monarch. His disciplined leadership was inspiring and unmatched and would set the example as a role model of those who would follow in holding the highest office in the land. The title 'Father of the Country' was well bestowed.

The time is now near at hand which must probably determine whether Americans are to be freemen or slaves; whether they are to have any property they can call their own; whether their houses and farms are to be pillaged and destroyed, and themselves consigned to a state of wretchedness from which no human efforts will deliver them. The fate of unborn millions will now depend, under God, on the courage and conduct of this army. Our cruel and unrelenting enemy leaves us only the choice of brave resistance, or the most abject submission. We have, therefore, to resolve to conquer or die. *George Washington-Address to the Continental Army before the Battle of Long Island August 27, 1776*

"The preservation of the sacred fire of liberty, and the destiny of the Republican model of Government, are justly considered as deeply, perhaps as finally staked, on the experiment entrusted to the hands of the American people." *George Washington- First Inaugural Address April 30, 1789*

"Whereas it is the duty of all Nations to acknowledge the providence of Almighty God, to obey His will, to be grateful for His benefits, and humbly to implore His protection and favor - and Whereas both Houses of Congress have by their joint Committee requested me "to recommend to the People of the United States a day of public thanksgiving and prayer to be observed by acknowledging with grateful hearts the many signal favors of Almighty God, especially by affording them an opportunity peaceably to establish a form of government for their safety and happiness." Now therefore I do recommend and assign Thursday the 26th day of November next to be devoted by the People of these

States to the service of that Great and Glorious Being, Who is the Beneficent Author of all the good that was, that is, or that will be – That we may then all unite in rendering unto Him our sincere and humble thanks – for His kind care and protection of the People of this country previous to their becoming a Nation – for the signal and manifold mercies, and the favorable interpositions of His providence, which we experienced in the course and conclusion of the late war –for the great degree of tranquillity, union, and plenty, which we have since enjoyed – for the peaceable and rational manner in which we have been enabled to establish constitutions of government for our safety and happiness, and particularly the national One now lately instituted, for the civil and religious liberty with which we are blessed, and the means we have of acquiring and diffusing useful knowledge; and in general for all the great and various favors which he hath been pleased to confer upon us. And also that we may then unite in most humbly offering our prayers and supplications to the great Lord and Ruler of Nations and beseech Him to pardon our national and other transgressions – to enable us all, whether in public or private stations, to perform our several and relative duties properly and punctually – to render our national government a blessing to all the People, by constantly being a government of wise, just, and constitutional laws, discreetly and faithfully executed and obeyed – to protect and guide all Sovereigns and Nations (especially such as have shown kindness unto us) and to bless them with good government, peace, and concord – To promote the knowledge and practice of true religion and virtue, and the increase of science among them and Us – and generally to grant unto all mankind such a degree of temporal prosperity as he alone knows to be best.Given under my hand at the City of New York the third day of October in the year of our Lord 1789."
George Washington-The Thanksgiving Day Proclamation Oct 3 1789

John Adams

"The Colossus of Independence"
Second President of the USA

Often overlooked and sometimes forgotten as a famous founding father, the life and works of John Adams make him and his contributions to liberty undeniably indispensable. His dedication to the cause of human dignity took him from his most valuable commodity; the loving surrounding of his family and his farm. Historians are fortunate that being a man of letters, his writings to his beloved wife Abigail, to his friend Benjamin Rush and later in life, Thomas Jefferson had survived the tumultuous times in which he lived and within the passages of those parchments we learned of a man who held high ethics, education, philosophy and love of country in high esteem, this coupled with his burning desire to be recognized for his diverse accomplishments. He appreciated the strengths in others, he put public duty ahead of self, he despised everything associated with slavery, he respected the law with moral virtue as his guiding conscience, and above all, his devotion and learned philosophy from those who came before was put to the good of the country by reconciling the extreme factions that sprang up during the beginning of our birth as a new republic.

John Adams was born in Braintree Massachusetts, the eldest of three sons to John Adams Senior and Susannah Boylston Adams on October 19, 1735. He descended from a proud Puritan family lineage going back to about 1636. His grandmother, Hannah Bass Adams, was the great granddaughter of John and Priscilla Alden, who were central figures in the historic chronicles of the *Mayflower* Plymouth landing. The salt box dwelling in which the family lived was simple and common in hard working farming Puritan communities. Young John was born to virtuous parents, and deeply admired his father. He would later write, "In wisdom, piety, benevolence and charity in proportion to his education and sphere of life, I have never known his superior."

His father's independent spirit and love of country were his lifelong inspiration.[63] He learned to read at home, entered a private school when a previous instructor was less than supportive and there he flourished.

John Sr. a member of the Braintree church, took his eldest son to hear sermons hoping he would follow the ministry. Young John was tutored by a local minister and passed the exams to enter Harvard College when only fifteen. There he discovered an affection for books and knowledge, he became proficient in understanding both Greek and Latin, reading the classics in those historic languages. He cherished the works of Cicero, studied moral philosophy and logic. His confidence had, by his own admission, made him conceited. He sought to improve himself of vanity.

Graduating Harvard in 1755, he returned home where he became a teacher and taught school for two years before deciding to practice law. He apprenticed for an attorney, writing out the documents and learning the complexities of law for two years, and was then ready to open his own law practice. In 1761 he met Abigail Smith and after a three year courtship, their loving companionship and deep felt devotion to one another was made eternal. They were married by her father, the Reverend William Smith and moved into a house next door to John's childhood home. Abigail would be his ardent supporter, his sounding block, his mentor and friend. Events were shaping at this time that would affect the daily routines of the colonists in ways they could not imagine, political upheaval surrounding the Adams home that would influence greatly on the young lawyer. The tax on sugar from the King of England and Parliament was met with protest in America, a year later the Stamp Act of 1765, placed a burdensome tax on all printed materials. These taxes were a result of the cost of the Seven Years War with the French, which put the liability of its debt on the American citizens by having them go to a local British Customs office to purchase stamps to make all documents legal, such as property deeds, wills, newspapers, pamphlets, ship's papers and the like. Citizens rebelled. John's cousin Samuel Adams would form the

Sons of Liberty, a group of men, who, reacting mostly by mob rule, targeted British officials sympathetic to the tax. They stoned the house of Andrew Oliver, who was assigned to distribute the stamps, and destroyed the home of Lieutenant Governor Thomas Hutchinson.

John Adams was appalled by the barbarism and saw this infringement as violation of English law and wrote *"A Dissertation on the Canon and the Feudal Law"* which was reprinted in England under the title, *"The True Sentiments of America."*[64] It was unsigned and untitled and printed in the *Boston Gazette* and was his first political essay, centering on the notion that liberty is a natural right "derived from our Maker." The public outcry was deafening and the Stamp Act was soon repelled, replaced by the Townshend Acts, which were taxes on paper, glass, paint and tea. British soldiers were dispatched to watch for smugglers and supply the muscle for payment, colonists were forced to house and feed them for nothing. Hostilities became glaring.

Adams now had a family to think about since becoming a father of a daughter named Abigail or "Nabby", a son John Quincy would follow two years later.

John Adams became a respected attorney, gifted by his stubbornness and high moral character, he traveled at times on horseback to other towns going as far as New Hampshire and Maine to handle law cases of all sorts. In 1768 he moved his growing family and his practice to a rented house within the city of Boston. March 5, 1770, would bring John Adams to the forefront of Massachusetts notoriety and the main topic of discussion to all the colonies scattered around America. A mob of angry Bostonians harassed a young British soldier guarding the Custom House, first with angry threats, then snowballs and ice were thrown. A call for more soldiers brought Captain Preston and seven more armed soldiers into the skirmish. The threatening crowd grew to hundreds, some wielding sticks and clubs, spouting vulgarities amidst rising anger with oyster shells and stones accompanying the flying snowballs and ice. The disturbance ended with five men, all citizens shot dead. The next day John Adams, now only thirty-four, was requested to defend the British captain and his men, which he accepted, knowing his reputation and the safety of his family rested on his decision. He reasoned that the law and fair trials must be enacted to everyone in a free country, no-matter how unpopular he knew he would become. After months of preparation, his devotion to impartial representation resulted in a trial performance where he told the jury, "Fact are stubborn things, and whatever may be our wishes, our inclinations, or our dictums of our passion, they cannot alter the state of facts and evidence."[65] The court outcome was the full acquittal of Captain Preston, who it was determined, did not give an order to fire into the crowd, and was found to be 'not guilty.' Six of the eight soldiers were also found not guilty, the remaining two were found guilty of manslaughter, not murder, their thumbs branded as punishment.

With his reputation soon growing, his law expertise brought him in contact with the wealthy shipping merchant, John Hancock, another outspoken voice for independence from British sovereignty. The unfair tax on tea escalated with the destruction of several ship's cargo, in a raid led by Samuel Adams and the Sons of Liberty, resulting in the Boston Tea Party on December 16, 1773. King George III of England was furious at the impetuousness of the Americans and ordered the closing of Boston Harbor, with his warships in place, all imports and exports ceased, business shut down, and town meetings were suspended. British tyranny was in full view and its impact spread to other colonies. The King's army swelled within Boston, tensions mounted, and a meeting of the American colonies was called to discuss current events.

In August 1774, John Adams, Samuel Adams and Robert Paine were chosen by the Massachusetts legislature to meet with other representatives from twelve of the thirteen colonies (Georgia abstained) at the First Continental Congress in Philadelphia, Pennsylvania. He accepted the position, but before leaving, moved his family, now expanded with two more sons, Charles and Thomas back to his home in Braintree.

This Congress would demonstrate a sign of unity against the king and Parliament and would discuss the current crisis. It ended with the assurance that the colonies will support Boston and that they will gather again the following year. When Adams and company met again in Philadelphia to attend the Second Continental Congress in May 10, 1775, America was now at war with the mother country. One month earlier, the British Governor Thomas Gage received orders from the king to seize the firearms and gunpowder from the colonists. Plans of the redcoat march to Concord, Massachusetts were relayed to patriot Paul Revere who rode off on horseback during the night to warn the townspeople. A militia was formed to head off the redcoat militia. An armed standoff was underway until the first shot of the American Revolution was fired at Lexington on the morning of April 19, 1775, followed later that day at Concord. Adams, who was home at the time would get a first hand look at the death and carnage.

The tone of the Second Continental Congress had now changed. Reunited with George Washington from Virginia and meeting Thomas Jefferson for the first time as well as the notably popular and highly respected Benjamin Franklin from Philadelphia impressed the delegation from New England. John Adams was of the mind and impatience that independence from Britain was now the only solution. He relied on his understanding of the works of Plato, Aristotle, Cicero and John Locke, a central figure of the great Enlightenment. Locke's view on the principles of nature and the right of people to revolution when those principles are violated coincided with his thoughts.

There were, however others like delegate John Dickinson from Pennsylvania that felt that making peace with England was in the best interest of all. The spirited debate, between the two exhibited in Adams an air that can best be described as pompous. It also produced a published insult of Dickinson which shamed Adams for a while. Confident in his ability to see leadership, he addressed the assembly and boldly recommended

George Washington as the best man to lead a Continental army against the formidable British forces. His decision was wisely admired as a sign of unity of the colonies and to demonstrate, especially to the powers of Britain that the conflict was not with Boston and New England alone. He was then elevated to the position as the Chairman of the Board of War, where his duties were mainly to find financing for combat and his recommendations to Congress to create a much needed navy. His duties were demanding, toiling away on the shipment of supplies to arm, feed and clothe an army. Adding to his burden was the prolonged absence from his family, his plentiful exchange of letters between himself and Abigail lessened the pain. He returned home for a few weeks in December but the new year and loyalty to the cause brought him back again to Philadelphia. Thomas Paine's well received pamphlet, *Common Sense* would revive a dispirited populace proclaiming that America should indeed split from Britain and in so doing, declare independence. Within that premise, Adams could not agree more, but as was his style he found room to criticize Paine. In his writing, *Thoughts on Government*, he outlined that Paine had talent for tearing down government than in having any thought on how it should be set up.[66]

The popularity of *Common Sense* combined with the news that General Washington had ousted the British navy from Boston harbor on March 17, gave a much needed push towards the drive for independence.

On June 7, 1776, within the confines of the State House, Virginia delegate Richard Lee rose, and made a motion to declare the colonies free states, and addressed the assembly:

"Resolved...That these United Colonies are, and of right ought to be, free and independent States, that they are absolved from all allegiance to the British Crown, and that all political connection between them and the State of Great Britain is, and ought to be, totally dissolved..."[67]

It was seconded by the domineering voice of John Adams, and argued forcefully over several days. Upon its passage, it was determined that a five-man committee be formed to frame the resolutions and the reasons for the separation. Benjamin Franklin, Thomas Jefferson, Robert Livingston, Roger Sherman, and John Adams would layout a declaration. Adams, with a good sense of character felt that Jefferson was the best choice to draft a declaration of independence. Both loved agriculture, shared a deep love of books, authors, and held a fond devotion to family, hearth and home. Adams keenly noted Jefferson had "the reputation of a masterly pen,"[68]

Adams would later recall that he insisted that Jefferson write the document.

"Why?" Jefferson asked.

"Reasons enough" Adams said. "What are your reasons?"

"Reason first: You are a Virginian and a Virginian ought to appear at the head of this business. Reason second: I am obnoxious, suspected and unpopular. You are very much otherwise. Reason third: You can write ten times better than I can"[69]

After the thoughts and ideas of the red headed Virginian, were put to parchment, Adams became the lead voice in promoting and supporting its contents. Declaring independence was easy. Achieving independence would be a grueling and demanding task. Washington's amateur army would face numerous defeats and hard earned victories. Being outmanned and outgunned the struggle would bring bloodshed, starvation, frostbite, heat exhaustion and self doubt to all who marched. Assistance from Europe was essential to aide the American cause. John Adams had returned home to renew his law practice, but within two months, succumbed to the need of urgency by the Congress, when asked to join Franklin, and Arthur Lee as diplomats to France to seek their financial and military support against the British. He set sail for the three thousand mile, two month journey on treacherous, rolling ocean waves during the winter of January 1778, joined by his ten year old son, John Quincy. The mission to bring the French aboard was made easier by the popularity of Ben Franklin, a fact that the envious Adams could not ignore. He suspected Franklin of being more concerned for fulfilling his own personal needs and self gratification and taking all the credit for their mission than on the mission itself; a timely procurement of American security. He recorded how the twenty-four year old King Louis XVI and his lovely queen Marie Antoinette possessed the power to determine the fate of his country. Communications between home and the diplomats took six weeks at best, leaving them to make vital decisions on their own. The personalities of these three men became less than harmonizing during the long absence from home. When France became an American ally, father and son voyaged home to join the family back in Braintree in the autumn 1778. He continued to his farming and law practice but later turned his attention and experience into writing the constitution for his home state. Within its contents he outlined his concerns for good government including the separation of powers, a declaration of rights and a governor with broad jurisdiction. The Massachusetts State Constitution was accepted by the legislature and ratified in late October 1780. It gave John Adams the distinction of helping produce the very first state constitution in America.

That same month, being ever restless, Holland would beckon to John Adams. Appointed by Congress as the ambassador to that country, he would seek their counsel for trade and financial support. Leaving for his new assignment he, along with his eldest son, would again travel abroad, stopping first in Paris to rejoin Franklin, resume his duties and put John Quincy into school. After his duties in Paris, both father and son rolled north by carriage to the Hague in Holland. This country was well known for its religious tolerance, the starting point for the Pilgrims, and the leader in shipbuilding with the busiest port. This provided the Dutch with wealth enough to lend. Persuading them to contribute to a new country would be strenuous until news that General Washington had defeated the King's army at Yorktown, Virginia in October 1781. The surrender of General Cornwallis secured both the loan and trade commerce Adams desired. The war was over, but his devotion to public service was not.

A peace treaty would have to be drawn up and to the credit of Adams, Franklin and the newly arrived diplomat John Jay, the three agreed that this pact with Great Britain must stipulate an acknowledgement of American independence. The Treaty of Paris of 1783 declared; "His Britanic Majesty acknowledges the said United States...to be free and sovereign, and independent states."[70] Coastal fishing rights and all territories were to fall within American jurisdiction. During the lengthy negotiations, The Adams family would be reunited in Europe. Young Charles came to Europe earlier and mother and daughter "Nabby" followed. John Adams took the position as Ambassador to Great Britain. Thomas Jefferson, who had become governor of Virginia after the signing of the Declaration of Independence now replaced him in his old position as Ambassador to France. In a historic meeting, an understandably tense Adams met with King George III in London on June 1, 1785, knowing he devoted his life to conquer him for over the last ten years, knowing also the list of the monarch's misdeeds against his countrymen were heralded in the American Declaration. With rehearsed, well chosen words and a respectful attitude of grace, Adams addressed the king, "I shall esteem myself the happiest of men if I can be instrumental in restoring the confidence and affection - or in better words, the good old nature and the good old humor, between peoples who, though separated by an ocean and under different governments, have the same language, the same religion, and kindred blood."

The king was impressed and responded, "...I wish you Sir, to believe, and that it may be understood in America, that I have done nothing in the late contest, but what I thought myself indispensably bound to do, by the duty which I owed to my People. I will be very frank with you. I was the last to consent to the Separation, but the Separation having been made and having become inevitable, I have always said, as I say now, that I would be the first to meet the Friendship of the United States as an independent Power."[71]

The three years that Abigail and John spent together were spent in lavish surroundings in Paris and London, but he was absent from home during the dismantling of the loosely knit Articles of Confederation and the writing and adoption of a new constitution, that designed not a monarchy, not a democracy but a limited centralized government, a republic, governed by law with coequal branches of authority. Each separate state debated the U.S. Constitution and each state ratified this document. When his role as foreign ambassador waned on his spirit, Adams sent word to Congress that he wished to be relieved from his position and return home to Braintree. When his ship docked in Boston he was given a hero's welcome, with cheering crowds and celebratory cannon fire. The overseas consul, who delivered a peace treaty that recognized America as independent and as the individual who won over the Dutch loaners was given a grand reception.

His name was submitted as a candidate for the office of Chief Executive. George Washington was elected overwhelmingly, Adams was second. At this time second place majority winners became the Vice President. Adams simply had to accept the office in which he was selected which he did nine days before Washington took the oath at Federal Hall in New York City on April 30, 1789.

The role of vice president was unsettling to Adams, having been relegated to a secondary position of overseeing every session of the Senate in a listening capacity, not as a vocal opinion maker. He was also out of an advisory role to the president that ex-minister to France and now Secretary of State Thomas Jefferson, and Secretary of the Treasury, Alexander Hamilton enjoyed. Adams in his quest to bring an air of dignity to the chief executive office both domestically and abroad, took a fair amount of criticism by spending long weeks in Congress discussing the proper title for the newly elected leader. How

Washington should be addressed was mulled over, Adams proposed, "His Highness the President," "His Esteemed Majesty, the President" and "His Excellency, the Supreme Commander in Chief" borrowing no doubt, from his decade long experience with the crowns of Europe. His critics found his choices to smell of monarchy. Due to his short height and stout physique he was slurred by them as "His Rotundity."

His vice presidential position was less than challenging for the brilliant mind he possessed and the lifetime experience he was more than willing to assert. He would lament to Abigail that he held "the most insignificant office that ever the invention of man contrived or his imagination conceived."[72] Nevertheless, he worked tirelessly and honorably in his title. During Washington's two terms as president, the nation was a distant spectator to the murderous reign of terror that tore the French government to its core, the French Revolution. When Adams first heard of the outbreak of revolution in France, he speculated what might happen "in a nation of thirty million atheists."[73] The British member of Parliament, Edmund Burke, saw the world as Adams did. Both men supported the American Revolution and warned of the bloody insurrection in the streets of France. The effects would trouble the shores of America.

Within the Washington cabinet, surrounded by the walls of the Philadelphia State House, the location of the new government, political parties were beginning to form. Alexander Hamilton, the former captain and confidant to General Washington during the Revolutionary War, fought bitterly for a strong centralized government. He concluded that America's progress depended on robust commerce with the ability of the government to regulate trade, control monetary policy through a federal national bank, and use the national debt as investment capital. Jefferson was livid of Hamilton's proposal. He reminded him that the Constitution did not grant the government the right to establish a federal bank. Jefferson believed in the individual, state rights and was worried that Hamilton was turning the country over to "Stock jobbers and King jobbers" and making America a replica of the British government."[74] The Hamiltonian and Jeffersonian factions drew in there admirers and critics alike and in so doing created a wedge in the system. Adams sided with Hamilton, convinced that America would rise as a respected world power.

The 1793 outbreak of yellow fever took thousands of lives in the city of Philadelphia and beyond. Adam's good friend and delegate, Doctor Benjamin Rush warned of the epidemic and treated the sick and dying. Washington and his cabinet left the city in early September to be reunited months later.

The rise of political parties, the Federalists, led by Adams and Hamilton and the Anti-Federalists or Republicans led by Jefferson, were a strain on President Washington's administration and at the end of his second term, he decided to leave his vaulted position for another leader and retire for good to his beloved Mount Vernon. As vice president, Adams served under that title the longest of any position he held previous. His contributions were honorable and of the highest caliber, his allegiance for the entire two terms of Washington unquestionable. John Adams was awarded the Presidency by a three vote margin in the electoral college in 1796, due largely by the fact that Alexander Hamilton was secretly promoting the candidacy of Thomas Pinckney of South Carolina in an effort to make him the president and possibly prevent his adversary Thomas Jefferson from becoming vice president. Hamilton reasoned that he could control Pinckney. On both counts his plan backfired.

Thomas Jefferson became his vice president. Once friends, bound to a single cause of establishing American independence and as cordial overseas ambassadors, their hardheaded political opinions turned them in opposite directions on matters of how the government should run. Adams would face stiff opposition within his own cabinet. He had made the mistake to hold onto those in the previous administration notably Alexander Hamilton who had high ambitions for himself and worked with others to discredit the new president. The troublesome French

Revolution armies had spread to fighting Britain, Spain, Austria and Prussia and wanted America to ally with them. Adams taking Washington's advice announced neutrality. French war ships starting taking American merchant ships and crew in the Caribbean trade waters. President Adams send three men overseas to Paris to engage the French Foreign Minister Count Talleyrand on a new treaty. Upon arrival the American diplomats were met by three Frenchmen, all who held no official title, and demanded a substantial amount of bribe money to meet with Talleyrand. They refused the pay off demands of the three unknown French conspirators named only as Monsieurs X, Y and Z.

"Y" delivered a naked threat to the Americans. If no money was forthcoming, France would bring the full force of her power against the United States, and the young republic, no more than two decades old.[75]

When Adams learned of the outcome he was outraged. The 1778 alliance with France was renounced, and the XYZ Affair, as it became known, resulted with the new navy vessels (that Adams had requested years before in Congress) to sail along and protect their fellow countrymen's merchant ships. The sailing vessel USS Constitution 'Old Ironsides' and other ships engaged French frigates when threatened and prevailed in many battles. This outcome joined with his decision against launching a full scale war, illustrated Adam's statesmanship and propelled his popularity at home. His high prestige would be short lived, the Alien and Sedition Acts that followed would blemish his record. The Alien Act signed by Adams required all foreigners to register with the United States government noting that they faced deportation without trial if they were here less than seven years. The Sedition Act was established to prevent the newspapers of the day to print anything that was unfavorable or critical of the government, and its officials. Failure to comply by newspapers writers and owners was punishable by fines and or imprisonment. Adams signature put it into law and he was understandingly accused of censorship. Vice President Jefferson and James Madison were publicly outraged and resented fully the idea behind the new laws. They composed the Virginia and Kentucky Resolutions that attempted to assert states rights to dismiss unconstitutional federal laws and defend first amendment rights of free expression. Resentment of the Sedition Act became a paramount issue as Adams sought a second term. Thomas Jefferson would run against Adams. The war of words that spilled onto the newspapers and into the minds of readers were utterances of character abuse and slander. Jefferson encouraged James Callender, a "foul-penned journalist"[76] writing for the *Richmond Examiner*, (who had printed scandal against Hamilton) to report on the shameful manner of President Adams. Calling him publicly, "repulsive pendant," a "gross hypocrite," and "in his private life one of the most egregious fools upon the continent," Callender went even further to note that he was "that strange compound of ignorance and ferocity, of deceit and weakness."[77] As predicted, under the mandates of the Sedition Act, Callender was arrested, later found guilty and sent to jail for nine months. His incarceration worked against Adams and for the Republican. It was during this time in a private meeting, that Adams famous temper dismissed two of his cabinet members loyal to Hamilton.

Hamilton retaliated and published in October, a character assassin pamphlet called *A Letter from Alexander Hamilton, Concerning the Public Conduct and Character of John Adams, Esq., President of the United States*. The printed pummeling, coupled with Hamilton loyalists withholding their votes for Adams sealed his political fate.

With the new home of the president under construction and nearing completion in the new government capital of Washington City. John and Abigail moved into the huge mansion that would become known as the White House on November 1, 1800. A week later he learned from a dispatch from France that a new peace treaty with France had been signed and that France's new emperor Napoleon Bonaparte had "declared the differences between France and America were no more than a family quarrel."[78] The good news that America was spared of war was a tremendous victory for Adams, unfortunately it came too late to make a difference for his reelection.

The day the electors met to review the voting for president, John and Abigail received tragic word that their son Charles had died as a financially ruined alcoholic at the age of thirty, leaving behind a wife and family. Later they learned of John's defeat to Thomas Jefferson and Aaron Burr both tied for first in Electoral College votes. The Constitution determined the tie-breaking vote would be decided by the House of Representatives, in the end, it was decided on February 17, 1801, that Thomas Jefferson would became the third president. Before leaving office and the President's House to head back to his old home he started to call Stoneyfield, he made judicial appointments that were loyal to his Federalist thinking. His Secretary of State John Marshall was named Chief Justice of the Supreme Court and was approved by the Federalist controlled lame-duck Senate, he would serve in the court for thirty-five years. It was Justice Marshall that emerged the idea of judicial review, making the Supreme Court the deciders over what is constitutional or not. President Adams also recalled his son John Quincy from his duties as diplomat in Europe. In a horse drawn coach, John Adams left Washington City as he had planned a week prior, at four o'clock in the morning giving him an eight hour head start away from Jefferson's inauguration ceremonies. His predawn departure, advertised to Adam's foes and friends alike that he was ungracious in the title he just vacated and seen as a bitter old man. He left behind a scandal free administration and a healthy country. A new title was awaiting him, that of farmer John.

He lavished his time following his service to his country, in the fields at home, repairing stone walls and tending to his crop and livestock. The years were spent reasonably quiet surrounded by his family and grandchildren. He reread energetically the works of Shakespeare, Cicero, and the Bible. He read in local papers of the difficulties of the Jefferson administration, but to his credit, did not publicly comment on such matters. On the topic of the huge territorial expansion of the Louisiana Purchase, the French peace treaty, credited to Adams, no doubt paved the way to its acquisition from Napoleon.

At his writing desk, he renewed his long time friendship with his Philadelphia friend and confidant, Doctor Benjamin Rush exchanging a flurry of letters that encapsulated his ideas, opinions, and emotions. Within the folds of correspondence, he learned of the whereabouts and goings on with others he long admired and served alongside of in the creation of the American republic.

At the urging of Rush, he wrote to the now retired Thomas Jefferson, to congratulate him as he returned to his cherished Monticello. He extended his best wishes to him and Thomas, moved by the letter, wrote back a letter of admiration for John. This began a rekindle of mutual admiration on their past achievements and current events, of family and acquaintances, of politics, books, religion, and his life long contempt for slavery. During the War of 1812 the American armada won victory after victory against British warships on the high seas, Jefferson wrote to Adams to give him praise for the navy. John had the difficulty of putting pen to paper to share the heartfelt loss of their daughter Nabby to breast cancer and later his despondency over losing his friend, mentor, and spouse Abigail. In a letter to Jefferson just eight days before she passed away on October 28, 1818 from typhoid fever, he grieved, "The dear partner of my life for fifty-four years as a wife, and for many years more a lover, now lies in extremis, forbidden to speak or be spoken to."[79] When Jefferson learned of her death he wrote back, "I know well and feel what you have lost, what you have suffered, are suffering, and have yet to endure. The same trials have taught me that, for ills so immeasurable, time and silence are the only medicine."[80]

The balance to his misery was the glorious knowing that he lived long enough to see his son John Quincy, add additional titles to an already notable career, namely that of Senator, Harvard professor, Secretary of State and later on March 4, 1825, the sixth president of the United States. In his eighty-ninth year his teeth were gone and decaying, his hearing and eyesight diminished, he could not walk unassisted, but his spirits remained high.

Leading up to the fiftieth anniversary milestone of the signing of the Declaration of Independence the old patriot's heath declined. Physicians were summoned to his home when he became too weak to function on July 1, 1826. His health deteriorated seriously. On the Fourth of July, as cannon fire sounded in the distance to mark the great occasion, John Adams was near death, meanwhile in Virginia at Monticello, bedridden Thomas Jefferson died at one o'clock in the afternoon. Hours later, Adams surrounded by family around his bedside would speak his last words, "Thomas Jefferson survives" followed by a plea to his granddaughter Susanna, "Help me child! Help me!"[81] John Adams grasp on life ended at six-twenty that evening.
He was ninety.
As news spread, eulogies to both Adams and Jefferson were delivered across the country, celebrating their steadfast resolve for their roles in establishing a new republic. The Adams eulogy recounted his career and his faith in the future of America.

"I always consider the settlement of America with reverence and wonder, as the opening of a grand scene and design in providence, for the illumination of the ignorant and the emancipation of the slavish part of mankind all over the earth."
John Adam Diary entry, February 21, 1765

"Facts are stubborn things;
and whatever may be our wishes, our inclinations,
or the dictates of our passions, they cannot alter
the state of facts and evidence."
John Adams- the Arguments for Defense of the Soldiers in the Boston Massacre Trials, December 1770

"The natural liberty of man is to be free from any superior power on earth, and not to be under the will or legislative authority of man, but only to have the law of nature for his rule."
John Adams-The Rights of the Colonists, November 20, 1772

"Yesterday the greatest question was decided which ever was debated in America; and a greater perhaps never was, nor will be, decided among men.
A resolution was passed without one dissenting colony,
"that these United Colonies are, and of right ought to be, free and independent States.
John Adams- letter to his wife Abigail, July 3, 1776

"The Second Day of July 1776,
will be the most memorable Epoch, in the History of America.
I am apt to believe that it will be celebrated, by succeeding Generations, as the great anniversary Festival.
It ought to be commemorated, as the Day of Deliverance by solemn Acts of Devotion to God Almighty.
It ought to be solemnized with Pomp and Parade, with Shews, Games, Sports, Guns, Bells, Bonfires and Illuminations from one End of this Continent to the other from this Time forward forever more."
John Adams letter to his wife Abigail July 3, 1776

"The judicial power ought to be distinct from both the legislative and executive, and independent upon both, that so it may be a check upon both, as both should be checks upon that."
John Adams- letter to George Wythe 1776

"Our Constitution was made only
for a moral and religious people.
It is wholly inadequate to the government of any other."
John Adams- Message to the Massachusetts Militia, Oct 11, 1798

"I Pray Heaven to Bestow The Best of Blessing on THIS HOUSE,
and on All that shall hereafter Inhabit it.
May none but Honest and Wise Men ever rule under This Roof!"

John Adams letter to his wife Abigail November 2, 1800
(inscribed over the fireplace of White House State Room)

Thomas Jefferson

"Father of the Declaration of Independence"
"Man of the People"
"The Sage of Monticello"
Third President of the USA

The very name of Thomas Jefferson has become synonymous with the precious ideals of independence, liberty and freedom. A shy boy raised from a life of privilege on the fringe of the Virginia wilderness grew to become one of our most renowned founding fathers. A man of many titles and talents, he was an architect, lawyer, writer, farmer, scientist, inventor, revolutionary, politician, ambassador to France, Vice President and President of the United States, but it was his authorship of the Declaration of Independence that gave birth to a remarkable republic in America and in so doing caught the attention of the rest of the world, not only for his generation but for generations to follow.

He was born April 13, 1743, in Shadwell, Virginia, the third child and eldest son of Peter Jefferson and Jane Randolph, the daughter of the wealthy and influential Randolph family. His father owned a tobacco plantation within his three thousand acre property. A plantation that depended on slaves to harvest the valuable crop. He was tutored at age five and at age nine he attended the school of a Scottish member of the clergy, Reverend William Douglas. There he learned Latin, Greek and French. Young Thomas inherited the plantation when his father died at age fourteen. He stayed with the well educated Reverend James Maury, whose schoolhouse was on his farm and whose well stocked library of over four hundred volumes were available to young Thomas's curiosity. Being excessively determined to educate himself, he was known to tear himself away from recreation to dive headlong into his studies. Along with his education in science and history he appreciated music and learned to play the violin. When he turned sixteen he entered

William & Mary College in Williamsburg which was the capitol of Virginia. There he met Dr. William Small who taught science and introduced him to the works of Isaac Newton, John Locke, and the Scottish Enlightenment. Deciding that the legal profession would be his career, he studied law from George Wythe, who would later be a signer of the Declaration of Independence. His devotion to his studies caught the eye of his mentor and he was invited to be in the company of Governor Fauquier, and the men who made up the Governor's Council. His mother's cousin Peyton Randolph was the king's attorney and Young Thomas would go to the General Court to listen to the debates and observe. He was presented before the General Court by Wythe and started his law practice in 1767. One case brought him much attention. It involved a man whose grandmother was a mulatto born from the union of a black man and white woman. According to a 1705 law, the grandmother was subject to servitude up to the age of thirty-one, since she had given birth to a daughter before that age, the daughter also was subject to servitude until age thirty-one and likewise her offspring, a man, who Jefferson represented for free. He argued before the judge that "under the law of nature, all men are born free" The judge ruled against his client before the other side presented its position.[82] It was the cold reality of the time.

It was easy to understand that the tensions between England and her colonies trickled into the daily dialog in Williamsburg and Jefferson was in the center of thoughtful political discussions. Practicing law in Albemarle County and the fact that he had come into his father's inheritance, he started the building of his home that would be a lifetime obsession and hobby; Monticello. In his new residence he would collect books for its extensive library.

He was elected to the House of Burgesses on May 8, 1769, and joined follow Virginians George Wythe, Patrick Henry and a fellow farmer, George Washington. On New Year's Day 1772 he married Martha Wayles Skelton, a young twenty-three year old widow. Their daughter Patsy the first of six children was born in late September. The following year Martha's father John Wayles died leaving her his estate and together the Jefferson's combined land holdings and slaves nearly doubled.

Before years end in 1773 the Boston Tea Party would occur and the closing of the harbor there soon followed. The members of the House of Burgesses voiced their support for their fellow colonists in the north and the Virginia governor Lord Botetourt reacted swiftly by dismantling that legislative body. The representatives countered this action by deciding to meet in Philadelphia with the representatives of other colonies to voice their growing concerns, this was the first Continental Congress. Prior to that meeting Jefferson penned for the Virginia delegation, *"A Summary View of the Rights of British America"* which became widely published without his name on it. In part he wrote, "To remind him, (his majesty) that our ancestors, before their emigration to America, were the free inhabitants of the British dominions in Europe, and possessed a right which nature has given to all men, of departing from the country in which chance, not choice, has placed them; of going in quest of new habitations, and of there establishing new societies, under such laws and regulations as to them shall seem most likely to promote public happiness..."[83] Influenced by the content in his collection of books were John Locke's *Two Treatise of Government* and the complete works of Montesquieu, including his *Spirit of Laws*. Algernon Sidney's book *Discourses Concerning Government* laid out republican principles of government based on natural rights. Though Jefferson himself was not a chosen delegate at the first Continental Congress, his *Summary View* pamphlet was highly regarded as was his writing skill and reputation.

In March 1775, Jefferson became the delegate to the Second Continental Congress when Peyton Randolph vacated his chair to return to matters in Williamsburg. A month later on April 19, the last chance for American and British reconciliation was cut off with the bloodshed at Lexington and Concord. He arrived in mid June in Philadelphia in time to see Washington, the newly named commander in chief of the continental forces head off to Boston. He met like minded liberty seekers, Benjamin Franklin, and Samuel and John Adams. He stayed at this time with a cousin, a respected cabinetmaker Benjamin Randolph. During his stay his pen and ink drafted the *"Declaration of the Causes and Necessity for Taking up Arms,"* a pamphlet so compelling, Washington's troops cheered upon hearing the contents.

Following the death of his mother in Shadwell, he returned to Philadelphia in May of 1776 and stayed again with Benjamin Randolph, however he had made a request of the craftsman, by asking his cousin to fabricate for him a portable writing desk of his own design. It was made of mahogany with satinwood inlay on the drawer front and back. True to his genius, it combined style and functionality, by featuring a hinged baize fabric covered writing surface, a locking drawer for papers quills, nibs, and a glass inkwell. A slanted book rest allowed for easier reading on his two hundred mile trips between Philadelphia and Virginia. Jefferson called it his writing box. In June, delegate Richard Henry Lee prompted by the Virginia government, moved a resolution that Congress call for a declaration of independence from England. Congress answered by appointing a committee of five to outline it. Ben Franklin, John Adams, Roger Sherman and Robert Livingston nominated Jefferson, the youngest member of the committee, to draft the declaration.

Thomas moved into the second floor bedroom of the Graff House on Market Street and on his writing box, he inscribed the reasons for the separation. He relied on his background in political philosophy and the common sense blessings of natural law. This document would be the first of its kind anywhere in the world.

As Jefferson noted in a letter to a fellow Virginian, James Madison; "it was intended to be an expression of the American mind, and to give to that expression the proper tone and spirit called for by the occasion." The immortal line from the declaration; "We hold these truths to be self evident that all men are created equal..." was written by a known slaveholder, however he accepted the Enlightenment position that all men were born free and slavery was contrary to the law of nature and he expected that in time the act of slavery would be revoked and slaves would regain their natural status as free men.[84] He borrowed the line, "long train of abuses" from John Locke's *Two Treatises of Government.* In his first draft of the Declaration he defined that free men included all men, including slaves held in bondage, he denounced the slave trade as a "cruel war against human nature itself."[85] He even stated that the king was guilty of the continuation of the slave trade. This would later be omitted by the delegates.

After forty-seven changes in committee, it was presented to general assembly in Congress where additional changes were made, some of which Jefferson rightly opposed, primarily slavery.

On July 4, 1776, Congress approved the Declaration of Independence and requested it be printed in handbills and sent to all units of the army and sent to towns large and small throughout the country. Four days later it was read out loud in the streets of Philadelphia. Copies were sent to General Washington to read to his troops.

Within that unrivaled document, four references to God had been inscribed. Inspired in part by the presence of the delegate from New Jersey, John Witherspoon, they are; "When in the Course of human events, it becomes necessary for one people to dissolve the political bands which have connected them with another, and to assume among the powers of the earth, the separate and equal station to which the Laws of Nature and of *Nature's God* entitle them, a decent respect to the opinions of mankind requires that they should declare the cause which impel them to the separation. We are endowed by *our Creator* with certain unalienable Rights, that among these are Life, Liberty and the pursuit of Happiness.....appealing to *the Supreme Judge of the World* for the rectitude of our intentions.....with a firm reliance on the protection of *divine Providence*, we mutually pledge to each other our lives, our fortunes and our sacred honor"

This Declaration of Independence proclaimed not only to the British empire but asserted to the world that our very lives and liberty are natural rights or the unalienable gifts from God, which no person or government can rightfully take away. It affirmed that the purpose of government is to equally secure and protect the people's individual rights no-matter their race, or religion. It was a radical departure from the mindset of the day, where at that time the wealthy, and influential controlled society, and the consent of the governed to have a say in their government and leaders was unheard of.

He returned to his family in Monticello in September but was back in the Virginia House of Delegates three weeks later. He was named to a committee on religion along with James Madison and seventeen others. The mutual respect and friendship between himself and Madison would endure till the end of their lives. It was the Virginia Statute for Religious Freedom that Jefferson drew up resolutions that called for total freedom of religion and the disestablishment of the Church of England, it was adopted not right away but ten years later in 1786.[86] His friend, James Madison's influence was crucial in it's passage. It was a model for the First Amendment to the U.S. Constitution.

Jefferson was elected Governor of Virginia on June 1, 1779, following Patrick Henry. He served for two years. When the British fleet landed the traitorous Benedict Arnold's troops near Richmond in January 1781, Jefferson notified nearby militias as there were no standing army there to defend the city. He was forced to evacuate his family and moved records and military stores to safety. Arnold's armies swept in and set fire to public and private buildings before leaving. In May he was forced to flee Monticello on horseback through wooded areas only minutes before the British butcher, Lieutenant Colonel Banastre

Tarleton ascended up the hill of Monticello. Jefferson's term as governor expired on June 2.[87]

The fortunes of the Americans turned in their favor when General Washington and French allies defeated the British at Yorktown, forcing their surrender on October 19, 1781, thus ending the Revolutionary War. Jefferson faced an emotional setback when his thirty-three year old wife Martha died on September 6, 1782, only months after delivering their sixth child. Heartbroken, he destroyed the love letters between them, depressed he spent weeks alone in forlorn isolation. Only two of their children, both daughters, the eldest Martha, and fourth child Mary, would live to adulthood. When Jefferson traveled to Europe with John Adams and Benjamin Franklin to negotiate with the French to open commercial trade with the victorious Americans, his eldest daughter now twelve accompanied him. He was elected as the Minister of France by Congress after Franklin retired in May 1785 and would remain there for four years. During that time he is kept aware of the political goings on at home, especially those events surrounding the creation of the Constitution by letters from his confidante, James Madison. Their regular back and forth correspondence across the Atlantic supplied crucial ideas and judgements vital to its adoption. Some topic matters discussed ranged from the placement of a 'Bill of Rights' into the document, the concerns of state rights and the limits of the federal government. The rotation of elected leaders was essential as Jefferson worried about the corruption of power with presidents holding lifetime appointments. His younger daughter now joined him in France, escorted by one of his slaves, Sally Hemmings. Following his stay and return home he learned that he has been appointed as the first Secretary of State under President George Washington.

As a member of Washington's cabinet, he was in close contact with Alexander Hamilton, the man who along with James Madison and John Jay, co-authored the *Federalist Papers*. Hamilton, who was Washington's Secretary of the Treasury, insisted that the new nation needed a strong central government at the expense of states rights. He reasoned that the national debt incurred from the Revolutionary war was to be picked up by the individual states which pitted states with small debts against states with larger ones. Taxes were placed on whiskey and imported goods, and through Hamilton's insistence Congress established the Bank of the United States. Jefferson's working relationship was severely strained due to Hamilton's principles, and their respective views on the Constitution. Jefferson had more confidence in the 'people' and believed the government should not do anything that the Constitution did not specifically outline. Hamilton thought the Constitution was only a loose framework of laws on which the government could build as it saw fit and do anything that the Constitution did not say it could not do.[88] The resulting rivalry resulted in a two party system that we still see today. Hamilton became the leader of the Federalist party and Jefferson headed the Democratic-Republicans. He resigned as Secretary of State in January 1794, returned to Monticello, but his stay was short lived. When John Adams sided with the Federalists and ran for president after the second term of George Washington was up, Jefferson ran against his old friend. Since no provision in the constitution allowed for political parties, Jefferson's loss by three electoral votes made him the vice president under Adams. Disagreements between them mounted, centered on direction of the new government. As head of the Senate, Jefferson wrote the manual for parliamentary procedures drawing on the British model. "His Senate Manual would stand as one of the most useful and enduring."[89] The John Adams presidency lasted only one term when four years later, Jefferson ran against him, due largely in part of his distaste of the Sedition Act approved under Adams in 1798. Seen as an attempt to silence views and opinions contrary to the Federalists, the Sedition Act amongst other things justified the punishment of any person writing, uttering, or publishing "any false, scandalous and malicious writing" against the president, Congress or the government of the United States.[90]

The lead up to this election provided for the citizens, an endless barrage of political attacks aimed at Jefferson's religious views of deism, accusing him of tearing down religion and introducing immorality. The Federalist party tried to tie him to the French Revolution, insulted his heritage, and in one newspaper described the man from Monticello as "a mean-spirited, low-lived fellow, the son of a half-breed Indian squaw, sired by a Virginia mulatto father ... raised wholly on hoe-cake made of coarse-ground Southern corn, bacon and hominy – with an occasional change of fricasseed bullfrog." Likewise there were vicious attacks on John Adams. Claims that the friends of war will vote for Adams and friends of peace for Jefferson. This marked the first presidential campaign. Jefferson and Aaron Burr were tied for first in the Electoral College thereby defeating Adams. The tie would be broken by a majority vote in the House of Representatives, in the end Thomas Jefferson became the third president in March 1801, with Aaron Burr winning the vice presidential seat. The peaceful transition of power was unique in the world, his inaugural speech called for unity, "We are all Republicans, we are all Federalists." Throughout his presidency, he made it a habit to consult his entire cabinet on all foreign affairs. He ignored any type of presidential pageantry and preferred common dress on all occasions. One of his first orders was to use the naval ships under his command to defend against and defeat the Barbary pirates attacking American trade vessels. He composed a letter to the Danbury Baptists in 1802 after receiving from them a gracious letter revering to his outspoken stance on religious liberty. The Baptists were a religious minority in New England where the Congregationalist church was legally established in Massachusetts and Connecticut. His letter would produce one of the most misunderstood and misused statement regarding the place of religion and government.

"Gentlemen,

The affectionate sentiments of esteem and approbation which you are so good as to express towards me, on behalf of the

Danbury Baptist association, give me the highest satisfaction. My duties dictate a faithful and zealous pursuit of the interests of my constituents, & in proportion as they are persuaded of my fidelity to those duties, the discharge of them becomes more and more pleasing.

Believing with you that religion is a matter which lies solely between Man & his God, that he owes account to none other for his faith or his worship, that the legitimate powers of government reach actions only, & not opinions, I contemplate with sovereign reverence that act of the whole American people which declared that their legislature should "make no law respecting an establishment of religion, or prohibiting the free exercise thereof, "thus building a wall of separation between Church & State. Adhering to this expression of the supreme will of the nation in behalf of the rights of conscience, I shall see with sincere satisfaction the progress of those sentiments which tend to restore to man all his natural rights, convinced he has no natural right in opposition to his social duties. I reciprocate your kind prayers for the protection & blessing of the common father and creator of man, and tender you for yourselves & your religious association, assurances of my high respect & esteem.

Th Jefferson
Jan. 1. 1802."[91]

The statement, "wall of separation between church and state" as Jefferson intended, never prohibited religious expression in public, but rather restrained the government from interfering with religious exhibitions. Jefferson had spent a political lifetime respecting state rights as a matter of federalism; his "wall" had the federal government on one side and state government and churches on the other.

That "wall of separation between church and state" reference has been falsely interpreted over the years, most notably by Supreme Court Justice Hugo Black in 1947 with *Everson vs. Board of Education*, a case involving the use of public transportation to take some children to Catholic parochial schools with taxpayer reimbursement to the parents. The "wall of separation…" does not appear in the U.S. Constitution, but no matter, Black's "high and impregnable" wall has separated religion from all government be it local, state and federal. "Black also declared that the religious clauses of the First Amendment, which were intended to be a check on the federal government, were now applicable to state and local governments. The term "wall of separation" was to attach thereafter to every case or controversy arising under the establishment clause or the free exercise clause."[92] This distortion has been dishonestly credited to Jefferson, but was not of his mindset, but rather that of Hugo Black and those like-minded jurists that followed. An interpretation, that Black issued to forward the idea of a secular society.

Proof of this can be found in Jefferson's "A bill for Appointing Days of Public Fasting and Thanksgiving" written before his presidency, and as governor of Virginia in 1779, he designated a day for "publick and solemn thanksgiving and prayer to Almighty God"[93]

The immense Louisiana Purchase in 1803, was a departure from Jefferson's firm stance on constitutional obedience, namely having the government involved with states' rights. He was strongly concerned that Spain would cede its holdings in Louisiana to France where political tensions were mounting and he knew that American security was in peril if an aggressive power became its neighbor. In addition, valuable access to the Mississippi River at New Orleans was in jeopardy. Jefferson sent envoys to France to negotiate for the purchase of the city. The French Emperor Napoleon Bonaparte was in dire need of money to fund his war effort and had abandoned any ideas of acquiring a new French empire in America. He was willing to sell the entire Louisiana territory for fifteen million dollars, a tremendous bargain, impossible to ignore. This strategically doubled the size of the United States and provided valuable commerce access to the Missouri and Mississippi rivers. The immensity of the land also provided a buffer between English possessions in the Canadian north. His personal secretary Meriwether Lewis and William Clark set out on an expedition to define the new borders, build friendly Indian relationships, and document the climate and the available natural resources for the growing country.

He was the last of the signers of the Declaration of Independence to serve as President, and after leaving the presidency having served two terms, he retired at last to his hill in Virginia. He busied himself into the workings of the fields which had fallen on hard times. Through mutual friends, one of which was fellow Declaration signer, Benjamin Rush, a correspondence between John Adams and Thomas Jefferson came about. Each of the ex-presidents learned from third parties of their respect for one another and after eleven years of silence between his old friend and political opponent, he received a letter written by Adams on January 1, 1812 wishing him happy new year. This was the beginning of a warm and respectful correspondence between the two old patriots lasting till the end of their lives. These letters exchanged between Quincy Massachusetts and Monticello detailed information on historical, scientific and religious topics.

The war of 1812 brought the British once again to the shores of America and in 1814 they descended on Washington and destroyed the Capitol building then housing the Library of Congress by setting it ablaze along with the Executive Mansion and other government buildings. Calling the acts of the British soldiers, "acts of barbarism which do not belong to a civilized age,"[94] Jefferson sold his personal library collection of 6,487 volumes to replace the lost books for a cost of $23,950.

Jefferson throughout his political career was proud of the thinking behind the Constitution and knew that its basic principles must be upheld in order for the nation to survive. He worried that a government that judged itself would eventually become unlimited in its power, that an unbridled judiciary could turn the Constitution into "a thing of wax." He expressed this matter in a number of correspondences, one notably to his former consul to Lisbon, William Jarvis.

"You seem to consider the judges the ultimate arbiters of all constitutional questions; a very dangerous doctrine indeed, and one which would place us under the despotism of an oligarchy. Our judges ... and their power [are] the more dangerous as they are in office for life, and are not responsible, as the other functionaries are, to the elective control. The Constitution has erected no such single tribunal, knowing that to whatever hands confided, with the corruptions of time and party, its members would become despots. It has more wisely made all the departments coequal and co-sovereign within themselves ... When the legislative or executive functionaries act unconstitutionally, they are responsible to the people in their elective capacity. The exemption of the judges from that is quite dangerous enough. I know of no safe depository of the ultimate powers of the society, but the people themselves..." -- *Letter to Mr. Jarvis, Sept, 1820*[95]

Always keenly aware that an educated populace was essential for holding onto a republic. He founded the University of Virginia, designed the buildings, oversaw construction, planned the curriculum and the courses of study. On the fiftieth anniversary of the signing of the Declaration, Jefferson was to be the guest of honor at the celebration at the University, but ill health prevented it, he sent a letter in his place. As fate would have it, he died on that historical day of observance, only hours before John Adams, now ninety years old died as well.

As he directed, the engraving on his tombstone says:

Here Lies
Thomas Jefferson
author of the Declaration of American Independence
of the Statute of Virginia for religious freedom
and the father of the University of Virginia.

"The God who gave us life, gave us liberty at the same time."
from "A Summary View of the Rights of British America" - 1774
Thomas Jefferson

"I prefer the tumult of liberty to the quiet of servitude."
Thomas Jefferson- letter to James Madison, January 30, 1787
from Latin translation:
Malo periculosam, libertatem quam quietam servitutem

"I consider the foundation of the Constitution as laid on this ground: That "all powers not delegated to the United States, by the Constitution, nor prohibited by it to the States, are reserved to the States or to the people." [10th Amendment]
"To take a single step beyond the boundaries thus specifically drawn around the powers of Congress is to take possession of a boundless field of power,
no longer susceptible of any definition."
Thomas Jefferson letter to George Washington 1791

"I would rather be exposed to the inconveniences attending too much liberty
than to those attending too small a degree of it."
Thomas Jefferson letter to Archibald Stuart, December 23, 1791

"I have sworn upon the altar of God,
external hostility against every form of tyranny
over the mind of man."
Thomas Jefferson letter to Dr. Benjamin Rush - September 23, 1800

"The last hope of human liberty in this world rests on us.
We ought, for so dear a state to sacrifice
every attachment and every enmity."
Thomas Jefferson letter to William Duane March 28, 1811

"No man has greater confidence
than I have, in the spirit of the people."
Thomas Jefferson to *James Monroe,* 1814

James Madison

"The Father of the Constitution"
Fourth President of the USA

The role James Madison held in establishing a new kind of government has few equals. He was a man of exceptional wisdom in concert with his tireless pledge for liberty and self government, accompanied by a fervent devotion to the creation of America's representative republic. Madison was an intellectual giant and a revolutionary statesman of the highest order. His often overlooked contributions to the American political landscape before his presidency outweighed what he accomplished during and after his role as Chief Executive.

He was born March 16, 1751, at Port Conway, Virginia and grew up the first of twelve children of which five would die in infancy, on the family plantation in Montpelier. He read the books in his father's library and by age eleven he was tutored by Donald Robertson and quickly learned literature, algebra, geometry, Latin, Greek, and French. Short, slight of build and shy at the age of eighteen he rode horseback to Princeton New Jersey where he entered the college there. The College of New Jersey was considered best for young James by his father and tutor for its high moral and religious principles.

He studied under the guidance of college president and Scottish Presbyterian minister, Dr. John Witherspoon, a future signatory of the Declaration of Independence and the only active clergyman to do so. Witherspoon was schooled in Scotland and was influenced by the thinkers of the Scottish Enlightenment and the works of Cicero, Hume, and John Locke, whose political philosophy mirrored his own and found its way into his teachings. Witherspoon as well as his students such as Henry Lee, Aaron Burr, Gunning Bedford Jr. would go on to play important roles in American political leadership.

Madison's commitment to his studies completed his four year curriculum in two years, received his diploma yet stayed on another six months to study Hebrew and theology Dr. Witherspoon. This overwork led to a severe nervous disorder that lasted many months.

By 1773 he studied law and was witness to the brewing revolution and the merits of freedom and self government. He cheered the actions of the Bostonians over the tea act and saw the distress of King George III Coercive Acts, but it was the cause of religious freedom that ignited a passion in young James for rebellion. He was elected in 1775 to the Orange County Committee of Safety and in 1776 he became a delegate to the Virginia Convention and General Assembly in Williamsburg, where he was put on a committee to formulate a new constitution and declaration of rights for the new government for Virginia. His contribution was the demand for religious freedom, it was in that committee that he met and became a loyal friend and ally of Thomas Jefferson. His articulation skills were highly admired and he was elected to the Council of State where he worked with governor Patrick Henry, a radical revolutionary and founding father who earlier spoke passionately to the Virginia legislature, "Is life so dear, or peace so sweet, as to be purchased at the price of chains and slavery? Forbid it, Almighty God! I know not what course others may take; but as for me, give me liberty or give me death!" A speech that mobilized Virginians against the British militia. The revolutionary wartime demands on the Council provided Madison the experience of dealing with finance and taxation, army and navy supplies, Indian affairs and the like. Later, Madison was elected as a Virginia delegate to the Continental Congress in 1779 where he worked with the new governor Thomas Jefferson. A respectful collaboration and friendship developed between the two that would last to their deaths. Two Virginians that would, through their thoughts, deeds, and actions would contribute to change a nation and challenge the world.

Soon after the war, the weakness of the Articles of Confederation became clearly evident. They proved good enough to unify thirteen colonies against a common enemy but feeble at controlling interstate trade and commerce. They could make laws but had no power to enforce them, request money to pay national debts but had no means of collecting it. Central government weakness was on display and soon foreign nations took advantage by limiting trade and failing to recognize the new congress as a government at all, even Barbary pirates threatened and overtook American ships and crew without fear of retaliation. A Constitutional Convention to establish the rules of the new nation were to be decided by delegates entering Philadelphia in May of 1787. The honorable George Washington left retirement at Mount Vernon and presided over the convention.

James, now thirty-six years old was the experienced delegate from Virginia who authored the Virginia Plan, the framework for the gathering. At five foot six inches, and reserved in voice, Madison made up for what he lacked in stature, by demonstrating a knowledge of the great thinkers of the Scottish Enlightenment as well as present and past monarchies, democracies and republics, such as ancient Greece and Rome, their strengths and failures.

In establishing the Constitution he was an energetic advocate for a strong central government with coequal branches equally sharing the control and power. His devotion to the cause and sense that the future of America depended on the outcome of what would take place within the walls of the State House, his daily notes of the debates provided the only known historical source of the proceedings (in keeping with the pledge of secrecy, these were not published until 1840, four years after his death).[96]

The impact of Baron de Montesquieu can be found in one of Madison's writings entitled, *Spirit of Government*. In it he wrote; "Montesquieu has resolved the great operative principles of government into fear, honor, and virtue, applying the first to pure despotism, the second to regular monarchies, and the third to republics. The portion of truth blended with the ingenuity of this system, sufficiently justifies the admiration based on its author."[97]

Weeks of argument centered on every possible circumstance surrounding the power of the central government, states rights, the limits of the Executive branch and state representation through their citizenry, some even put forth the notion that the chief Executive should serve a lifetime appointment, like a monarch. One of the largest pitfalls was the uncertainty of state representation in Congress. Larger states wanted more representation based on population. The smaller states were against it as their voice would be diminished, they wanted equal representation. The adoption of the 'Connecticut Plan' solved the problem by creating two houses of Congress, The House of Representatives and the Senate. The House of Representatives was filled by elected state leaders based on population. The Senate would be composed of two delegates from each state regardless of the size. The compromise satisfied all. Likewise the slavery question created a divide. Northern states looked to abolish slavery while the Southern states economy depended upon them. By counting slaves as three-fifths of an individual, designed to penalize the slaveholder and not dehumanize the slave, and equally as important, it reduced the representation of the slave states and proportioned its share of taxes. Borrowing from John Locke's idea that the purpose of government is to protect the rights of it's citizens, the Constitution outlined in detail, the limits the new government would have on its inhabitants. It would consist of three coequal branches of government, the Executive, Legislative and Judicial. State chosen Electors whose numbers are equal to its representation in Congress, would be enacted to choose a President based on the votes of the citizens. On September 17, 1787, the Constitution of the United States was adopted by the delegates and needed ratification by only nine of the thirteen states.

At the conclusion of the Constitutional Convention, Madison penned to his friend Thomas Jefferson, now overseas as the ambassador to France, a detailed summary of the proceedings in a letter dated October 24, 1787. In part he wrote; "This ground work being laid, the great objects which presented themselves were 1. To unite a proper energy in the Executive and proper stability in the Legislative departments, with the essential characters of Republican Government. 2. To draw the line of demarcation which would give the Central Government every power requisite for general purposes, and leave to the States every power which might be most beneficially administered by them. 3. To provide for the different interests of different parts of the Union. 4. To adjust the clashing pretensions of the large and small states, each of these objects were pregnant with difficulties. The whole of them together formed a task more difficult than can be well conceived by those who were not concerned in the execution of it. Adding to these considerations, the natural diversity of human opinions on all new and complicated subjects, it is impossible to consider the degree of concord which ultimately prevailed as less than a miracle."[98]

Antifederalists opposed the new Constitution on the basis of they believed state rights and individual rights would be totally diminished. Patrick Henry was the most audible critic. Rallying against its ratification, he believed a monarchy would result from a too powerful central government. George Mason, the delegate from Virginia and author of the 1776 '*Virginia Declaration of Rights*' along with Elbridge Gerry from Massachusetts were persuasive voices at the convention, dead set against signing the Constitution unless a 'bill of rights' for the people were added to it. The defenders of the Constitution were called the Federalists and the collaboration of John Jay, Alexander Hamilton, and James Madison (using the pseudonym "Publius") in producing *The Federalist Papers*, a series of eighty-five published articles that explained the groundbreaking features of the Constitution made great strides in justifying their positions. In *Federalist No. 10* authored by Madison, he stated the advantage of a large republic is better equipped in dealing with troublesome factions as well as the setbacks of pure democracy. This was plain as day after reading *Idea of a Commonwealth* by the

Scottish philosopher David Hume. In *Federalist 10* he explained, "....democracies have ever been spectacles of turbulence and contention; have ever been found incompatible with personal security or the rights of property; and have in general been as short in their lives as they have been violent in their deaths."[99] "In the next place, as each representative will be chosen by a greater number of citizens in the large than in the small republic, it will be more difficult for unworthy candidates to practice with success the vicious arts by which elections are too often carried; and the suffrages of the people being more free, will be more likely to centre in men who possess the most attractive merit and the most diffusive and established characters."[100]   He also worried over the "tyranny of the majority" based on his (and John Locke's) realistic understanding of the inherent conflicts in society expressed by Madison who considered "the various and unequal distribution of property" the "most common and durable source of factions."[101]

Federalist No. 51 laid out the composition of the new government by explaining the separate but equal Executive, Legislative and Judicial branches.   This is vital to preserving liberty and protecting the rights of the people. "If men were angels, no government would be necessary. If angels were to govern men, neither external nor internal controls on government would be necessary. In framing a government which is to be administered by men over men, the great difficulty lies in this: you must first enable the government to control the governed; and in the next place oblige it to control itself. A dependence on the people is, no doubt, the primary control on the government..."[102] Madison having won a seat in the House of Representatives, drafted the outline of the first ten amendments to the Constitution, which would become known as The Bill of Rights. It must be known that Madison and his fellow Federalists were concerned about including a 'bill of rights' as they reasoned these rights may be confused as coming from the government instead of being 'natural law.' Why set them down again when the words from the Declaration of Independence, "endowed by their Creator with certain inalienable rights" did so. Also there was concern that any right not listed, may not be protected. However Madison changed his mind by concluding their insertion would demonstrate to the public a knowledge of their individual liberty and a reason to defend them.

The *Bill of Rights* were introduced in September 1789, less than four months after the election of George Washington, to herald the 'natural rights' of all Americans, to quell the concerns of the antifederalists, and blaze the trail to ratification to all the states. Originally twelve amendments were proposed, the first two were not ratified. The ten amendments confirmed the limits of the new government and safeguarded the fundamental freedoms of the individual such as the freedom of speech, religion, the press and the right to bear arms. It prevented the quartering of troops, protected against unreasonable search and seizure, allows for the right of due process by law, and trial by jury, and proclaim the powers of States and people. The *Bill of Rights* were ratified on December 15, 1791. Our U.S. Constitution was undoubtably the finest piece of parchment paper the world has ever witnessed. Beyond the words in the preamble; 'We the People of the United States, in order to form a more perfect Union,...' there lies the rules and regulations to allow an informed American people to decide on the course their government will take, not the other way around, and in addition, an amendment mechanism was put in place that could allow for changes that in time may prove necessary. Madison knew as did many of the founding fathers that there existed a human flaw that the desire to obtain power and dominate others was a fact of life. This document guarded against self imposed tyranny by a strong central government. George Washington was present during Madison's articulate debates on the Constitution and referred to him for advice often during his presidency.
In 1794 he married Dolley Payne Todd and left the House of Representatives in 1797 after eight years of service, disgusted with the John Jay treaty with England. During our American

Revolution, France was undergoing its own revolution. The French people rose up against King Louis XVI and large portions of his army joined the rebellion. The King and his Queen, Marie Antoinette were overrun and beheaded. The old French methods were so reviled, riotous mobs created a bloody reign of terror that lasted for years and caused the death of thousands. After France became a republic, Frenchmen surged into outside European countries to preach the cause of freedom. Fearing that similar rebellions could topple their kings and regimes, war was declared on France by a combination of European powers led by Great Britain. The newly formed United States remained neutral. Great Britain was infuriated, believing Americans were blood relations and spoke the same language should come to their aid. France was outraged as well, reminding the American leadership that several years earlier they assisted them with money, men and ships to help them gain their independence. American cargo and trading ships and their crews became the victims of their ire and were taken as prizes with no discussion of justice. To relieve the angry concerns of the American people, Washington sent John Jay, author of the *Federalist Papers* and the first Chief Justice to England to arrange for a treaty to dissolve the situation. He received few concessions from England, no release of the men and ships, no agreement to free the oceans for safe passage of our sea vessels. England decided only to give up the forts they occupied following the revolution. James Madison was infuriated at the terms of the treaty. Likewise, the 'Alien and Sedition Laws' under the presidency of John Adams were deemed unconstitutional, and Madison's pen warned of his concerns, "...this bill contains other features, still more alarming and dangerous. It dispenses with the trial by jury; it violates the judicial system; it confounds legislative, executive, and judicial powers; it punishes without trial; and bestows upon the President despotic power over a numerous class of men."[103]

He became Thomas Jefferson's Secretary of State in 1801 and served with Jefferson for his two terms in office. During this time he oversaw the monumental Louisiana Purchase. In 1809 he was inaugurated the forth President of the United States. His administration was plagued by foreign policy missteps. The war in Europe continued and along with it came blockades of ports. Americans attempting to squeeze through the blockades were overrun with their captured crewmen forced to serve on England's ships. When the captain of the American ship *Chesapeake* refused to be boarded, the British opened fire killing twenty sailors, they boarded the ship took four sailors prisoners killing three. This event lead to the war of 1812 also known as "Mister Madison's War." British troops stormed Washington DC in August 1814. Just ahead of the invading army, President Madison was out rallying troops, and seeing the situation as serious, he sent word to his wife Dolley to flee the Executive mansion. She heeded his words, but not before she saved the Gilbert Stuart painted portrait of General George Washington. One month later the British attack on Fort McHenry in Baltimore harbor spawned our national anthem, "The Star Spangled Banner" penned by lawyer Francis Scott Key.

The Battle of New Orleans in January 1815 was a crushing American victory led by General Andrew Jackson ending the war a month later. Unbeknownst to those soldiers, a peace treaty had been drafted weeks earlier on Christmas Eve. The 'Second War for Independence' ended with the Treaty of Ghent signed in February 1815. As a result, America proved once again to Great Britain that we were a force to be reckoned with and trade and commerce became agreeable. After leaving the office of the presidency he retired to Montpelier. Following the death of Thomas Jefferson on July 4, 1826, he took over the office as second President of the University of Virginia, and would hold that title until his death.

He attended a convention to rewrite the Virginia Constitution. In the autumn of 1834, he composed a letter entitled, "*Advice To My Country*," in this written communication he pronounced his heartfelt desire, "the advice nearest to my heart and deepest in my convictions is that the Union of the States be cherished and perpetuated."[104]

When James Madison died in 1836 at the age of eighty-five he was the last surviving member of the Constitutional Convention. He was buried on his Montpelier plantation. The Congress paid their respects to this champion of freedom by shrouding the chairs of the Speaker of the House and Senate president in black and wore black crepe armbands for thirty days.

"Americans have the right and advantage of being armed-unlike
the citizens of other countries whose governments are afraid
to trust the people with arms."
James Madison- The Federalist No. 46

In framing a government which is to be administered
by men over men, the great difficulty lies in this:
you must first enable the government to control the governed;
and in the next place oblige it to control itself.
James Madison- Federalist No. 51, Feb. 6, 1788

"..Liberty may be endangered by the abuse of liberty,
as well as by the abuses of power.."
James Madison- Federalist No. 63

"Where an excess of power prevails, property of no sort is duly
respected. No man is safe in his opinions, his person,
his faculties, or his possessions."
James Madison- Papers March 29, 1792

"We are teaching the world the great truth
that Governments do better without Kings and Nobles
than with them.
The merit will be doubled by the other lesson that
Religion flourishes in greater purity, without
than with the aid of Government."
James Madison- letter to Edward Livingston July 10, 1822

"The right of the people to keep and bear...arms
shall not be infringed. A well regulated militia, composed of the
body of the people, trained to arms,
is the best and most natural defense of a free country..."
James Madison, I Annals of Congress 434 June 8, 1789

I believe there are more instances of the abridgment of the
freedom of the people by gradual and silent encroachments of
those in power, than by violent and sudden usurpations.
*James Madison speech at the Virginia Convention
to ratify the Federal Constitution, Jun. 6, 1788*

Alexis de Tocqueville

Alexis de Tocqueville was born July 29, 1805, in Paris, France, the third son of aristocratic parents. Schooled until he was sixteen by his own father's tutor, an elderly Catholic priest named Abbe LeSueur, he entered the College Royale in the northeastern city of Metz. For two years he studied philosophy and at eighteen he returned to Paris to study law, as was the tradition of his family. When Alexis reached twenty-one he, like his father, entered civil employment and became a magistrate at the Versailles court of law. It was here that he met Gustav Beaumont who would become a traveling companion and lifelong friend. Events in France were noteworthy as the July Revolution of 1830 saw the ascendency of Louis-Philippe to the throne and the change in power jeopardized Tocqueville's position. A generation before, his maternal grandmother and aunt were executed, his own parents narrowly escaped beheading by guillotine during the Reign of Terror of the French Revolution. The American model of government intrigued Alexis, to the point that he wanted the study it up close. He presented the excuse to study the prison system there in order to obtain passage for him and Gustav. In the spring 1831, after a thirty-seven day voyage, the twenty-five year old Tocqueville entered America. Warmly received throughout their journey, Tocqueville met with ex-president John Quincy Adams and current president Andrew Jackson. The last surviving signer of the Declaration of Independence, Charles Carroll of Carrollton, Maryland, granted them an audience as well as bankers, lawyers, settlers and prisoners. His observations and interviews provided the framework for what was to become a major literary accomplishment.

Democracy in America appeared in two volumes, Part I in 1835 and Part II in 1840 and was a compilation of sociology and political observances he noted as he traveled around the United States. It was a classic mostly optimistic commentary of our government from the eyes of a foreigner and touched on societal subjects as race and religion, class structure and money, the judicial system and role of government. The future of America showed serious pitfalls down the road. In a nation conceived on liberty for all, he also witnessed the hypocrisy of slavery and predicted the coming conflict between slaves and anti-abolitionist slave owners which did evolve into the War between the States in 1861. On the subject of centralization, he insisted that in the wrong hands (a tyrannous majority) could be fatal to liberty, while emphasizing that no such threat yet existed in the U.S. He was a warm admirer of American federalism and local-self government, and his doctrine of decentralization was perhaps the most characteristic part of his message.[105]

Tocqueville's insight made him cognizant of the importance of moral qualities of the individuals that make up a democratic government and he placed his hopes in education of the people in order to comprehend and foresee the invisible shackles of tyranny on the judgement and conduct of the society. In *Democracy in America,* he warned of "Unlimited power is in itself, a bad and dangerous thing: human beings are not competent to exercise it with discretion."

"Over this kind of men stands an immense, protective power which is alone responsible for securing their enjoyment and watching over their fate. That power is absolute, thoughtful of detail, orderly, provident, and gentle. It would resemble parental authority if, fatherlike, it tried to prepare its charges for a man's life, but on the contrary, it only tries to keep them in perpetual childhood. It likes to see the citizens enjoy themselves, provided that they think of nothing but enjoyment. It gladly works for their happiness but wants to be the sole agent and judge thereof. It provides for their security, foresees and supplies their necessities, facilitates their pleasures, manages their principal concerns, dissects their industry, makes rules for their testaments, and divides their inheritances. Why should it not entirely relieve them of the trouble of thinking and all the cares of living? Thus it daily makes the exercise of free choice less useful and rarer, restricts the activity of free will within a narrower compass, and little by little robs each citizen of the proper use of his own faculties. Equality has prepared men for this, predisposing them to endure it and often even regard it as beneficial. Having thus taken each citizen in turn in its powerful grasp and shaped him to its will, government then extends its embrace to include the whole of society. It covers the whole of social life with a network of petty, complicated rules that are both minute and uniform, though which men of the greatest originality and the most vigorous temperament cannot force their heads above the crowd. It does not break men's will, but softens, bends, and guides it; it seldom enjoins, but often inhibits, action; it does not destroy anything, but prevents much being born; it is not at all tyrannical, but it hinders, restrains, enervates, stifles, and stultifies so much that in the end each nation is no more than a flock of timid and hardworking animals with the government as its shepherd."[106]

"If ever freedom is lost in America that will be due to omnipotence of the majority driving the minorities to desperation and forcing them to appeal to physical force. We may then see anarchy, but it will have come as the result of despotism."[107] Tocqueville was in no doubt, a dedicated admirer of several of our founding fathers, referring to James Madison's thoughts in *Federalist No. 51* as well as the ideas and opinions of Thomas Jefferson. He regarded Jefferson "as the most powerful apostle of democracy there has ever been."[108] Morality was front and center in places of worship and both Tocqueville and Beaumont were impressed by the fact that American republicans saw religion as an essential support to democracy and liberty.[109] The American separation of church and state played a strong role on the strength of religion. He saw the importance of the relationship between humanity and God, their souls and duty to God and to their fellow man.

He saw the value of religion in forming a moral society and hence a republican democracy. In his tour de force he observed;

"I sought for the greatness and genius of America in her
commodius harbors and her ample rivers -- and it was not there,
in her fertile hills and boundless forests -- and it was not there,
in her rich mines and vast world commerce -- and it was not
there, in her democratic Congress and her matchless
Constitution and it was not there. Not until I went to the
churches of America and heard her pulpits aflame with
righteousness did I understand the secret of her genius and
power. America is great because she is good, and if America
ever ceases to be good, American will cease to be great."

In regards to commerce, which revolved mostly around
seafaring vessels, Alexis reported on the American national
character:
"Any American, taken at random, will be found to be hot in his
desires, enterprising, adventurous, above all an innovator. This
spirit stows itself, indeed, in all he does; it is part of his laws, his
politics, his religious doctrines, his economic and social theories,
his private business; it goes everywhere with him, to the depths
of the forests as much as to the heart of the cities. The same
spirit, applied to seaborne trade, makes the American sail faster
and sell cheaper than all other merchants."[110] Tocqueville, like
others who understand freedom, proclaimed the virtues of
individualism and their 'pursuits of happiness' contribute
greatly to economic success.

He died young at age fifty-three of tuberculosis on April 16, 1859
and was buried in Normandy France.

"Liberty cannot be established without morality,
nor morality without faith."
Alexis de Tocqueville - Democracy in America Vol.I

"Despotism may govern without faith, but liberty cannot."
Alexis de Tocqueville- Democracy in America, Volume I Chapter XVII

"The greatness of America lies not
in being more enlightened than any other nation,
but rather in her ability to repair her faults."
Alexis de Tocqueville- Democracy in America, Vol. I Chapter XIII

"In America the principle of the sovereignty of the people is
neither barren nor concealed, as it is with some other nations; it
is recognized by the customs and proclaimed by the laws; it
spreads freely, and arrives without impediment at its most
remote consequences If there is a country in the world where the
doctrine of the sovereignty of the people can be fairly
appreciated, where it can be studied in its application to the
affairs of society, and where its dangers and its advantages may
be judged, that country is assuredly America."
Alexis de Tocqueville 'Democracy in America' Chapter IV

"The Americans combine the notions of Christianity
and of liberty so intimately in their minds, that it is impossible to
make them conceive the one without the other…
Religion in America…must…be regarded as the foremost
of the political institutions of that country."
Alexis de Tocqueville 'Democracy in America' Chapter IV

Abraham Lincoln

The Great Emancipator
Honest Abe
The Liberator

There is little doubt that of all the occupants who have held the title of president of the United States, the name of Abraham Lincoln ascends above them all as the most revered. His unyielding devotion to hold the country together during its most trying times of a bloody civil war and with a steadfast adherence to the founding principles has placed his life and presidency into immortal homage. Rising from humble beginnings, this self taught man educated himself to convey and communicate to his fellow countrymen a love for all mankind and a devotion to the principles of the founding fathers to reunite a divided country.

He was born in a small log cabin on February 12, 1809, in Hardin County Kentucky, the second child to Thomas and Nancy Hanks Lincoln. His sister Sarah was born two years and two days earlier. Named after his grandfather who was killed by Indians when his father was six years old, the young Abraham was required at a very young age to perform all the manual labor necessary to keep the family warm and fed. When better farmland was found in Indiana, the family loaded all their belongings on a raft and navigated on the Ohio River to Little Pigeon Creek, where a temporary shelter was constructed until Thomas and young Abraham could construct a new log cabin. They lived there only a year when his mother died of milk poisoning. Nancy's sister and her husband living nearby, having met the same fate days earlier, concluded with his cousin Dennis moving into the Lincoln cabin. The loss of his mother was shattering to Sarah and Abraham. Thomas remarried a woman named Sara Bush Johnston the widowed mother of three children and together the seven family members crammed into the small log shelter. Sarah adored Abraham, and wholeheartedly supported his craving for books and an eagerness for knowledge, to escape the constant manual labor for basic survival. Unlike his new tender mother, who influenced his sense of humor, his father was a harsh taskmaster, making him feel like he was a slave to his demands. He insisted his son work his family farm and in addition work for neighbors and then turn over every penny that he earned, to solve Thomas Lincoln's financial problems.[111] Those early deep rooted memories had much to do with his later views on the heinous acts of human bondage.

Having little formal education, (less then a year in his lifetime) Abraham managed to teach himself reading, writing and spelling. He borrowed books and read whenever he could between chores, his favorites being *Aesop's Fables*, *The Life of Washington*, *Arabian Nights* and *Robinson Crusoe*.[112] He would face personal tragedy again when his sister Sarah, now married, died at age twenty-one during childbirth. At twenty-one he came to Illinois where he helped his father build another log cabin and split rails for fencing. Soon after he settled in New Salem, where he found work as a clerk in a general store. His duties there brought him in contact with many of the towns folks who were attracted to Lincoln's honest work and ability to seize their attention with jokes and vivid storytelling. His quest for knowledge and an increasing interest of law brought him into the local court where he learned to draw up simple legal documents and become skilled at debates. When the Black Hawk War broke out, Lincoln enlisted and was chosen captain of his unit, although he saw no fighting during this Indian land dispute, he was attracted to the leadership role he held. He returned home and ran for the state legislature with only two weeks before election day. He lost that race and returned to the general store. Friends helped him become the postmaster in New Salem which, as an added benefit to being paid, brought him in contact with various newspapers which he readily absorbed.

With his confidence growing he ran for the state legislature again and won at the age of twenty-five. He read everything he could about law and after getting reelected to the state legislature two years later, he left New Salem for good and headed to Springfield, obtained his law license on March 1, 1837, and commenced practice. In the legislature he became a member of the Whig Party and voted against proslavery resolutions, a brave move as he was well in the minority in his thinking. The firestorm surrounding slavery had begun to build bitter walls between the North and South. Lincoln believed the nation was best served proceeding with "reason, cold, calculating, unimpassioned reason."[113] In Springfield, Stephen A. Douglas, a Democrat attorney in the legislature as well, became one of Lincoln's political rivals.

He met Mary Todd, a well educated young woman from a wealthy family and ten years younger than Abraham. They both shared strong personalities and a love of politics and were married in November 1842, with their first son Robert joining them the following August. His unique charm and personality and love of practicing law continued to grow. He earned two more terms in the legislature and he opened his own law firm leaving it in charge of his junior partner William H. Herndon when he decided to run for Congress. Another son, Edward, was born in March 1846 and he was elected to Congress five months later, beating his democratic opponent, Peter Cartwright, a popular Methodist circuit rider and evangelist. During their campaigns, Cartwright labeled Lincoln an "infidel" knowing that he did not belong to any Christian church even though Lincoln was an avid reader of the Bible. There is a popular story of an interchange between the two candidates in church during the campaign. Cartwright, after failing to get a response from his opponent whether or not he wanted to go to heaven or hell, said, "May I inquire of you Mr. Lincoln, where you are going?" "I am going to Congress" was Lincoln's reply.[114]
He lived in Washington D.C. during his two year term and after completion, returned back to Springfield to his law practice. Tragedy struck again, when Eddie almost four, died after two months of illness, most likely tuberculosis, although it may have been a hereditary disease. Abraham was understandably

depressed and Mary's mourning developed into erratic behavior. Ten months later, another son, William was born and a fourth son Thomas, nicknamed 'Tad' was born in April 1853 joined the household.

The return to public life can best be revealed in a letter Lincoln wrote to his good friend Jesse W. Fell, "...From 1849 to 1854, both inclusive, practiced law more assiduously than ever before-- Always a Whig in politics, and generally on the Whig electoral tickets, making active canvasses--I was losing interest in politics, when the repeal of the Missouri Compromise aroused me again..."[115] The Missouri Compromise had made slavery illegal in those territories in 1820, but now that area under the Kansas-Nebraska Act, overturned the compromise to become slave states. Stephen A. Douglas, now a senator, had sided with this new resolution, and antislavery abolitionists were furious. The Republican party was formed in 1854 to stop the steady expansion of slavery and the old Whig Party soon dissolved. Lincoln joined the Republicans in 1856. Violence broke out between pro-slavery and abolitionists groups and the dividing line between these factions grew. The Dred Scott Supreme Court decision in 1857 tightened the tensions, when Supreme Court Justice Roger B. Taney ruled that a slave named Dred Scott, whose master moved into a 'free' state could not sue for his freedom. Deemed by many to be the worst Supreme Court decision in history, it established that black slaves were not citizens and a slave was a slave no matter where they lived. The antislavery North's ire was boosted. Lincoln reentered politics, challenging Senator Douglas for the seat in the Senate in June 1858. His nomination speech centered on his idea that "A house divided cannot stand. I believe this government cannot endure permanently half slave and half free." Confronting the short, rotund Douglas, known as 'The Little Giant,' face-to-face in a series of seven debates throughout Illinois on the slavery issue. Douglas was the leading supporter of popular sovereignty where Lincoln defended "all men are created equal" in the

Declaration of Independence and opposed slavery as 'a moral, a social and a political wrong.'[116]

It must be noted that the general opinion of the population of the time was that blacks were inferior to whites and Lincoln was no exception to that thinking, but he passionately rejected the idea that whites had the right to rule blacks. The great black abolitionist, Frederick Douglass had many encounters with Lincoln throughout his presidency and remembered him, "In all my interviews with Mr. Lincoln I was impressed with his entire freedom from popular prejudice against the colored race. He was the first great man that I talked with in the United States freely, who in no single instance reminded me of the difference between himself and myself, of the difference of color... I felt as though I was in the presence of a big brother, and that there was safety in his atmosphere."[117]

The fondness Lincoln had for the Declaration of Independence, the Constitution and its authors was no secret and was revealed in many of his speeches. He understood that holding together the great republic that they had forged was paramount to his decision making. He knew that his compatriots were first 'political slaves' to King George III and pursued freedom above all else, how could this not be so for the black citizens? At Lewistown, Illinois just days before the Lincoln-Douglas debates, he beseeched his onlookers to return to the words in the Declaration.

"...representatives in old Independence Hall, said to the whole world of men: 'We hold these truths to be self-evident: that all men are created equal; that they are endowed by their Creator with certain inalienable rights; that among these are life, liberty, and the pursuit of happiness.' This was their majestic interpretation of the economy of the Universe. This was their lofty, and wise, and noble understanding of the justice of the Creator to his creatures. Yes, gentlemen, to all his creatures, to the whole great family of man. In their enlightened belief, nothing stamped with the Divine image and likeness was sent into the world to be trodden on and degraded, and imbruted by its fellows. They grasped not only the whole race of man then living, but they reached forward and seized upon the farthest posterity. They erected a beacon to guide their children, and their children's children, and the countless myriads who should inhabit the earth in other ages. Wise statesmen as they were, they knew the tendency of prosperity to breed tyrants, and so they established these great self-evident truths, that when in the distant future some man, some faction, some interest, should set up the doctrine that none but rich men, or none but white men, or none but Anglo-Saxon white men, were entitled to life, liberty, and the pursuit of happiness, their posterity might look up again to the Declaration of Independence and take courage to renew the battle which their fathers began, so that truth and justice and mercy and all the humane and Christian virtues might not be extinguished from the land; so that no man would hereafter dare to limit and circumscribe the great principles on which the temple of liberty was being built...do not destroy that immortal emblem of Humanity — the Declaration of American Independence."

Lincoln lost that Senate race narrowly but the debates brought him into national recognition and he was invited to speak at the Cooper Union in New York City in early 1860. His closing remark, "Let us have faith that right makes might, and in that faith, let us to the end, dare to do our duty as we understand it." made such an impact he was nominated to run for the office of the president. The Democrats had two candidates to run for the highest office, Stephen Douglas and John Breckinridge, who was vice president to President James Buchanan. A forth candidate, John Bell from the Constitutional Union Party ran as well. The Republican Party campaign slogan 'Wide Awake' was used to promote Lincoln.[118]

In November of 1860, Lincoln won, becoming the sixteenth president without a single vote from the South, an outcome that infuriated the slave states. Their newspapers rang out with chilling words such as, "the evil days..are upon us" and "the South should arm at once." Between the time of the election results and four months later on March 4, 1861, at Lincoln's inauguration, two changes took place, seven southern states seceded from the Union forming the Confederate States of America, under their president, Jefferson Davis and Lincoln changed his appearance by hiding his boney face with a beard. The facial hair was recommended in a letter from a little girl named Grace Bedell. The Lincoln family left Springfield and traveled by train to Washington, DC under threat of assassination. They entered the city during the dark of evening. At his inaugural speech, Lincoln spoke of the troubles that awaited the country and his duty to uphold the Constitution, "... I hold that in contemplation of universal law and of the Constitution, the Union of these States is perpetual. Perpetuity is implied, if not expressed, in the fundamental law of all national governments. It is safe to assert that no government proper ever had a provision in its organic law for its own termination...one of the declared objects for ordaining and establishing the Constitution was *"to form a more perfect Union."* But if destruction of the Union by one or by a part only of the States be lawfully possible, the Union is *less* perfect than before the Constitution, having lost the vital element of perpetuity...We are not enemies, but friends. We must not be enemies. Though passion may have strained it must not break our bonds of affection..."

The South scoffed him. Lincoln's attempt to hold the country together and avoid conflict fell on deaf ears. Several weeks later on April 12, the Civil War began when the South fired upon Fort Sumter in the harbor of Charleston, South Carolina, forcing it into Confederate hands within two days. Lincoln called for a militia and 75,000 men volunteered. Events moved quickly with Virginia seceding from the Union and establishing the Confederate capital at Richmond. Arkansas, Tennessee and North Carolina soon followed Virginia's lead and Union troops moved in quickly to protect Washington, DC. The troops in the North grew, ships were dispatched to place blockades around southern ports and the writ of 'hapeas corpus' was suspended to arrest any southern sympathizers. The suspension of 'hapeas corpus' was politically extreme. It eliminated the right of a court to insist that a citizen who has been arrested to be either charged with a crime or released and in this case allowed the military to hold individuals indefinitely where martial law had been imposed. It started in Maryland where Lincoln doubted the loyalty of state officials who burned wooden bridges, preventing Federal troops from crossing over them on the way to protect Washington D.C. The action was seen as a pro-Confederate plot. Lincoln authorized General Scott to suspend hapeas corpus in Maryland, the rest of the East would soon follow.

Lincoln was careful to explain this conflict was about keeping the union together and not to malign four northern slave-holding border states, Maryland, Delaware, Kentucky and Missouri. Lincoln understood that losing these states through secession would seriously jeopardize northern strength, he also knew that although he opposed slavery, he also believed it was unconstitutional to interfere with states rights. He was committed to stop the expansion of slavery.

The Battle of Bull Run on July 21, 1861, was the first major battle of the Civil War and the defeat suffered by the Union troops crushed any idea that this conflict would be over soon. The casualties were disturbing, so George B. McClellan was made commander of the troops on the Potomac River to protect the capital. McClellan was an excellent organizer but an unenthusiastic fighter, and many months went by without him taking the battle to the Confederates; time wasted that allowed them to create havoc. President Lincoln buried himself into his work, reading and responding to war department reports and gaining experience as commander-in-chief. He was taking a great interest from the field reports of Brigadier General Ulysses S. Grant, who led his union troops in successful triumphs over the Confederates by capturing two of their forts, Fort Henry and Fort Donelson in western Tennessee. These victories had the added bonus of opening the Cumberland River, a strategic entrance point to the South.

At the White House, Mary Lincoln became excessively extravagant in decorating the executive mansion, and the cost overruns weighed heavily of Lincoln's famous patience. They argued over the expense and he offered to pay back the government. He did find time during this stressful period to be with his sons, Willie and Tad. Robert Lincoln was at Harvard University. The joy the boys gave the president would be short lived. Days after Grant's taking of Fort Donelson, Willie died of typhoid fever on February 20, 1862, after weeks of illness. The loss of their second son was devastating. The president was heartbroken, he sobbed, "He was too good for this earth, it is hard, hard to have him die."[119]

Mary, grief stricken as well, could not get out of bed for a month. Abraham broke down into tears. To avoid depression over his son's passing, according to his wife, he found himself becoming closer in faith to God and devoted himself fully into reuniting the country. Combat ensued and casualties mounted into the thousands in places called Shiloh, Seven Pines, Fair Oak Station. The Seven Days Battle near Richmond Virginia found McClellan in retreat from General Lee's military expertise. The newspapers labeled McClellan as "Mac the Unready" and the general lashed out publicly at the war department, headed by Secretary Edwin Stanton and at the president himself. Lincoln knowing the misfortune of infighting within the ranks defended his secretary and general and took the blame for the squabble in a departmental meeting on August 6th. It was said that on the winding staircase of the War Department building, a young officer carrying reports to Secretary Stanton rushed along one evening taking three steps at a time, and butted his head full force into the President's body about the point of the lower vest pocket. Seeing whom he had hit, he groaned, "Ten thousand pardons." Lincoln responded: "One's enough, I wish the whole army could charge like that."[120] The recent events however, weighed on the president and Lincoln became desperate. In order to hit the South in the heart he would change the direction of the war by freeing the slaves.

*"If I could save the union without freeing any slaves, I would do it,
and if I could save it by freeing all the slaves, I would do it."*

After discussing with black leaders the idea of separating the races by relocating black citizens to the Caribbean, and elsewhere, this colonization was met with indignity from Frederick Douglass, the leading black voice of abolition. Lincoln realized his error and the Emancipation Proclamation was laid out in September 1862, to his cabinet members as a vital war measure, it outlined, "all persons held as slaves within any State or designated part of a State, the people whereof shall then be in rebellion against the United States, shall be then, thenceforward, and forever free." In short, it made slavery illegal in rebel states only.

The battle at Antietam was a union victory but McClellan's failure to pursue and finish off the rebel army was the last straw for the president. McClellan was replaced. Lincoln, however used the occasion for the win at Antietam to announce his Emancipation Proclamation. It was signed into law on January 1, 1863 and brought jubilation to abolitionists, outrage in the South and unrest to some amongst union troops, who believed that the purpose of the war had changed. There was desertion within the Union ranks. The confederate army crushed the union forces under the command of General Ambrose Burnside in one of the worst defeats in army history at Fredericksburg, Virginia, and later another brutal union defeat was presented at Chancellorville, now under the leadership of Joseph Hooker.

To gain troop strength, a union draft was put into place to recruit young men and by reason of the Emancipation Proclamation, abolitionists pushed the president into forming all black armies to fight alongside union troops. The bravery of the black regiments proved beneficial, they were excellent fighters for as a group they had the most to gain. Lincoln took notice of their valor and never mentioned colonization again. Twin victories boosted the north's morale that summer, General Pemberton surrendered the city of Vicksburg to General Grant and thus opened up the Mississippi River, and General Meade defeated Robert E. Lee at the three day battle of Gettysburg, Pennsylvania. Both came on July 4th.

The Gettysburg campaign robbed the Confederates from taking northern strongholds and the loss of life by both armies was staggering, but the war was turning the north's way. In the aftermath of the Emancipation Proclamation, Abe was quoted as saying, *"If my name ever goes into history, it will be for this act."*[121]

Lincoln, in a brief moment of elevated spirits, was impressed with a letter to him from Sarah J. Hale, the editor of the 'Lady's Book' Magazine.' The subject of her correspondence was "to have the day of our annual Thanksgiving made a National and fixed Union Festival...for some years past, there has been an increasing interest felt in our land to have the Thanksgiving held on the same day, in all the States; it now needs National recognition and authoritive fixation, only, to become permanently, an American custom and institution..." On October 3, Lincoln issued a proclamation that urged Americans to observe the last Thursday in November as a national holiday of Thanksgiving. The following month, a battlefield cemetery was dedicated at Gettysburg on November 19, 1863, and President Lincoln was invited to speak. His two minute address to the assembled crowds would be forever known as one of the most memorable speeches in American history. Following the orator Edward Everett, Lincoln rose and spoke,

"Four score and seven years ago our fathers brought forth on this continent, a new nation, conceived in Liberty, and dedicated to the proposition that all men are created equal.
Now we are engaged in a great civil war, testing whether that nation, or any nation so conceived and so dedicated, can long endure.
We are met on a great battle-field of that war.
We have come to dedicate a portion of that field, as a final resting place for those who here gave their lives that that nation might live.
It is altogether fitting and proper that we should do this.
But, in a larger sense, we can not dedicate, we can not consecrate,

we can not hallow this ground. The brave men, living and dead, who struggled here, have consecrated it, far above our poor power to add or detract. The world will little note, nor long remember what we say here, but it can never forget what they did here. It is for us the living, rather, to be dedicated here to the unfinished work which they who fought here have thus far so nobly advanced. It is rather for us to be here dedicated to the great task remaining before us that from these honored dead we take increased devotion to that cause for which they gave the last full measure of devotion that we here highly resolve that these dead shall not have died in vain, that this nation, under God, shall have a new birth of freedom and that government of the people, by the people, for the people, shall not perish from the earth."

The war pushed on through the remainder of 1863 and into 1864. Relentless, bloody and no end in sight. Locations like Chickamauga, Chattenooga, Spotsylvania, Cold Harbor and Petersburg filled the newspapers. The stench from the battlefields was unforgettable. Bullets, bayonets, and cannonball disfigured their targets beyond recognition, horseflies swarmed the discarded piles of blood-soaked limbs outside of makeshift medical tents. Devastation to homes and fields were a mainstay. The names of the war dead and the wooden coffins that followed ranged well into the thousands. More recruits were needed, and hundreds of thousands were requested. The war report images had a sickening effect on the president. He became depressed and exhausted from lack of sleep, and the evidence was plain to see in the photographs of Matthew Brady, yet he spent endless time at the War Department across from the White House, visited army hospitals, wrote letters and speeches. The presidential election were to be held despite the war and Lincoln wanted to be reelected to finish the task and restore the union with peace. He chose Andrew Johnson, a southern democrat to join his ticket. George McClellan was nominated by democrats under the influence of Copperhead policies to go against his commander-in-chief. With his popularity running low, Lincoln worried that his election loss would be his old adversary's gain and the South would gain their independence and the union would be forever divided. Union Generals Grant and William T. Sherman moved their troops into southern strongholds. Sherman's successful taking of the city of Atlanta, Georgia on September 2, 1864, propelled the morale of the people of the North and contributed enormously to the Republican success that Election Day. Lincoln beat McClellan and was reelected.

He now turned his attention to taking the war enacted Emancipation Proclamation to its rightful conclusion by abolishing slavery forever throughout the entire United States and its territories by establishing the thirteenth Amendment to the Constitution. Lincoln used all his influence to rally Congress to this cause and success came on January 31, 1865, when it passed by a vote of 119 to 56. The start of 1865 found the president of the Confederate States of America Jefferson Davis facing a situation rapidly spiraling out of control. Food and clothing shortages were forcing large numbers of his armies to abandon their weapons and head home. Riots and demonstrations broke out on southern cities. On February 3, Davis sent his Vice-President Stephens and other representatives to meet with Lincoln and his Secretary of State William H. Seward at the Hampton Roads Conference aboard the Union transport *River Queen*. He stubbornly insisted on recognition of Southern independence, which was of course unacceptable to Lincoln and the conference broke up.[122] General Sherman troops proceeded northward. A large part of Columbia, the South Carolina State capital was burned, as were other towns. When Columbia fell into the Union's hands, Charleston was evacuated and fell also.

Lincoln delivered his second inaugural speech on March 4, and appealed for unity, and openly embraced religion, having made fourteen references to God and quoted the Bible four times as well. The address ended immortally, "...With malice toward none, with charity for all, with firmness in the right as God gives us to see the right, let us strive on to finish the work we are in, to bind up the nation's wounds, to care for him who shall have borne the battle and for his widow and his orphan, to do all which may achieve and cherish a just and lasting peace among ourselves and with all nations." It was in that address that he contended that the Civil War might be the punishment of God to both the North and South for the evil of slavery and that the bloodshed might not end.[123]

The end of the war was now within reach. Richmond, the capital of the South, was abandoned after Grant defeated Lee near Petersburg. Union troops tore up the train tracks to prevent enemy reinforcements from entering. Confederate soldiers set bridges ablaze to slow the advancing union troops and winds sent the flames into many of the buildings. Richmond, was for the most part demolished. Lincoln wanted to see Richmond, and on April 4, an Army attachment on horseback, escorted him into the charred city. He was met by jubilant black citizens crowding eagerly to see "their Liberator." One man pushed a five dollar confederate note into Lincoln's hand telling him that he was saving up to buy his freedom and since Lincoln did it, the money was his. Lincoln carried the five dollar currency in his pocket from that day on to remind him of the sacrifices on both sides to obtain this historic occasion.

Days later, General Lee's forces were cut off by union troops near Appomattox Virginia and Grant asked Lee to surrender. Lee sent word that he wanted the terms of surrender and word was returned, "there is but one condition I would insist upon, namely; that the men and officers surrendered shall be disqualified from taking up arms again, against the Government of the United States."[124]

On April 9, Lee met with Grant at the Appomattox courthouse and surrendered. Lee's men were paroled to return to their homes, all equipment was surrendered, their rifles stacked, and the union issued 25,000 rations to the Confederate troops.

At long last the war was over.

The death toll was astronomical, new estimates bring the total dead to about 750,000.

Celebration rang through the streets of Washington D.C. and Lincoln spoke to the crowd from the White House on April 11. He spoke of a new unity between the North and South and a peaceful reconstruction. He spoke also of giving ex-slave citizens the right to vote, an utterance that would enrage one member of the crowd, a loyal Confederate sympathizer and well known actor named John Wilkes Booth. That claim was the last straw. His hatred for Lincoln had surpassed all reason, he plotted to kill the president.

Finally feeling relaxed, Abraham had a Cabinet meeting on the morning of Friday, April 14, and later he joined Mary on a carriage ride together. That evening they would attend Ford's Theatre. They arrived at 8:30 PM for the stage presentation of *Our American Cousin* and as they entered the presidential box overlooking the stage, the audience stood and applauded while the orchestra played 'Hail to the Chief' in honor of the president. They were accompanied by Major Henry Rathbone and Clara Harris, a friend of Mary. Booth, having retrieved his mail earlier the theatre, learned that the president would be attending the show that evening, this gave him the information he needed to get close to him. At 10:15 PM while the president sat in a rocking chair next to his wife, Booth quietly entered the box, blocked the door and shot the president in the back of his head at close range with a small derringer. The president collapsed, Mary screamed and Major Rathbone was slashed by Booth with a knife he carried. The assassin jumped from the balcony onto the stage, catching his booted spur in a decorative flag, thus badly injuring his leg upon landing, he raised his knife shouting, "Sic semper Tyrannis" which is Latin for "thus always to tyrants." With pandemonium overwhelming the crowd, Booth fled on horseback out of Washington. At the same time, co-conspirators were to kill Vice President Johnson and Secretary of State Seward, in order to create government disorder and chaos. Neither were successful. Seward was stabbed but recovered.

Lincoln was alive but unconscious and doctors summoned to his side knew the wound was incurable. He was carried to a bed in the Peterson rooming house across the street. Physicians, family and his cabinet members gathered into the parlor, the hallway and the bedroom where Lincoln clung to life until 7:22am the next morning when the Great Emancipator, struggling for breathe, took his last and died. He was fifty-six years old.

It was reported that Secretary of War Edwin M. Stanton remarked famously, "Now he belongs to the ages."

The nation mourned the passing of this incredible man who gave everything to save the country and abolish the scourge of slavery. His open casket was on public view in the White House the following Tuesday. Hundreds lined up to pay respects in the black draped room. Mary was uncontrollably grief stricken and could not attend the funeral Thursday where the casket was removed to the Capitol building, to lay in state, for additional mourners to file past. The Friday following the assassination, Lincoln's body along with the remains of his son Willie, were reverently placed on a train bound for Springfield, tracing the path he took four years earlier when he took the oath of office. The locomotive was draped in bunting, presidential flags with black fringe and on the front a portrait of Lincoln. In between Washington and Springfield, eleven more funeral events were held during the thirteen day trek traveling through major cities. Father and son were finally laid to rest on May 4th.

The gunman having escaped on horseback from Ford's theatre was soon accompanied by co-conspirator David Herold, stopping the morning after the killing to receive treatment for his mangled leg at the home of Doctor Samuel Mudd. After twelve days in hiding, on April 26, Booth was caught and killed in a struggle in a Virginia tobacco barn. Herold surrendered, but he and the other conspirators were rounded up, trials were held, and verdicts were declared. Four of them were given prison sentences and four guilty members were hung on the grounds of the Old Arsenal Penitentiary in Washington on July 7th.

Abraham Lincoln would be forever immortalized as a simple, principled man who rose from dirt floor poverty to achieve epic greatness as an eloquent speaker who could win the hearts and minds to all that heard him. A trailblazing leader dedicated to preserving the principles laid out by our founding fathers in the Declaration of Independence and the Constitution and who put the welfare of the country well above himself.

"Let reverence for the law be breathed by every American
mother to the lisping babe that prattles on her lap;
let it be taught in schools, in seminaries, and in colleges;
let it be written in primers, in spelling-books, and almanacs;
let it be preached from the pulpit, proclaimed in legislative halls,
and enforced in courts of justice. And, in short, let it become the
political religion of the nation; and let the old and the young, the
rich and the poor, the grave and the gay of all sexes and tongues
and colors and conditions, sacrifice unceasingly at its altars."
Abraham Lincoln-the Young Men's Lyceum in Springfield Illinois 1838

"Let every American, every lover of liberty, every well-wisher to
his posterity swear by the blood of the Revolution never to
violate in the least particular the laws of the country, and never
to tolerate their violation by others. As the patriots of seventy-six
did to the support of the Declaration of Independence, so to the
support of the Constitution and laws let every American pledge
his life, his property, and his sacred honor—
let every man remember that to violate the law is to trample on
the blood of his father, and to tear the charter of his own
and his children's liberty."
Abraham Lincoln-Young Men's Lyceum, Springfield, Illinois 1838

"A house divided against itself cannot stand.
I believe this government cannot endure, permanently half slave
and half free. I do not expect the Union to be dissolved — I do
not expect the house to fall —
but I do expect it will cease to be divided.
It will become all one thing or all the other."
Abraham Lincoln- Speech at Republican Convention, Springfield
Illinois, accepting the Senate nomination, June 16, 1858

"Don't interfere with anything in the Constitution.
That must be maintained, for it is the only safeguard of our
liberties. And not to Democrats alone do I make this appeal,
but to all who love these great and true principles."
Abraham Lincoln Speech at Kalamazoo, Michigan, August 27, 1856

The people of these United States are the rightful masters of
both Congresses and courts, not to overthrow the Constitution,
but to overthrow the men who pervert the Constitution.
Abraham Lincoln Speech at Cincinnati, Ohio September 17, 1859

"Neither let us be slandered from our duty by false accusations
against us, nor frightened from it by menaces of destruction to
the government nor of dungeons to ourselves.
Let us have faith that right makes might, and in that faith,
let us, to the end, dare to do our duty as we understand it."
Abraham Lincoln- Address at the Cooper Institute 1860

"I have always thought that all men should be free; but if any should be slaves, it should be first those who desire it for themselves, and secondly, those who desire it for others. When I hear anyone arguing for slavery, I feel a strong impulse to see it tried on him personally."

Abraham Lincoln- Statement to an Indiana Regiment passing through Washington, March 17, 1865

Frederick Douglass
The Lion of Anacostia

Slavery was his birthmark, freedom from oppression a long held dream. Courage comes in many forms, but the bold ability to speak out against atrocities inflicted on a certain race of people because their skin color was different was not only a gift to the black race but an inspiration to all humanity. In a tumultuous time in America, his rise from hopeless bondage to be an educated advocate for abolition is all the more glorious in his achievement to overcome the odds.

He was born Frederick Augustus Washington Bailey in Tuckahoe, Maryland, in February 1818, the slave son of Harriet Bailey and a white father of which he was unacquainted with. The exact date of his birth was unknown to him as well and together supplied a stigma that forever robbed him of his true identity. As an infant his mother, a field slave, was separated from him to work at a nearby plantation, he was taken care of by his grandmother, Betty Bailey, also a slave. He saw his mother on rare occasions when she walked twelve miles at night to lie down with him only to slip back unseen to the fields before sunrise. She would die by the time he was seven. At age six being old enough to work, he was chosen to go in the Wye House mansion owned by the wealthy plantation owner Edward Lloyd V. He was to be a companion for his twelve year old son Daniel Lloyd. Aaron Anthony was the chief overseer of the Lloyd plantation, he was Frederick's master and most likely his father. He witnessed from a hiding spot, the savage whipping of his young aunt, by Anthony, the cries of tortuous pain, the flowing blood from sliced flesh now zig zagging across her naked back and torso. Other slaves bore the scars and humiliation at the sadistic whim of the whip. Hopelessness was their existence. Human beasts of burden, cognizant of their role in society, made to feel inferior to white superiors. They had no say in what they could do or where they could go, including religious services. Families were divided up at auctions never to be seen again. These revelations sowed the seeds of a purpose driven life, to escape the dishonor of bondage. When Aaron Anthony died, his estate and belongings were equally divided between his three living children. Frederick would later recall that the slaves were put into categories of men and women, old and young, married and single ranked for valuation along with the livestock of sheep, horses and swine.

When he turned eight, he was sent to the Baltimore home of Hugh and Sophia Auld, a brother of Aaron's son-in-law named Thomas Auld. He was to be a companion for their two year old son Tommy. It was there that the "pious, warm and tenderhearted" Sophia patiently taught the light skinned slave child the alphabet and how to read. However, her husband reminded her that such instruction was unlawful and dangerous to the slave. In time she ceased to follow up in her teaching but his inquisitiveness took over, he wanted more. He reinforced his quest for knowledge with the help of white boys he befriended in the city streets. At about age twelve he was introduced to the book, *'The Columbian Orator,'* a collection of speeches, poems and dialogues. In it he read of an account between a master and his slave and the conversation regarding the runaway slave's return after the third time. "In this dialogue the whole argument in behalf of slavery was brought forward by the master, all of which was disposed of by the slave. The slave was made to say some very smart as well as impressive things to reply to his master--things which had the desired though unexpected effect; for the conversation resulted in the voluntary emancipation of the slave on the part of the master.[125] The book's content would reveal to him the blessings of knowledge and the plague of slavery. He noted that learning to read exposed him to his "wretched condition, without the remedy." To say he merely read the book would be an understatement, he memorized by heart the speeches and writings.

At fifteen he was taken out of Baltimore and returned to Thomas Auld, where he resisted his authority. His dissent found him hired out and put to work as a field hand on a farm outside of St. Michaels, Maryland. For six months he worked whenever sunlight availed itself, sustaining severe beatings and whippings from the farmer Edward Covey. On an extremely hot August afternoon he fainted from heat exhaustion and crawled to the shade of a fence post to rest, he was violently kicked in the side by Covey's boot that shook his body then kicked again. Taking up a sharp hickory stick the "heartless monster" savagely struck his skull resulting in a bloody head wound. Fearing he could be killed, he staggered for miles back to his master Thomas Auld to complain of the cruel atrocity he faced, but was met with no sympathy for his condition, going so far as to make excuses for Covey's conduct. The discussion ended when he was told to return back and take whatever discipline was handed him. When brutal punishment was to be administered for fleeing, Frederick fought back. What followed would be the focus of attention of Frederick's later writings where he recalled the two hour scuffle in '*The Narrative of the Life of Frederick Douglass*' and a later work, '*My Bondage and My Freedom*.' The fighting ceased when the bloody Covey gave up, never to physically mistreat him again, possibly ashamed that his reputation as a 'Negro breaker' was 'mastered by a boy of sixteen.' Frederick recalled the fight with Covey, "was the turning point in my life as a slave. It rekindled in my breast the smoldering embers of liberty...I was a changed being after that fight. I was nothing before; I was a Man Now. It recalled to life my crushed self-respect and my self-confidence, and inspired me with a renewed determination to be a FREEMAN."[126]

At eighteen he was again reunited with Hugh and Sophia Auld where he found work at the Baltimore shipyards. Employed as a 'chalker' sealing the seams in ships hulls, he worked alongside other black workers, some slaves and some free blacks, he secured friendships, attended political meetings, religious and social groups apart from the white establishments. It was at one such meeting that he met Anna Murray, a free black woman sympathetic to Frederick's undeserved title. After some time he made a deal with Hugh establishing that he would pay him weekly to move out of the house, find steady work and arrange for all his necessities. He was enjoying his new found independence until he was late with his weekly payment and his self reliance was in jeopardy. His master wanted him to move back home and in the course of their heated altercation a suggestion was put forth of selling him to the hopelessness of back breaking plantation work in the deep south. Frederick rebelled. Escape to freedom in New York City would become his obsession. Dressed as a sailor with money Anna supplied from the sale of a bed, along with forged papers allowing him to travel, he went by train to Wilmington, ferried to Philadelphia then made his way to New York City. Anna soon joined him there and they married in the print shop of David Ruggles, a well known abolitionist and guardian for slaves escaping through the Underground Railroad. They married on September 15, 1838, just twelve days after his flight to freedom began. Together they traveled northward to New Bedford, Massachusetts to find employment in the shipyards there.

There existed a real fear that slave catchers acting like bounty hunters could capture and return him to Maryland. Two days after his arrival, Frederick decided to change his name. His friend chose the name Douglas from a lead character in a poem entitled *"The Lady of the Lake."* He liked the name but changed the spelling, Frederick Bailey was now Frederick Douglass. The couple settled into a black community, attended a Methodist church and he found odd jobs at the docks. Early the following year, in 1839, Frederick subscribed to the abolitionist paper, '*The Liberator*' and reveled in its contents. It was a weekly newspaper, edited by William Lloyd Garrison that was dedicated to the sole purpose of ending slavery immediately. Frederick's admiration for Garrison was second to none, and of his work he noted that it, "detested slavery..preached human brotherhood, denounced oppression, and with all the solemnity of God's word demanded the complete emancipation of my race."[127] From *The Liberator* he learned that Garrison's Bible was his text book, and the principles for abolition were laid out plainly.

In the Douglass home, *The Liberator* and the *Bible* lay together side by side. For three years he worked to support his family, attended anti-slavery meetings, and spoke of his rising spirit of those who opposed the way of the taskmasters.

On Nantucket Island in August 1841 'The American Anti-Slavery Society' held a rally headed by William Lloyd Garrison and like minded speakers. Twenty three year old Douglass, now the father of two children, Rosetta and Lewis Henry, traveled there to listen to the rally and was unexpectedly asked to speak to the crowd as a recipient to the cruelty of slavery. He did not disappoint.

Standing tall and speaking with a rich baritone voice he was introduced as a 'chattel' or a piece of property, he delivered his recollection of slavery, his desire to educate himself and escape to a free state. The listeners were captivated by his two hour monologue. Promoted by Garrison, Frederick Douglass was hired by the American Anti-Slavery Society to go on the speaking circuit as a "fugitive slave lecturer" and tell his story traveling throughout different towns and into states like New York, Ohio, Indiana and Pennsylvania. It was known as the Hundred Conventions Project. In 1842 he moved his family to Lynn, Massachusetts, a third child, Frederick Douglass Jr. would join the family that year as well. As his popularity grew so did the likelihood of being threatened and harmed by those who supported slavery as well as the perilous possibility of being caught by bounty hunters. In Indiana, he and fellow speakers had their good clothes spoiled by 'evil-smelling eggs' and in the town of Pendleton, unable to obtain a building in which to speak an outside platform was erected and trouble began. "As soon as we began to speak a mob of about sixty of the roughest characters I ever looked upon ordered us, through its leaders, to "be silent," threatening us, if we were not, with violence."[128] The platform was knocked down, the teeth of one speaker were knocked out, another suffered head injuries, Frederick was knocked unconscious and his hand broken.

After years of speaking at all types of gatherings, some were suspicious that Frederick Douglass was even a slave at all since he left out information in his talks that could lead to his discovery. To remove doubt from listeners of his true heritage, he used his writing and verbal style and continuing self betterment to write down his one hundred and twenty-five page autobiography entitled, *The Narrative of the Life of Frederick Douglass*, published in 1845 by the Massachusetts Anti-Slavery Society. It detailed the names, places and torturous eyewitness accounts of slavery and became a huge success selling thousands of copies nationally. The greater exposure demanded greater protection, so within months of unveiling *The Narrative*, he sailed to Great Britain for a twenty-three month stay to give speeches there, in Ireland and Scotland as well. He was treated respectfully, gained favorable distinction and sold hundreds of copies of his book, however, back in Maryland, Hugh Auld, who had bought Frederick from his brother Thomas for one hundred dollars, was incensed over his family's less than honorable exposure in the Douglass autobiography. Two female British abolitionists raised money to pay off Hugh Auld for his freedom and he accepted the amount of one hundred and fifty pounds of sterling about ten times the amount he paid, freeing him forever on the fifth of December 1846, "from all manner of servitude..."[129]

He returned to the United States, moved to Rochester New York and with money raised by his friends in England, he started to publish his own newspaper called the *North Star* in December 1847. Named after the celestial north star that slaves followed as they fled southern plantations by way of the underground railroad, he wanted a publication different from all others, one written and run by "the colored people." In his judgement, "a tolerably well-conducted press in the hands of persons of the despised race would by...enkindling their hope of a future and developing their moral force, prove a most powerful means of removing prejudice and awakening an interest in them."[130] His eldest daughter Rosetta and son Charles would assist in the operation of his tabloid, later the name of the paper would be changed to the *Frederick Douglass Papers*. As a writer and speaker he became engaged in politics. His views were changing from his mentor William Garrison, no longer did he believe like Garrison that the U.S. Constitution was to be abhorred as a pro-slavery document and the union dissolved between slave holding and non slave holding states but instead the Constitution was 'the warrant to abolish slavery in every state of the union.'[131]

True to his convictions of equality for all, he attended and spoke at a Women's Rights Conventions where the right to vote was paramount to their concerns. In his paper he wrote of the relevance of their opinions. National events were taking hold that would take the emotions of its populace to new levels on both sides of the slavery issue, situations were coalescing towards war. Harriet Beecher Stowe's anti-slavery novel, *Uncle Tom's Cabin* is a story about a sympathetic, Christ believing, Bible reading slave named Tom and the tribulations he faces. The book published in 1852 was a phenomenal best seller, respected in the North and despised in the South.

In 1854, the Illinois Senator Stephen A. Douglas sponsored the Kansas-Nebraska Act permitting the spread of slavery into the new Kansas and Nebraska territories and thus repealing the provisions of the Missouri Compromise. Abraham Lincoln was so incensed over this decision, that he would put his law practice on the side, entered politics and challenged him to the famous debates for his Senate seat. In response to the Kansas-Nebraska Act, the formation of the Republican Party was created by anti-slavery abolitionists. Frederick Douglass wrote his second autobiography, *My Bondage and My Freedom* in 1855.

Then on March 1857, the Dred Scott Decision was handed down by the Supreme Court of the United States. Considered the worst Supreme Court ruling ever made, it determined that a slave named Dred Scott was considered the property of his slave owner and as such was not subject to the rights of US citizenship or protected under the rights of the Constitution. Douglass called it "The cold-blooded decision by Chief Justice Taney...wherein he states, as it were a historical fact that

"Negroes are deemed to have no rights which white men are bound to respect."[132]

The John Brown raid on the federal armory at Harpers Ferry, Virginia October 17, 1859 was designed to steal weapons and arm slaves for revolt against their masters resulted instead in the killing of the raiders and the hanging of Captain John Brown and his fellow conspirators. John Brown had enlisted the help of Frederick Douglass in his insurrection, but Douglass refused, concluding that it would not help in the abolitionist movement.

The threat of violence was mounting and the slavery question dominated the presidential campaign. The election of Republican Abraham Lincoln in November 1860, provoked political tensions in the southern states which held firm to slavery. They sent word to Congress that those states were succeeding from the union, to establish their own president and government. Weeks after Lincoln's inaugural speech in March 1861, the attack of Fort Sumter on April 12, began the War between the States. As the machines of war were brought into the conflict and the bloody casualties mounted up, Douglass puts pen to paper and became a vocal critic of President Lincoln charging that the war should be an anti-slavery crusade insisting that black soldiers should be recruited. Lincoln insisted it was to keep the union together. The president knew that slave labor was vital to the southern economy and Confederate cause, if they were freed it would hurt the southern states. Colonization as a means of separating the races by relocating black citizens to the Caribbean, and elsewhere, was met with discredit from Douglass.

The slaughterous battle of Antietam provided Lincoln a victory and the reason to announce his Emancipation Proclamation on the first day of the new year in 1863. "The proclamation itself was throughout like Mr. Lincoln. It was framed with a view to do the least harm and the most good possible in the circumstances...it was thoughtful, cautious and well guarded at all points."[133]

The outcome was the freeing of the slaves in the southern states that had succeeded from the union. Their escape to the North became a burden on jobs that were scarce in places, but allowed them to enlist and be accepted into the army. In New York City attempts to enforce the draft were met with rioting violent mobs that quickly turned into a savage race rampage bringing bloodshed to many black individuals for three days straight until disbanded by federal militia.

Douglass used his oratory gift to become a bombastic vocal recruiting officer for black soldiers. The Massachusetts 54th army regiment was an all black unit with white officers and two of his sons within the ranks, Charles R. Douglass and Lewis H. Douglass who would see promotion as a sergeant major. This fighting force would make history in July 1863 in their epic battle against the Confederate held Fort Wagner. Their bravery would resonate and bring forth many others to serve in the union cause. His other son, Frederick Jr. would recruit black troops in the Mississippi Valley. By war's end the contribution of Douglass recruitment efforts for the victory of the North was indisputable. A month later, would find him in Washington, D.C. where he met with President Lincoln at the White House. During their cordial meeting, both men gained each others mutual respect. Douglass claimed, "My interviews with President Lincoln and his able secretary greatly increased my confidence in the antislavery integrity of the government, although I confess I was greatly disappointed at my failure to receive the commission promised me by Secretary Stanton. I, however, faithfully believed, and loudly proclaimed my belief, that the rebellion would be suppressed, the Union preserved, the slaves emancipated, and the colored soldiers would in the end have justice done them."[134] They would meet again in the same place a year later. Lincoln requested Douglass's help in going into the South and spreading the message of emancipation. Douglass recollected his admiration of the president, "Mr Lincoln was not only a great President, but a great man-too great to be small in anything. In his company I was never in any way reminded of my humble origin, or of my unpopular color."[135]

In the course of the Civil War, Douglass was impatient with Lincoln having waited eighteen months to declare emancipation but after the war ended he realized he judged Lincoln erroneously. "He noted that from the point of view of the abolitionist, "Lincoln seemed tardy, cold, dull, and indifferent." Lincoln was president, however and had to be measured "by the sentiment of his country." By that standard, Douglass admitted that Lincoln was "swift, zealous, radical and determined.""[136]

The Thirteenth Amendment to the Constitution took the Emancipation Proclamation to its final conclusion by abolishing slavery in the entire country. The president signed it on February 1 of 1865 and was sent to the states for ratification.

Douglass would be in the audience during Abraham Lincoln's second inaugural speech in March having won reelection months earlier, and met with the president afterwards. Lincoln recognizing him in the crowd of well wishers grabbed him by the hand and told those near him, "Here comes my friend Douglass, I am glad to see you. I saw you in the crowd today, listening to my inaugural address; how did you like it?" Frederick replied, "Mr. Lincoln, that was a sacred effort."[137]

Forty-two days later, Douglass was in Rochester N.Y. when news was transmitted that his friend for freedom was felled by an assassin's bullet. Stunned by the calamity, he along with the nation mourned its loss. He delivered a eulogy at a memorial service the day Lincoln died on April 15, and months later was presented the sixteenth president's walking stick as a memorial gift from Lincoln's widow Mary Todd Lincoln

The Thirteenth Amendment became law on December 18, 1865. Douglass would campaign for voting rights to black citizens. He was met with rudeness from President Andrew Johnson, Lincoln's Vice President who entered the high office after Lincoln died. Johnson accused Douglass as being ungrateful for demanding the right to vote, and suggested that leaving the country was in the best interests of the newly freed people. Relentless in his pursuit of total equality, and shrugging off the racist comments from Johnson, he attended an *American Equal*

Rights Association meeting in Philadelphia to argue for voting rights of both blacks and women.

The Fourteenth Amendment, added in 1868, overturned the appalling Dred Scott decision by declaring all people born in the United States were citizens of the country, the Bill of Rights provided equal protection under the law to everyone in the state regardless of color. The right to participate in electing leadership in a reunited country was vital to the beliefs of Douglass, who lectured heavily throughout the country for ballot rights. Public sentiment mirrored his opinion and in February 1870, the third post Civil war Reconstruction Amendment was ratified by the states and added to the Constitution. The Fifteenth Amendment fulfilled his dream. It stated, "The right of citizens of the United States to vote shall not be denied or abridged by the United States or by any State on account of race, color, or previous condition of servitude." On the strength of that measure the American Anti-Slavery Society having met all its obligations voted to dissolve the organization. He moved his family to Washington D.C after his home in Rochester was destroyed by fire and arson was suspected. His family escaped without injury but within the charred remains were the ashes of the complete archives of his newspapers the *North Star*, *The Frederick Douglass Papers* and the *Douglass' Monthly,* a loss of historic proportions. He campaigned for Republicans Ulysses S. Grant, Rutherford B. Hayes and other candidates, lecturing at the same time to protect black suffrage and promote their leadership in the South where is was not warmly received.

In 1877 he was appointed to the position of U.S. Marshal of the District of Columbia by President Hayes, and visited his old slave owner Thomas Auld, now eighty-two years old and in failing health, in a meeting at his former home in Maryland. Slave and slave master now "stood upon equal ground." Their face to face encounter began with formal greetings, the shaking of hands and the release of deep down burdens. Auld told Marshal Douglass, "Frederick, I always knew you were too smart to be a slave, and had I been in your place, I would have done as you did" to which he replied, "Captain Auld, I am glad to hear you say this. I did not run away from you, but from slavery..."[138] His return to Washington D.C. soon had him moving to the Anacostia area to a huge twenty room home with gardens on acres of land overlooking the capitol city in a home he called Cedar Hill.

His third and last autobiography, *The Life & Times of Frederick Douglass*, was published in July 1882, the same month his wife Anna suffered a paralyzing stroke that took her life weeks later. Her body was buried in Mt. Hope cemetery in Rochester. He would suffer with depression over the loss of his wife but would marry again in January 1884 to Helen Pitts, a white woman's rights activist who was twenty years his junior and who worked in his office as a clerk. The mixed marriage carried mixed emotions by both the black and white races and was met with public prejudice. Frederick's response was his first spouse's complexion matched his mother's and his second wife's skin tone was like his father's. He was made the Minister of the Republic of Haiti in 1889 by President Benjamin Harrison for the purpose of negotiating a location for a U.S. naval base, but was unsuccessful to secure the site and resigned from the position two years later. He struggled to the end of his life to end segregation with the passing of 'Jim Crow' laws in southern states.

He died at his home on February 20, 1895, at age seventy-eight years old following his attendance earlier at a women's rights meeting. His body was laid to rest beside his first wife Anna. His presence and lifetime devotions would suffer a tremendous setback with the arrest of Homer Plessy for sitting in a "whites only" New Orleans railroad car in 1892. The incarceration would result in the Supreme Court dealing race relations in the country a severe blow with the passage of the *Plessy vs. Ferguson* ruling by creating facilities throughout the South that separated blacks from whites with so called equal facilities. It grew to include railroad cars, buses, drinking fountains etc. The term "Separate but equal" was considered to be no threat to the U.S.

Constitution. Racial tensions remained high for nearly sixty years, when in 1954, the Supreme Court would undo its ruling against state sponsored segregation in *Plessy vs. Ferguson* by ruling in favor of *Brown vs. Board of Education*, which argued that state laws that set up separate public schools for black and white students was unconstitutional. The Civil Rights Law of 1964 would make it illegal to discriminate against anyone in public and in employment surroundings based on sex, color, ethnic or religion ideals. Of this, Frederick Douglass would have been proud.

"The man who is right is a majority. We, who have God and conscience on our side, have a majority against the universe"
Frederick Douglass- letter to William Lloyd Garrison, January 1, 1846

"I would unite with anybody to do right
and with nobody to do wrong."
Frederick Douglass- Lecture at the The Anti-Slavery Movement, 1855

"The limits of tyrants are prescribed
by the endurance of those whom they oppose."
Frederick Douglass - speech Canandaiqua, New York, August 3, 1857

"I end where I begin, no war but an abolition war,
no peace but an abolition peace.
Liberty for all, chains for none."
Frederick Douglass- Speech at the Women's Loyal League at the Cooper Institute, New York City, January 13, 1865

"The life of the nation is secure only
while the nation is honest, truthful, and virtuous."
Frederick Douglass-Speech on the anniversary of Emancipation,
Washington, D.C. April 1885

"To those who have suffered in slavery
I can say I too have suffered.
To those who have battled for liberty, brotherhood
and citizenship I can say I too have battled."
Frederick Douglass- The Life and Times of Frederick Douglass

"To suppress free speech is a double wrong.
It violates the rights of the hearer
as well as those of the speaker."
Frederick Douglass- 'A Plea for Free Speech,' Boston 1860

"I recognize the Republican party as the sheet anchor
of the colored man's political hopes and the ark of his safety."
Frederick Douglass- letter in response to a
Congressional candidate inquiry, August 15, 1888

Mister Lincoln was not only a great President,
but a great man- too great to be small in anything.
In his company I was never in any way
reminded of my humble origin,
or of my unpopular color.
Frederick Douglass-The Life and Times of Frederick Douglass
Part 2, Chapter 12

Harriet Tubman

The Moses of her People
Underground Railroad Conductor

Love for your fellow citizen has different degrees of recognition. Love brought about by boldness despite unimaginable physical hardship stands by itself. It is one thing to stand on principle and take charge of circumstances that defy righteousness in surroundings that are safe and secure, it is quite another to spend a good portion of your life witnessing anguish, suffering torment, and physical hardships while defying death at every turn. Harriet Tubman and her faith never retreated in the face of extreme peril during her multiple midnight escapes to lead the downtrodden people of her race out of the bondage of slavery and into the arms of freedom. She serves as the finest example of true heroism.

Entering the world under the scourge of slavery, she was born Ariminta "Minty" Ross in 1820 or 1822, in Dorchester County, Maryland and who like Frederick Douglass, suffered the humiliation of never knowing for sure their birthdate as exact records for slaves were not kept. Her parents were Benjamin Ross and Harriet 'Rit' Green, the 'property' of different owners. Ben was owned by Anthony Thompson, a plantation owner in Madison, Maryland and Rit was the chattel property of Mary Brodess, a widow with a two-year old son, Edward. When Anthony and Mary married, their assets including their slaves were combined and Ben and Rit met, married (though not legally) built a home on the Madison plantation and raised a family of nine children, with Minty being the fifth child. When Edward turned twenty-one, he inherited his mother's estate (she died when he was just nine or ten years old) which included Rit and all her children as was the practice at the time. The family was split up when their father Ben was forced to remain in Madison to oversee the cutting and logging of timber, while Edward moved the others to his plantation in Bucktown,

Maryland where he married a woman named Eliza Ann and together they began to raise a family of their own. Rit and any offspring she had were all promised their freedom when she turned forty-five, in accordance with his mother's wishes that were written in her grandfather's will. Edward Brodess failed to honor the agreement his mother had, and decided instead to increase his income by selling off Minty's siblings. Rit's sixteen year old daughter Mariah was the first to be sold to a slave trader in Mississippi, a son James was sold as well. Rit threatened a Georgia trader who wanted her youngest son Moses. She hid the boy with other families over a month until the sale was abandoned. Her other brothers Ben and Robert became field hands, oftentimes "hired out...to others, some who proved to be tyrannical and brutal to the utmost limit of their power."[139] When Minty was only five years old, she was recruited to care for an infant of a woman known as Miss Susan. If the baby cried, despite sitting up all night rocking the child, Minty was whipped across the face and neck. Once caught taking a lump of sugar, and fearing a lashing, Minty fled and hid in a neighbor's pigsty for five days, eating what she could that came into the trough until hunger forced her home for food and a whipping.

When she was six, she was hired out to a man named James Cook to learn weaving and to wade into the marshes to trap and catch muskrats. The cold December wetlands made her sick with the measles, but she was forced to return into the frigid swamps to catch more rodents. Becoming gravely ill she was returned home and nursed back to health by her mother only to be hired out again when she recovered. As she grew, Minty worked the fields, plowed them, cut and chopped wood, gaining strength the whole time. In 1834, she along with the plantation cook, went to a dry goods store to buy items for the home, when a slave belonging to a man named Barnett left his work without permission and entered the store with his overseer in pursuit. The slave resisted apprehension and the overseer demanded Minty to help and to tie him up, but she refused and the slave broke free. The overseer grabbed an iron two-pound counter weight and threw it at the escapee, missing him but striking her in the forehead, severely gashing open her skull. She was carried home fainting and gushing blood and remained there two days without medical attention. She was returned to the fields sweating and bleeding. The head injury would forever torment her with severe headaches, seizures, vivid dreams and bouts of lethargy. It was also at this time she was becoming deeply religious having learned Bible stories from her mother, and exposure to various Christian faiths. The evangelical emphasis on spiritual freedom was part of the core theology of many black denominations...such as the African Methodist Episcopal Church.[140] She prayed all the time. She had 'visions' which she was convinced were messages from God. At age eighteen, Minty changed her slave name from Ariminta to "Harriet Ross" taking the name of her mother.

Around 1844 Harriet received permission from her slave owner to marry John Tubman, a free black man, and in so doing, attempted to obtain her freedom through the courts when a lawyer she hired found in the Dorchester County Records, the last will and testament stating the freedom of her mother and her offspring. Edward Brodess had ignored the will and his own mother's desires. Strapped for cash, he was successful in ending her claim, and decided on the sale of two more sisters, Linah and Soph. Harriet watched helplessly and remembered the "agonizing expression on their faces, heard their weeping as they turned and took one last look at their home."[141] Linah's two daughters were separated in the sale. The paralyzing trauma of losing her sisters and witnessing the injustice of slave trading stayed with her all her life. Regardless of the fact that she was married, the threat with sale into the deep south was genuine.

On March 7, 1849, Edward Brodess died leaving behind numerous debts for his wife Eliza to pay off. It appeared the likelihood of selling Harriet, her family and other slaves looked evident. Harriet decided it was now time to escape to freedom.

John Tubman, cautious about the dangers appealed to her to stay put but on September 17, she escaped with her two brothers Ben and Henry. After arguing amongst themselves as to the direction and methods for safely reaching the free north, they forced a reluctant Harriet to abandon the mission and return to enslavement. In October, Harriet escaped alone, knowing the demands on her body and spirit to avoid capture would be demanding beyond comprehension. Being unable to read or write, she suffered illiteracy, had no money, traveled during the night following the north star, rested in the marshes and woods by day. Constantly looking over her shoulder, she learned who could be trusted in her secret to reach the promised land. Free blacks pointed out hidden paths to follow and aided by a white Quaker woman, she was supplied names of supporters to her cause and hidden in a wagon and taken away from Maryland to the Delaware border by her husband. Delaware was a free state but dangerous, as it was also home to 'slave catchers.' The Eastern Shore Underground Railroad provided a pathway of sympathetic abolitionists to help her and others of like mind with safe houses (also known as depots) to protect them and covertly deliver messages and vital information to the next 'stop' along the escape route. Heading north to the free state of Pennsylvania, ninety miles away was the goal.

The Underground Railroad had its roots in the partnership of free blacks and antislavery groups, notably the *Religious Society of Friends* (Quakers) whose theology emphasized the spiritual equality of all human beings regardless of race.[142] The free black community was not immune from the 'slave catchers' who would kidnap a free black and put him or her back into bondage for a bounty. That fear and an obligation to the enslaved of their race gave them the commitment to act clandestinely to house, transport and safeguard those seeking freedom. After possibly three weeks of weary travel, Harriet finally reached Philadelphia, Pennsylvania. She later remembered, "I looked at my hands to see if I was the same person. There was such glory over everything; the sun came like gold through the trees, and over the fields, and I felt like I was in Heaven."[143] She found work, saved money and made important contacts. During the summer she stayed and worked in Cape May, New Jersey earning a salary as a cook and maid. The *Fugitive Slave Law* passed in September of 1850 was a callous federal ruling that protected slave owners of their human property by demanding all federal marshals arrest any alleged runaway slave or face a $1000 fine if they refused. Free states were not exempt. Harriet became more determined to bring her family north.

Her first rescue took place in December 1850, when she learned her niece Kessiah and her children were to go on the auction block in Maryland. Aided by her niece's spouse and friends in Baltimore they were able to secure the family and with Harriet's help, got them all together and safely into Philadelphia. Later that Spring she returned to Baltimore by way of the Underground Railroad depots and rescued her brother Moses and two other men with him. With saved money on her person, confidence in her planning abilities, and a new suit of men's clothes, she took a huge risk by traveling back to her old home in Dorchester County to bring her husband back with her to Philadelphia in the autumn of 1851 after their two year absence. When she arrived, she discovered her husband had married a free woman named Caroline and rejected her offer. Distressed by the outcome she opted to forget him, but keep his last name, and dedicate herself to help others shackled by slavery. She mobilized slaves to escape back north and then returned later to gather eleven more, including another brother and his wife. With the *Fugitive Slave Law* in full affect, she now moved her people out of the country into Canada. Frederick Douglass would recall how his home in Rochester, New York was a depot in the Underground Railroad possibly for Harriet's eleven. Driven by ambition and her prayers, she returned to Philadelphia, worked for more money then ventured back for more slaves. As was the routine she traveled mostly during the winter when the nights were longer, rested by day avoiding bounty hunters in both directions and enduring agonizing headaches. As a fugitive aiding other fugitives, she carried a gun for protection and made it clear to all that joined her expedition that the journey was deadly serious and each member was not to return to the plantation or risked being shot. One member low on morale, threatened to leave but faced Harriet's revolver and her words, "You go on or die."[144] The chance of having the groups whereabouts revealed was too hazardous. They all made it to Canada. In 1852 she made one, possibly two trips to slave country and by the winter of 1853-54 she made five trips liberating thirty slaves to freedom.[145] Clever in her methods, she would start her escapes on Saturday evenings as slaves were not missed on Sundays, their only day off, and runaway newspaper advertisements were not printed. She paid free blacks to tear down reward posters to gain an advantage as well. Her back and forth trips now ended in St. Catharines in Ontario, Canada, and her notoriety grew behind-the-scenes in established abolitionist circles. Harriet's 1854 Christmas Eve arrival back in Dorchester reunited her with three of her brothers, Ben, Robert and Henry, a girl named Jane (the fiancee of brother Ben) and two other slaves. They made their way forty miles to the farm in Poplar Neck, Maryland where their parents, Ben and Rit were united again after Ben purchased his wife from Eliza Brodess for twenty dollars. They ate well and rested there before leaving Christmas night, it would be the last time they could rest. without torment until they arrived safely in St. Catharines, connecting with other family members who had settled there. Now free, the Ross brothers changed their last name to Stewart. Later, an attempt to liberate her sister Rachel failed when she would not leave without her children who were hired out and separated. This failure with Rachel would repeat itself again, but others would join "Moses" as she was called out of her resemblance to the Biblical man of the same name who freed his people from the cruelty and bondage of Egypt's pharaoh. When word reached Harriet that her father faced possible arrest for aiding runaways, she proceeded to bring them north. It was May of 1857 and this trip was fraught with peril with increased armed bounty hunters heavily armed with bloodhounds to aid in the captures, but the warmer weather made it tolerable for her seventy-year old parents to survive. Harriet rigged an old horse with a straw collar and a wheeled rig and brought her folks north to Wilmington Delaware, then to Philadelphia, on to New York City, northwest to Rochester and finally into St. Catharines to be reunited with their children, grandchildren and great grandchildren. Years later, the brutal Canadian winters proved to difficult for Ben and Rit so Harriet moved them to the outskirts of Auburn, New York on a piece of property that New York Senator and strong abolitionist, William H. Seward sold to her. She went in search of money to pay back her land and home by giving lectures and speeches of her exploits as a conductor on the Underground Railroad. In Boston she met John Brown, the radical abolitionist who was raising money for his attack on Harpers Ferry, Virginia. They met several times discussing his armory takeover and his aim to steal weapons and lead an armed slave revolt. The Brown raid would end in failure for him, many of his co-conspirators including two of his sons were killed in the attack. John the leader, and his surviving raiders were later tried and executed by hanging.

Harriet Tubman dubbed "General Tubman" by John Brown delivered more folks to freedom. A captured slave in Troy, New York was carried out of a judge's chambers on Harriet's shoulders with police bullets fired at them and a crowd of her supporters aiding in their escape. In 1860, her travels south brought her the heartbreaking news that her sister Rachel had died, saddened by sorrow of her loss, she was unwilling to head back empty handed and found a married couple and their three children ready to go with her. This trip was faced with scant clothing, exposure to bitter snow and rain, little food and greater risks of capture. Saved by a Quaker when they were forced to escape to an island in a swamp after they were exposed by a man who alerted the authorities. The bold trek north took longer than expected but as always the group, exhausted and stressed from armed pursuit made it to their final destination. Her safety reaching the breaking point, this dangerous mission would be her last. In her lifetime, it was estimated that she made about nineteen round trips and saved over three hundred slaves.

Following the election of Republican Abraham Lincoln in 1860, seven southern states seceded from the Union, maintaining their opposition to the Republican platform that stated in part that it was the right of Congress to end the spread of slavery in the territories and the Dred Scott decision was unjustified. The new Confederate states hold on slavery was at the root of the separation. After the attack on Fort Sumter on April 12, 1861, the War between the States would divide the country in an event like no other before it.

Harriet Tubman's title "The Moses of her People" along with her daring accomplishments became the topic of interest to many including Massachusetts Governor John Andrew, who arranged passage for her to go to the Union camps at Port Royale, South Carolina, where her skills of going undetected could be beneficial to the Union army in obtaining valuable information behind enemy lines. There was much for Harriet to think about; "there were the old folks in the little home up in Auburn, there was the little farm of which she had taken the sole care; there were the many dependents for whom she had provided by her daily toil. What was to become of them all if she deserted them? But the cause of the Union seemed to need her services, and after a few moments of reflection, she determined to leave all else, and go where it seemed that duty called her."[146] Upon her arrival in May 1862, she distributed food, clothes, and books from donations up north. She taught newly freed women to do washing, sewing, and baking for the Union soldiers, so they could support themselves with wages instead of depending on Government support.[147] She spied on Confederate troop movements relaying the information to officers stationed at Hilton Head. She worked as a cook and nurse, following the troops into battle, working to keep them alive through bloody engagements and disease which included smallpox. Her experience in crawling around the woods and marshes was vital in procuring necessary remedies to the sick and dying through her knowledge of life saving roots and herbs. The Emancipation Proclamation on January 1, 1863 was an Executive order from President Lincoln proclaiming that all those enslaved in the Confederate States to be forever free. It was a war decision to break the South's spirit and grasp on holding onto slavery. It allowed the Union army, as it took over parts of the Confederacy, to emancipate those people rather than return them to their masters. The Proclamation did not apply to slave states under Union control. In short, it made slavery illegal in rebel states only. Ex-slaves from the South quickly joined the Union army and Harriet assisted in the recruitment, creating African American regiments.   Six months after the Proclamation's release, she became the first woman to plan and lead a Civil War battle when she joined forces with Colonel James Montgomery and about three hundred black soldiers, sailing up South Carolina's Combahee River in the lead gunboat. Her espionage located several valuable Confederate warehouses holding weapons and supplies. The object of the expedition was to take up torpedoes placed by the rebels..to destroy railroads and bridges and cut off supplies to the rebel troops.[148] The Combahee River raid was successful, in that it was a boost for the Union war effort and more importantly, it freed seven hundred and fifty slaves. Her collaboration with the army was noticed and the name "Harriet Tubman"appeared in northern newspapers. She returned to her nursing and cooking to supply her an income.   She assisted the famed 54th Massachusetts black regiment as a scout, cook and nurse. Late in 1863, exhaustion overcame her and went home to Auburn to check on her parents and rest up. In time, she returned to her battlefield nursing tasks until the end of the war. At war's end she stayed on to labor as a nurse in a hospital at Fort Monroe, Virginia that treated black soldiers. Lack of medical supplies prompted her to visit her old friend, William Seward, Lincoln's Secretary of State in Washington D.C., who having recovered from the assassination attempt on his life, the night Lincoln was shot and killed, provided her with a meeting with the U.S. Surgeon General to voice her concerns. While in the nation's capitol, she applied for back pay for her unfaltering service to the army as a spy, cook, laundress and nurse. Both her requests were lost in government bureaucracy.

She traveled home to New York to be with her family, and as a member of the armed services was given a soldier's pass to ride the train for half fare. A racist train conductor in New Jersey believing the 'pass' she carried was either stolen or forged, ignored her polite explanation that she worked for the government and cursed her, "Come hustle out of here! We don't carry niggers for half-fare."[149] He tried to move her into the smoking car, but she refused the indignity to leave her seat. Two male passengers supporting the conductor pried her fingers loose from the train interior and threw her forcibly into the smoking car, hurting her ribs and shoulder and breaking her arm in the process. She recovered in New York City, then made her way home to Auburn. To raise money for her family she took in boarders, and allowed Sarah Bradford, a white abolitionist and author from Auburn to write her biography. Sarah and Harriet became familiar through correspondence while she served the Union cause. She prepared her biography by interviewing her subject and by contacting other well known abolitionist leaders for additional background material. One such letter was from Frederick Douglass dated Rochester, August 29, 1868 -

"Dear Harriet: I am glad to know that the story of your eventful life has been written by a kind lady, and that the same is soon to be published. You ask for what you do not need when you call upon me for a word of commendation. I need such words from you far more than you can need them from me, especially where your superior labors and devotion to the cause of the lately enslaved of our land are known as I know them. The difference between us is very marked. Most that I have done and suffered in the service of our cause has been in public, and I have received much encouragement at every step of the way. You, on the other hand, have labored in a private way. I have wrought in the day - you in the night. I have had the applause of the crowd and the

satisfaction that comes of being approved by the multitude, while the most that you have done has been witnessed by a few trembling, scarred, and foot-sore bondmen and women, whom you have led out of the house of bondage, and whose heartfelt, "God bless you," has been your only reward. The midnight sky and the silent stars have been the witnesses of your devotion to freedom and of your heroism. Excepting John Brown - of sacred memory - I know of no one who has willingly encountered more perils and hardships to serve our enslaved people than you have. Much that you have done would seem improbable to those who do not know you as I know you. It is to me a great pleasure and a great privilege to bear testimony for your character and your works, and to say to those to whom you may come, that I regard you in every way truthful and trustworthy.
Your friend,
Frederick Douglass."[150]

Her book, *Scenes in the Life of Harriet Tubman* was printed, and published in 1869 and provided for her a much needed source of income. That same year she married a Civil War veteran, named Nelson Davis who was a boarder in her home. (two years earlier she had learned that her estranged husband John Tubman was murdered in a fight in Maryland.) Nelson and Harriet celebrated a highlight in their lives when they adopted a baby girl named Gertie in 1874. The year earlier, Harriet's brother John was introduced to two men that spoke of a buried box of gold coins smuggled out of South Carolina that they could not be seen with. John, Harriet and a friend of hers, who she convinced in lending her two thousand dollars in paper currency for the transaction and a share in the profits. The gold was reported worth over five thousand dollars. On the day of the business deal, Harriet was taken to the wooded area where the gold box was buried. When she failed to return in a reasonable time, brother John and friend went looking for her all night, finding her the next morning, bound and gagged, the money gone and a box of rocks for their trouble in its place. Her good sense of who to trust failed her.

Taking responsibility for her family and others monopolized her time, and several setbacks would again befall her. In 1880 her mother Rit passed away, surviving her husband Ben by nine years. Her wooden house burned to the ground, destroying her cherished letters and possessions. Money was needed to rebuild a new brick home in its place. Her repeated requests through paperwork to petition the government for back pay fell by the wayside. Harriet asked Sarah Bradford to reissue her biography. A second book entitled, *Harriet Tubman The Moses of Her People* was published in 1886, and like the first book that held some fact fallacies, the updated book, "played to the stereotypical characterizations of blacks that were popular in post-Reconstruction America. Bradford, in her effort to accommodate a racist reading audience, gave Harriet the dialect of an ignorant field slave."[151] Despite the shortcomings, the book again provided Harriet with much needed money for herself and her charities.

She maintained a faithful devotion to her prayers to God and to a committed attendance at the African Methodist Episcopal Church. The AME Episcopal Zion Church provided a social haven for mutual support. The war was over, slavery was abolished, but segregation was still the order of the day. Black Americans were still held prisoners in their dark skin. Harriet engaged her congregation to assist in raising funds to build a shelter and hospital for aging blacks, mostly old slaves without any family.

With a revived exposure from her biography, she entered the public speaking forum associating with the women of the suffrage movement. Names like Susan B. Anthony, Lucretia Mott, Elizabeth Cody Stanton, and Harriet Beecher Stowe were educated women seriously involved with women's rights and reform campaigns. They brought their 'talking points' across by invoking parallels between women's rights and slavery. Harriet spoke at these suffrage meetings in New York and Boston, her new found passion was to get women the right to vote.

Her husband Nelson died (most likely of tuberculosis) in October 1888, and two years later Congress passed a law to grant pension for Union soldier widows. After a complicated paper trail, Harriet was finally granted a pension five years later in 1895. It was eight dollars a month. In 1897 a New York Congressman rallied support to recognize her unselfish contributions to the war effort and the benefit was increased to twenty dollars a month. The twelve additional dollars was a result of her nursing duties.

Harriet was close to eighty years old.

In 1896 She bought a twenty-five acre plot of land next to her home for the purpose of building a home and hospital strictly for destitute, aged and sick African Americans. In 1903, she donated that plot of land to the AME Episcopal Zion Church on the condition that it be maintained for the conditions she pledged. The Auburn community funded the project and the Harriet Tubman Home opened in 1908. Now in her nineties, she became a permanent resident in the home that bears her name in 1911.

She died of pneumonia on March 10, 1913 and was buried with full military honors at the Fort Hill Cemetery in Auburn. Her lifetime allegiance to seek liberty for everyone makes Harriet Tubman a patriot of the highest order.

"I had reasoned this out in my mind;
there was one of two things I had a right to,
liberty, or death; if I could not have one, I would have the other;
for no man should take me alive; I should fight for my liberty
as long as my strength lasted, and when the time came for me to
go, the Lord would let them take me."
Harriet Tubman- 'The Moses of her People'
on her decision to escape from slavery

"I had crossed the line. I was free;
but there was no one to welcome me
to the land of freedom. I was a stranger in a strange land; and
my home, after all, was down in Maryland;
because my father, my mother, my brothers, and sisters,
and friends were there. But I was free, and they should be free.
I would make a home in the North and bring them there,
God helping me. Oh, how I prayed then, I said to de Lord,
I'm going to hold steady on to you, an' I know
you'll see me through."
Harriet Tubman- 'Scenes in the Life of Harriet Tubman'
-recollections of her first step into free territory

"We saw the lightning and that was the guns;
and then we heard the thunder
and that was the big guns;
and then we heard the rain falling
and that was the blood falling;
and when we came to get in the crops,
it was dead men that we reaped."
Harriet Tubman-'The Moses of her People'
recalling the Massachusetts 54th Army battle against Fort Wagner

"On my Underground Railroad
I never ran my train off the track and I never lost a passenger."
Harriet Tubman-'The Moses of her People'

Milton Friedman

Father of Economic Freedom

When one thinks about personal freedom, smaller less intrusive government and the betterment of humankind through the field of economic theory, the name Milton Friedman rises above the rest. He was an author, a professor of economics and an intellectual, who used the lectern and television to educate for free market capitalism in a manner that was self-assured, concise, instructive and entertaining.

He was born in Brooklyn New York on July 31, 1912, the fourth child of Jeno and Sarah Friedman, both Hungarian immigrants. They moved to Rahway, New Jersey where he attended Rahway High School, won a state tuition scholarship and enrolled in Rutgers University in the autumn of 1928, having just turned sixteen. One year later, in October, America witnessed the Wall Street Crash of 1929, the beginning of the Great Depression. It was at Rutgers that Milton turned his attention to the study of economics. Milton held several jobs to pay for non-tuition expenses which included working as a clerk and waiter. It was "his experience waiting tables that he gained better insight into the importance of entrepreneurial abilities and skills. The restaurant at which he worked changed hands while he was employed, and he experienced firsthand the difference between effective and ineffective management, a lesson that he remembered throughout his life."[152]

He graduated from Rutgers in 1932 and enrolled in the University of Chicago in September of that year to pursue his master's degree in economics, which he earned in a year. It was in his Economics 301 class that he was seated next to his classmate and future wife, Rose Director. His second year in graduate study took him to Columbia University in New York, an educational combination that benefited him immensely. Milton reflected later in his *Memoirs*, "the ideal combination for a budding economist was a year of study at Chicago, which emphasized theory, followed by a year of study at Columbia, which emphasized institutional influences and empirical work."[153]   He returned to Chicago University for another year and became an economics research assistant while deepening his relationship with Rose.   He took employment in Washington D.C. in the National Resources Committee in 1935 during the time of Franklin Roosevelt's New Deal and followed it in 1937 by becoming a research staffer in New York City with the National Bureau of Economic Research.   With a firm income in place, Milton and Rose were married on June 25, 1938.   Together they traveled to Wisconsin where he attended the University of Wisconsin as a visiting professor of economics in the 1940-41 academic year.   In the fall of 1941, with the United States entry into the second world war on the immediate horizon, Milton returned to Washington D.C. to work at the Treasury Department.   There he was exposed first hand to the inner workings of government, testified before congressional committees and helped develop the federal tax withholding system we use today.   In the winter of 1943 he joined the Statistical Research Group, headquartered at Columbia University where an accomplished group of mathematicians and statisticians worked out military supply effectiveness.

He was awarded a Ph.D from Columbia in 1946 and his thesis, *Income from Independent Professional Practice,* was published. That same year he returned to the University of Chicago to teach in the Department of Economics and remained there for thirty years, his last class being in the fall of 1976. In addition, he held a staff position in the Bureau of Economic Research. During his time in Chicago, Milton Friedman contributed many writings in the form of books and articles. *Capitalism and Freedom* published in 1962 was co-authored by Milton and Rose Friedman followed by a work written in collaboration with Anna J. Schwartz entitled; *Monetary History of the United States.*

In *Capitalism and Freedom*, he asserted that, "the role of competitive capitalism-the organization of the bulk of economic activity through private enterprise operating in a free market-as a system of economic freedom and a necessary condition for political freedom."[154] Also, the limited role that government should play in a free society is throughly documented and examined. This was in sharp contrast to Keynesian economics, the budgetary model used by the United States government leading up to and including the Great Depression and beyond. Formulated by economist John Maynard Keynes, who theorized in part, that government could borrow money and then spend it to boost a poor economy. It was a form of wealth redistribution that expanded government intrusion and impeded capitalism. Friedman's persuasive free market ideas took hold and brought him into conservative Barry Goldwater's 1964 presidential campaign as an economic advisor. Later his articles appeared regularly in *Newsweek* magazine. In 1968 he advised the Richard Nixon presidential campaign, having met Nixon during the Eisenhower administration. Friedman sat on a the committee that ended the military draft and turned it into an all-volunteer army. When Nixon imposed wage and price controls in 1971, Milton was not impressed and later commented on the harm that policy did to the country. He traveled outside the United States, visiting and lecturing on free market economics in the military dictatorship of Chile in 1975, in South Africa, and Rhodesia (now Zimbabwe). His teachings at home and abroad brought him world wide recognition that concluded with him being awarded the Nobel Peace Prize in Economics in 1976.

In 1977, Milton and Rose Friedman were approached to showcase his free society economic beliefs in a PBS television series. *Free to Choose* was a ten part one hour series of public lectures, followed by question and answer sessions and various location filmings with such titles as; *The Power of the Market*, *The Tyranny of Controls*, *The Anatomy of Crisis*, *Cradle to Grave*, *Cradle Equal*, *What's Wrong with our Schools*, and others. In passionate, plain spoken voice his ability to explain and educate the virtues of the free market enhanced his appeal to a much broader audience.

He was a strong supporter of the wisdom of Adam Smith and referred to the solid judgement of this remarkable 18th century visionary often in his television series *Free to Choose* as well as the book of the same name, that was written in conjunction with the ten part series. He noted that in Smith's *Wealth of Nations*, the market system was best served when individuals were free to pursue their own goals, and emphasizing "that both parties to an exchange can benefit and that, so long as cooperation is strictly voluntary, no exchange will take place unless both parties do benefit."[155] Smith's free-market capitalism metaphor of the "invisible hand" projects the simple idea that when any individual engages in the freedom to pursue interests of their own choosing, society benefits. Throughout the book, he references Smith's opinions on the role of government and trade, on public education, and the freedom to choose goods and services. Milton Friedman resuscitated the monetary philosophy of Adam Smith to a new generation.

"The fundamental principal of the free society is voluntary cooperation. The economic market, buying and selling, is one example. But it's only one example. Voluntary cooperation is far broader than that. To take an example that at first sight seems about as far away as you can get; the language we speak; the words we use; the complex structure of our grammar; no government bureau designed that. It arose out of the voluntary interactions of people seeking to communicate with one another. Or consider some of the great scientific achievements of our time the discoveries of an Einstein or Newton, the inventions of Thomas Alva Edison or an Alexander Graham Bell or even consider the great charitable activities of a Florence Nightingale or an Andrew Carnegie. These weren't done under orders from a government office. They were done by individuals deeply interested in what they were doing, pursing their own interests, and cooperating with one another. This kind of voluntary cooperation is built so deeply into the structure of our society that we tend to take it for granted. Yet the whole of our Western civilization is the unintended consequence of that kind of a voluntary cooperation of people cooperating with one another to pursue their own interests, yet in the process, building a great society."[156]

In *Free to Choose*, he also acknowledged the contributions of Thomas Jefferson, by his writings in the Declaration of Independence, which "proclaimed a new nation, the first in history established on the principle that every person is entitled to pursue his own values: "We hold these truths to be self-evident, that all men are created equal, that they are endowed by their Creator with certain unalienable Rights, that among these are Life, Liberty and the pursuit of Happiness."[157] The foundation and support system of economic success. "I Pencil: My Family Tree as Told to Leonard E. Read"[158] was retold by Milton Friedman on *Free to Choose*. It explained Adam Smith's vision of voluntary trade and commerce. In this case it allows many thousands of people to work together to create a simple pencil. It went this way.

"Look at this lead pencil, there is not a single person in the world who could make this pencil. Remarkable statement? Not at all. The wood from which it's made, for all I know, comes from a tree that was cut down in the state of Washington. To cut down that tree, it took a saw. To make the saw, it took steel. To make the steel, it took iron ore. This black center, we call it lead but it's really compressed graphite, I am not sure where it comes from but I think it comes from some mines in South America. This red top up here, the eraser, a bit of rubber, probably comes from Malaya, where the rubber tree isn't even native. It was imported from South America by some businessmen with the help of the British government. This brass ferrule, I haven't the slightest idea where it came from or the yellow paint or the paint that made the black lines, or the glue that holds it together.

Literally thousands of people cooperated to make this pencil. People who don't speak the same language; who practice different religions; who might hate one another if they ever met. When you go down to the store and buy this pencil, you are, in effect, trading a few minutes of your time for a few seconds of the time of all of those thousands of people. What brought them together and induced them to cooperate to make this pencil? There was no Commissar sending out orders from some central office. It was the magic of the price system. The impersonal operation of prices that brought them together and got them to cooperate to make this pencil so that you could have it for a trifling sum. That is why the operation of the free market is so essential, not only to promote productive efficiency, but even more to foster harmony and peace among the peoples of the world."[159]

President Ronald Reagan entered the White House in 1980, the same year that *Free to Choose* premiered. He complimented Milton Friedman on his television program, as a major influence of the correct course for economic survival and prosperity. The two men met for the first time in 1967, when Reagan was the governor of California and then later in 1973 when Reagan spent the day with Friedman, going from one campaign stop to another to initiate a proposition to limit state spending. After Reagan's election, Milton Friedman held a chair in the president's Economic Policy Advisory Board. His influence on the president was intense and Reaganomics, with its limited government, tax cutting principles, quickly and flawlessly put into effect, demonstrated that Friedman's philosophies turned America's capitalistic fortunes and respect skyward. President Reagan would later honor his contributions by awarding him the Presidential Medal of Freedom.

Great Britain's new conservative Prime Minister Margaret Thatcher was also an admirer of Friedman. His steadfast message of free market, free trade, smaller government, fair international exchange rates, lower taxes and reduced government regulations was reaching worldwide attention and acclaim.

When interviewed in 1984 by professors from the University of Stockholm and the University of Iceland on Icelandic State television, he was asked his views on the "ideal society" and of his "personal utopia." He responded, "My personal utopia is one that takes the individual or the family if you will, as the key element in society. I would like to see a society in which individuals have the maximum freedom to pursue their own objectives, in whichever direction they wish so long as they don't interfere with the rights of others to do the same thing. In such a society, I believe, you do need a government, but the government has a very limited role. Its role should be to provide for the national defense, to provide for protecting one individual from coercion by other individuals and finally to provide a mechanism whereby we can formulate the rules that will govern us, the rules that decide what we regard as private property, what we regard as the rights of individuals, legislative processes, and as part of that, a mechanism for judging differences in opinion so you will have essentially in my good society a very limited government devoted to the tasks of defense, of justice, of legislating rules and very little else. The rest would be left to the free individual activities of individuals joined together through the operation of a private and competitive market."[160]   His devotion to monetary economics fueled by the importance of the quantity of money influences government conduct (or misconduct) to the business cycles and inflation. The year 1988 bestowed on Friedman multiple accolades, namely, the Presidential Medal of Freedom award as well as the National Medal of Science award. Milton Friedman put to rest the belief that the Great Depression of the late 1920s through most of the 1930s was a failure of American private business and that government had to step in and save the economy from failure. His attentive research in scrutinizing the annual reports of the Federal Reserve over a fifty year period, produced the firm position that the Great Depression was a result of government failure of monetary policy and the Federal Reserve system to act in the manner in which it was established, that is, to prevent banks from closing and to squelch panics in their institutions. In the beginning of the 1930s, the Federal Reserve did neither. By 1933 one-third of the nation's banks closed their doors and the total amount of U.S. currency which included bank deposits declined by one-third as well. Friedman was a strong unwavering advocate of personal responsibility, knowing the best way to reduce poverty is in the free market and free enterprise system. Government interference by out of control welfare programs encourages poverty by rewarding it. He strongly supported an educational school voucher system which would allow schools to be competitive with each other for the financial credits the parents would pay to the school that performed the best for their children. He was convinced that school vouchers were a freedom issue. The schools that performed the best would get the better share of student attendance and money, they would have to work harder and deliver solid teaching consistently in order to get its share of parental support. Vouchers would provide the free market approach to education. In 1992 he wrote, *Money Mischief: Episodes in Monetary History,* which was a history of monetary practice and the influences that surround that system. Milton and Rose collaborated on their memoirs, writing *Two Lucky People* in 1998. The first 'Milton Friedman Prize for Advancing Liberty' was awarded in 2002 by the Cato Institute in recognition for the individual who greatly contributed in promoting freedom. Milton Friedman passed away on November 16, 2006, following a hospital stay for a viral infection. His loss was immeasurable in his capacity to see the world's inhabitants, not as a mish-mosh of separate nations but with the possibility of a unified free market storehouse, trading goods and services for the betterment of all mankind.

"The Great Depression, like most other periods of severe unemployment, was produced by government mismanagement rather than by any inherent instability of the private economy."
Milton Friedman-'Capitalism and Freedom' 1962

"One of the great mistakes is to judge policies and programs
by their intentions rather than their results"
Milton Friedman- Interview with Richard Heffner, December 7, 1975

"The world runs on individuals pursuing their self interests.
The great achievements of civilization have not
come from government bureaus.
Einstein didn't construct his theory
under order from a bureaucrat.
Henry Ford didn't revolutionize the automobile industry that
way. The only cases in which the masses have escaped
from the kind of grinding poverty...
in recorded history, are where they have had
capitalism and largely free trade."
Milton Friedman- Interview on The Phil Donahue Show 1979

"The society that puts equality before freedom
will end up with neither,
The society that puts freedom before equality
will get a high degree of both."
Milton Friedman- 'Free to Choose' the television series
'Created Equal' episode

"Economic freedom is an essential requisite for political freedom.
By enabling people to cooperate with one another
without coercion or central direction,
it reduces the area over which political power is exercised.
In addition, by dispersing power, the free market provides
an offset to whatever concentration of political power may arise.
The combination of economic and political power
in the same hands is a sure recipe for tyranny."
Milton Friedman- Free to Choose 1980

"Freedom is a tenable objective only for responsible individuals"
Milton Friedman- Free to Choose 1980

"Only government can take perfectly good paper, cover it with perfectly good ink and make the combination worthless."
Milton Friedman- Tyranny of the Status Quo Chapter 3 1984

"The only way that has ever been discovered to have a lot of people cooperate together voluntarily is through the free market. And that's why it's so essential to preserving individual freedom."
Milton Friedman- 'The Indispensable Milton Friedman'; On Freedom and Free Markets page 233

Ronald Wilson Reagan

The Great Communicator
Fortieth President of the USA

What are the attributes that shape leadership? President John Adams once said, "If your actions inspire others to dream more, learn more, do more and become more, you are a leader." John Adams would have approved of Ronald Reagan. His communication skills evolved over a lifetime and perfected at a time when they were needed most; as the 40th president of the United States. His immortal words inspire us today and will for years to come.

Ronald Wilson Reagan was born in Tampico, Illinois on February 6, 1911, to John and Nelle Reagan and joined an older brother Neil. According to family legend he earned the nicknamed "Dutch" from his father's observation that the young Ronald resembled a fat little Dutchman. John, known to all as "Jack" was the product of a tough upbringing, losing both his parents to tuberculosis before he reached the age of six. Raised by an elderly aunt, he became cynical, especially living through the prejudice of "Irish Need Not Apply" signs and the occasion of drinking too much at times. He became a shoe salesman, an exceptional storyteller, and a fiercely outspoken critic towards anyone who displayed any tendencies for prejudice, bigotry and intolerance. Ronald's father established this household value, "We care about things outside of us, we don't just talk about our wants and the ambitions in this family, we talk about what's needed in the world."[161] His mother Nelle was a deeply religious homemaker of the Protestant faith. Her deep beliefs in the blessings of God coupled with her eternal optimism had a lifelong lasting affect on her two sons. Neil and Ron regularly attended church and Sunday school.

Seeking better employment opportunities, the Reagan family moved five times in seven years. When Ronald turned nine, they moved to Dixon, Illinois. In small town Dixon, he learned the value of neighbor helping neighbor, the advantages of hard work and love of country. In High School he was president of the Dramatic Club, participated on the football team, and became a lifeguard at Lowell Park where he racked up seventy-seven lives saved over seven years. In his senior year, politics came calling and he was elected the student class president. In 1928, he entered Eureka College in Illinois to study economics. He played football and was chosen as the leader in a student revolt against critical college cutbacks. His words achieved the desired results, and the cutbacks never materialized. He worked washing dishes to offset tuition costs. Following college he landed a job as a sports announcer at radio station WOC in Davenport, Iowa, later getting national exposure on radio station WHO in Des Moines, broadcasting Chicago Cubs baseball games. Blessed with a distinctive voice that exuded honesty, self confidence and the ability to create images with words, his radio days helped to hone his communication skills. He joined the Army Reserve as a private in 1935 and two years later he traveled to California to attend the Chicago Cubs spring training session. While there, he took a screen test for the Warner Bros. studios and a month following, signed a contract with them. His first role was that of a radio announcer in a movie called *Love Is on the Air*. Later, in the movie, *Brother Rat* he met actress Jane Wyman and married her on January 26, 1940. That same year he won critical acclaim for his role of "George 'The Gipper' Gipp" in the biographical film about legendary Notre Dame football coach, Knute Rockne entitled, *Knute Rockne, All American*. The phrase he uttered, "...Win just one for the Gipper." would follow him well into his political career where in addition to being called 'Dutch' he was affectionately called 'The Gipper.' Other good roles would follow, including the role of father when a daughter, Maureen was born, but months after the bombing of Pearl Harbor and America's entry into World War II, his motion picture acting career would be put on hold. Reagan's was called to active duty in the Army Air Corps. Poor eyesight kept him stateside where throughout the war he produced hundreds of training films for the G.I.'s and was promoted to captain. He had seen classified films from Hitler's Nazi Party, detailing the horror and butchery of the death camps with the strewn disfigured bodies of Holocaust victims. The flickering celluloid images were a source of perpetual disgust. Months before the war ended, an adopted son, Michael joined the household, and he returned to acting and a multi million dollar contract. At this time in his life, Reagan, politically, was like his father, a Democrat. He supported President Roosevelt's New Deal programs and the rights of unions. He spoke up for America and rallied about his distain for fascism. He joined several groups including the American Veterans Committee and the Hollywood Democratic Committee. When he became aware that communist sympathy and suggestion was rampant at the meetings, he resigned from those organizations. There was growing concern that Communist influence was sweeping through Hollywood, backed up by FBI investigations. He became a board member of the Screen Actors Guild and devoted himself to that labor union. When studio strikes threatened the industry, Reagan became part of a fact finding group that determined the Guild's bylaws must be maintained and the strikes must not be respected. He received a call from an unidentified man warning him that if he spoke up with his findings, "Your face will never be in pictures."[162] The threats were serious but Reagan was unwavering. He was fitted with a shoulder holster carrying a 32 caliber Smith & Wesson pistol, and a twenty-four hour armed guard.

During a prolonged union labor strike in 1946 between the Screen Actors Guild and a Communist backed, Conference of Studio Unions, physical violence sprang up outside the studio gates. Bodies were beaten and cars were firebombed. Members of the Communist Party responsible for the unrest went public and admitted that Moscow had directed much of the action.[163] Vladimir Lenin, the creator of the Soviet Communist Party was accredited with the quote "Of all the arts, the cinema is the most important for us." It was unquestionably a vital visual art form that had a powerful impact on society.

The more Reagan learned about communism and the threat it posed to individual freedoms and the destruction of religion, the more he spoke out against it. He was relentless to this cause, doing all he could to draw attention to the curse of that philosophy. In March 1947 he was elected the President of the Screen Actors Guild, and later in October he testified at the House Committee on Un-American Activities hearings in Washington, DC. Before the Congress he remarked, "...In opposing those people, the best thing to do is make democracy work. In the Screen Actors Guild we make it work by insuring everyone a vote and by keeping everyone informed...however, if it is proven that an organization is an agent of a foreign power, or in any way not a legitimate political party – and I think the government is capable of proving that – then that is another matter...I do not believe the Communists have ever at any time been able to use the motion picture screen as a sounding board for their philosophy or ideology." Reagan was not pleased by over ambitious members of the House Un-American Activities Committee to blacklist innocent Hollywood activists, and set up a system where those falsely accused could openly voice their opposition to Communism and clear their names. His leadership and negotiation abilities were noticed, he would be reelected as President of SAG for five consecutive terms. Sterling Hayden, was a Communist who was part of the attempt to change Hollywood, and later left the Communist Party. When testifying before the Congress under oath, he was asked why the Communists did not succeed in taking Hollywood. He revealed, "We ran into a one-man battalion named Ronnie Reagan."[164]

At home, his relationship with his wife Jane deteriorated to a point where they divorced in the summer of 1949. Three years later he married another actress, Nancy Davis, who he met when she approached him as the president of the actor's guild to have her good reputation restored, when her name appeared accidentally on a 'blacklist.' Their first child, Patty was born in 1952. They appeared together on screen only one time in the movie entitled, *Hellcats of the Navy*, and a year later in May 1958, Nancy gave birth to their son Ron Jr.

Ronald Reagan's guidance on free market principles and capitalism were brought to fruition by his association with General Electric's Vice President, Lemuel Boulware. Boulware was an extraordinary manager and distinguished negotiator when dealing with labor unions. When in 1946, General Electric suffered the consequences of a crippling nationwide strike, none of the 16,000 employees under Boulware walked out.[165] He was a hands on teacher who visited all the company plants working closely with his executives and more importantly the blue collar staff. He learned of their concerns and taught the necessity of economics, free market concepts, and the stranglehold of government spending. With his movie career winding down, General Electric hired Reagan in 1954 to host a weekly television dramatic series which became known as *General Electric Theatre*. As host to the *GE Theater*, which soon became the country's top-rated Sunday evening prime-time program.[166] Reagan's personality became well known. In his contract, he would become a company goodwill ambassador, to travel and visit with company employees throughout the country. Boulware provided Reagan with his unique negotiating skills and introduced the works of Hayek, Hazlitt, Milton Friedman and others. The GE Vice President knew the advantages of educating his employees on the virtues of economics by taking this message directly to them and sidestepping politically motivated union officials in the process. Traveling predominately by train across the country, allowed Reagan time to absorb his reading material, the setbacks of big government intervention, overtaxation and the misfortune of socialism. He met with thousands of employees, spoke with them, but more significantly he listened to their concerns and researched each question he was unsure of, only to follow up by using his fact finding in the next meeting. His speeches at assembly lines and various plants recognized the respect and value for the individual. He saw firsthand the virtues of non-government interference and free market choice. The warehouse floor question and answer sessions that concluded each gathering tremendously amplified his skill as a 'great communicator.'

During his stint with GE he officially changed his political party affiliation from Democrat to Republican. He observed his old party of being for higher taxes and antibusiness leaving him to often repeat, "I didn't leave the Democratic party, the Democratic Party left me."[167] When Reagan and GE parted ways in 1962, he stood on the threshold of his political life. He had read Republican Arizona Senator Barry Goldwater's book, *The Conscience of a Conservative* and endorsed his candidacy in his 1964 presidential run against President Lyndon Johnson, in a televised address which became known as "The Speech" and "A Time for Choosing." It aired on October 27 of that year. All he had learned and held dear to his heart was proclaimed in that presentation. He spoke of the communist threat to the American way of life. He outlined the menace of an ever expanding central government, and bravely gave examples of elected representatives who supported those dangerous ideas. In part he told the audience:

"You and I are told increasingly that we have to choose between a left or right, but I would like to suggest that there is no such thing as a left or right. There is only an up or down--up to a man's age-old dream, the ultimate in individual freedom consistent with law and order--or down to the ant heap of totalitarianism, and regardless of their sincerity, their humanitarian motives, those who would trade our freedom for security have embarked on this downward course. In this vote-harvesting time, they use terms like the "Great Society," or as we were told a few days ago by the President, we must accept a "greater government activity in the affairs of the people." But they have been a little more explicit in the past and among themselves--and all of the things that I now will quote have appeared in print. These are not Republican accusations. For example, they have voices that say "the cold war will end through our acceptance of a not undemocratic socialism." Another voice says that the profit motive has become outmoded, it must be replaced by the incentives of the welfare state; or our traditional system of individual freedom is incapable of solving the complex problems of the 20th century. Senator Fullbright has said at Stanford University that the Constitution is outmoded. He referred to the president as our moral teacher and our leader, and he said he is hobbled in his task by the restrictions of power imposed on him by this antiquated document. He must be freed so that he can do for us what he knows is best. And Senator Clark of Pennsylvania, another articulate spokesman, defines liberalism as "meeting the material needs of the masses through the full power of centralized government." Well, I for one resent it when a representative of the people refers to you and me--the free man and woman of this country--as "the masses." This is a term we haven't applied to ourselves in America. But beyond that, "the full power of centralized government"--this was the very thing the Founding Fathers sought to minimize. They knew that governments don't control things. A government can't control the economy without controlling people. And they know when a government sets out to do that, it must use force and coercion to achieve its purpose. They also knew, those Founding Fathers, that outside of its legitimate functions, government does nothing as well or as economically as the private sector of the economy."

He concluded "The Speech" by detailing the high moral character of candidate Goldwater ending with a challenge of utmost importance to the nation's survival, "You and I have a rendezvous with destiny. We'll preserve for our children this, the last best hope of man on earth, or we'll sentence them to take the last step into a thousand years of darkness..." His articulation was flawless.

Soon after, Reagan's political career was launched. He ran for governor of California in 1966 coming out on top of several Republican nominees and soundly defeated the popular two term governor, Edmund G. "Pat" Brown by nearly a million votes. The Brown administration had spent nearly a million dollars a day more than it was taking in with revenues leaving Reagan with deficit of at least a $167 million.[168] Forced to temporarily increase taxes, he took his message directly to the people and explained how he would proceed in seriously controlling state spending, and at the same time vowed to return any state surplus money to the taxpayers. As promised, in 1968 and three other occasions, over five billion dollars in taxes were returned to the people of California during his eight years as governor.[169] He called out the National Guard when asked by college administrators to bring order to the University of Berkeley when violent rioters brought injury, destroyed property and denied others their education. He signed the Welfare Reform Act to stop fraud and waste in that program saving millions more. His hands-on attitude in harmony with the confidence in his ideas and ability to win over skeptics were bedrock values in setting his sights to national attention. In the two-hundredth year since America's declaration for liberty, Reagan focused at the highest office of the land by challenging President Gerald Ford for the party's nomination. He campaigned enthusiastically but lost the nomination; despite the outcome he confidently told his supporters that, "the cause goes on." The party lost the presidential election to the Governor of Georgia, Jimmy Carter. Four short years later he would face President Carter, whose favorability rating was dreadful due to his stumbling in both domestic and international arenas. Overseas, the Soviet invasion of Afghanistan and the televised taking of American hostages in Iran for four hundred and forty days topped the list, and at home things were worse. The energy crisis, double digit inflation, high interest rates and unemployment were the topics of conversation. Despite the media polls showing him and Carter in a dead heat in the last week of the presidential campaign, Reagan won in a landslide taking 44 of 50 states[170] making him the fortieth president of the United States. Following his oath of office on January 20, 1981, he took the opportunity to address the pitfalls facing the American people, namely high taxation and the ever growing and expanding government. "In this present crisis, government is not the solution to our problem; government is the problem." He went on to outline that the real strength of the United States lie with its people, a refrain that he would refer to often during his presidency.

"If we look to the answer as to why, for so many years we achieved so much, prospered as no other people on Earth, it was because here in this land we unleashed the energy and individual genius of man to a greater extent than has ever been done before. Freedom and the dignity of the individual have been more available and assured here than in any other place on Earth. The price for this freedom at times has been high, but we have never been unwilling to pay that price."[171]

Following his inaugural speech, President Reagan learned that the Iranian hostage crisis was finally over, the fifty-five Americans held in captivity for almost fifteen months were being released and en route to a U.S. Air Force hospital in Wiesbaden, Germany prior to coming home. He sent Jimmy Carter the next day to meet with them. This high point in Reagan's presidency would be shattered months later when on March 30, an assassination attempt was made on his life. Reagan had just delivered a speech in Washington D.C. to the Construction Trade Council when walking outside past reporters and camera crews, shots were fired from the handgun of a neurotic young man named John Hinckley Jr. His shots hit the president's press secretary James Brady, a secret service agent, a police officer and the gunman's target, President Reagan. The bullet ricocheted off of the door of the presidential limousine and entered Reagan's body under his left arm puncturing his left lung and lodging close to his heart just as a secret service agent flung him inside the vehicle. He was sped to George Washington University Hospital and as his Attorney General Edwin Meese III recalled, "there was a meeting of emergency room doctors at the hospital that very day, and the President received the finest medical attention one could possibly obtain."[172] In the days that followed this tragedy the American people were enamored with reports of the president's wit and humor, joking with the surgeons before the operation to remove the bullet and afterwards with his wife Nancy, telling her, "Honey..I forgot to duck." The courage, prayers and positive attitude exhibited by Reagan lifted all spirits, and endeared him to the country. Steadfast in his determination to push forward his economic recovery plans, he held a bipartisan conference of Congressional leadership in the White House during his recovery in his bathrobe. Comical as this image may conjure up, it was definitely unique. Throughout his presidency, upon entering the Oval office he was respectfully dressed in a business suit and never took off his jacket while there. His reverence for the office and the historical decisions that took place there were humbling, he saw the presidency as something much larger than himself.[173]

Following his recovery, Reagan's presidency was faced with a national altercation that would confront his leadership. The Professional Air Traffic Controllers Organization (PATCO) was threatening to strike unless wages for their members doubled. The cost to taxpayers for such an action would have been devastating, not to mention the resulting economic setbacks in grounding airline passenger and cargo flights. Reagan reminded their leadership that he was a former union president himself, he understood the clout they held, but their strike was illegal. Each member of the union had signed a sworn affidavit not to walk off their jobs. Reagan answered the PATCO strike demands in a Rose Garden press event on August 3, 1981 that demanded their members have forty-eight hours to end their strike plans or be fired. Period. It was a matter of national security that the skies over America be always protected. The deadline passed and 30 percent of the PATCO members returned to work but 70 percent stayed out resulting in the termination of 11,400 employees. Reagan held fast to the law and those that stayed plus the new controllers that were hired developed a new and safe air control system faster than the administration had hoped.[174] It was certain the Soviet Union was watching how the president of the US handled this national crisis. The PATCO union head lost his job as a result.

He had trust in the power of his ideas, the skills to make the complex simple and the sense of humor to charm any and all within earshot, all the prerequisites for captivating communication. His deeply held religious beliefs molded his leadership decisions and his ability to seek out experts in the field of economics such as Milton Friedman only enhanced his confidence in explaining issues of major importance to the American people such as supply-side economics. "Supply–side economics fit well with Reagan's fundamental view that the American people could solve the country's problems if government simply got out of the way."[175] On August 13, 1981 Reagan signed a tax cut bill known as the Economic Recovery Tax Act as a mechanism to bring a growing government under control and put more money back into the hands of the people who earned it. His faith in the American people was his eternal belief as was the optimism of his economic policies and he would reference it often.

It paid off.

In two years his "stay the course" slogan brought about for the nation "the longest and strongest peacetime economic expansion in history, an expansion that would eventually bring more than twenty-million new jobs..."[176] The naysayers in the media, in the Democratic party and some in his own party were wrong about their criticism of Reaganomics. When he first took office the top marginal rate was seventy percent, when he left the White House it was twenty-eight percent.

When it came to America's Cold War opponent the Soviet Union, Reagan negotiated with them on the basis of holding economic and military strength over a communist system that could not mask its domination over its people. As a keen observer that regimes resolute in the use of tyranny to control its masses with machine gun towers, concrete walls, barb wire fences lined with patrolling soldiers and attack dogs had to deal with endless attempts by their populace to flee to democratic freedom loving societies, it was communism's weakness on full display. Comfortable in his assessment, he ignored his critics at every turn and spoke openly and directly at every major speech on the sufferings of communist expansionism. Reagan did not approach the threat of the Soviet Union the same way his Oval office predecessors had in the past. He did not believe that we could deny any longer that Communist morality was a far cry from religious morality. Reagan understood the thinking in the minds of the leaders of the communist movement. He spoke openly and directly about the threat of Soviet expansionism and the perils it presented to every person caught in its wake by denying them freedom. He called them the "evil empire" when addressing a group of Evangelical Christians on March 8, 1983, and explained;

"...I pointed out that, as good Marxist-Leninists, the Soviet leaders have openly and publicly declared that the only morality they recognize is that which will further their cause, which is world revolution. I think I should point out I was only quoting Lenin, their guiding spirit, who said in 1920 that they repudiate all morality that proceeds from supernatural ideas—that's their name for religion—or ideas that are outside class conceptions. Morality is entirely subordinate to the interests of class war. And everything is moral that is necessary for the annihilation of the old, exploiting social order and for uniting the proletariat. Well, I think the refusal of many influential people to accept this elementary fact of Soviet doctrine illustrates a historical reluctance to see totalitarian powers for what they are. We saw this phenomenon in the 1930s. We see it too often today. This doesn't mean we should isolate ourselves and refuse to seek an understanding with them. I intend to do everything I can to persuade them of our peaceful intent,....At the same time, however, they must be made to understand we will never compromise our principles and standards. We will never give away our freedom. We will never abandon our belief in God. And we will never stop searching for a genuine peace." Within the contents of that speech he went on to praise the men who words and deeds he idolized, Abraham Lincoln, Thomas Jefferson,   Alexis de Tocqueville and George Washington who said that "of all the dispositions and habits which lead to political prosperity, religion and morality are indispensable supports."[177]

On Election Day in 1984, Reagan won his second term in a forty-nine state landslide victory over Carter's Vice President, Walter Mondale due mostly to the economic turnaround in the country. Later, Reagan met with Mikhail Gorbachev in 1985 in Geneva, Switzerland after three Soviet leaders died in office during Reagan's first term. The meeting was to start a dialogue in improving U.S. and Soviet relations and to dismantle Cold War tension and political hostility. Reagan and Gorbachev met to open communications on the reduction of nuclear arms within their respective countries and developed a civil association. Reagan suspected accurately that the Soviet interest was entirely economic in nature. To compete with American capitalism and buildup of the military technology, the Soviets were holding a weak negotiating hand, either buildup their military or feed their people. When they met again, this time in Reykjavik, Iceland on October 11, 1986 to further talks in arms reduction, Gorbachev made known his ironclad intention that the U.S. must, before any more talk of arms reduction could take place, cease any future development of SDI, known as the Strategic Defense Initiative, a system that would lock on and destroy any incoming warhead missiles aimed at America or its allies. It was here in these meetings with his Soviet adversary that all his communication and bargaining skills learned over his lifetime would coalesce into history changing events. The President refused Gorbachev's terms. SDI or 'Star Wars' (as the press called it) was not a bargaining chip. It was an insurance policy for the U.S. against any present or future enemies with nuclear weaponry. Reagan announced, "The meeting is over," and got up and left with his Secretary of State George Schultz.[178] The Soviet leader had misread Reagan's strength and commitment and calculated he would succumb to the media pressure at home to accept the Soviet's gracious offer of substantial reductions of weapons. Reagan remained resilient against all critics of which there were many and remained faithful to his ideals.

The Berlin Wall was erected by the Communists in 1961 to keep East Berliners from escaping to the free democratic West Berlin. President Reagan traveled to West Germany on June 12, 1987, and standing a few feet away from the Berlin Wall near the Brandenburg Gate delivered a memorable speech that reverberated around the world. He again challenged the folly of communist rule by telling the assembly,

"...We welcome change and openness; for we believe that freedom and security go together, that the advance of human liberty can only strengthen the cause of world peace. There is one sign the Soviets can make that would be unmistakable, that would advance dramatically the cause of freedom and peace. General Secretary Gorbachev, if you seek peace, if you seek prosperity for the Soviet Union and Eastern Europe, if you seek liberalization: Come here to this gate! Mr. Gorbachev, open this gate!

Mr. Gorbachev, tear down this wall!..."[179]

The challenge to Soviet domination seriously delivered by the 40th president brought the Soviet leader back to the negotiating table, which resulted in a signing ceremony in the East Room of the White House on December 8, 1987. The historic INF (Intermediate-Range Nuclear Forces) Treaty ended a class of nuclear weapons, reduced political tensions between the two countries, and ended the Cold War. The Prime Minister of Britain, Lady Margaret Thatcher was a like minded conservative leader whose friendship and alliance with Reagan changed the world. She noted that Reagan ended the Cold War without firing a shot. His strong spine and faith in doing what was right despite the pressures of the naysayers ended Soviet supremacy, and Eastern Europe flourished with new found freedom. The Gipper strongly accepted the expression of "trust but verify."

The 'wall' would come down a short two years later, on November 9, 1989, and with the dismantling of it came the reunification of Germany and the collapse of the Soviet Union. Reagan would travel back to where he gave his "Tear down the

Wall" speech after he left the presidency to take a few whacks at the wall himself. Years later, Reagan dedicated the first Ronald Reagan Freedom Award to Mikhail Gorbachev at the Ronald Reagan Presidential Library on May 4, 1992. Eight months later, on January 13, 1993, he was awarded the Presidential Medal of Freedom from his successor, President George H.W. Bush.

As the Great Communicator, it was easy to see why this man from humble beginnings was able to touch so many hearts. His verbal deliveries were always full of humorous one-liners, historical references, and honest patriotic pride that spoke to Republicans, Independents and Democrats as well. He was confident to discuss solutions to the nation's problems directly with the American people, and did so occasionally by side stepping the media sources that were in large part, hostile to his his thinking. He was comfortable with the camera, poised, truthful and sincere. His speech induced witticisms were from a thick collection of 4-by-6 hand written note cards that he kept in his desk back from his days as a spokesman for General Electric. On each one he jotted down jokes, one-liners and quotes from the minds of John and Samuel Adams, Edmund Burke, Cicero, Churchill, Edison, Thomas Jefferson, James Madison, George Washington, Patrick Henry, John F. Kennedy, Abraham Lincoln, Montesquieu, Adam Smith, Mahatma Gandhi and many others. Certain cards held lifelong reminders of phrases about religious faith, free markets, freedoms of each and every kind, and forgiveness. Self deprecating gags about government, socialism and his age were microphone mainstays. "You'll always stay young if you live honestly, eat slowly, sleep sufficiently, work industriously, worship faithfully and lie about your age." [180]

The 'notes' were placed into proper categories and were a vital part of his public speeches, their purpose was to inject the right ideas at exactly the right time with the proper inflection for the desired impact. A seasoned professional, he depended on memory needing no teleprompter. There were times when Americans needed a laugh or two, and Reagan was quick to deliver. Other times demanded spiritual reflection when somber situations arose and he did not disappoint. ."

At a moments notice, national and world headlines would shout out tragic events that would dispirit the emotions of the American people, and all eyes would fall on Reagan for answers. The terrorist bombings of the American embassy and the U.S. marine barracks in Beirut, took the lives of embassy assigned Americans and 241 Marines respectively. The Soviet Union attack on a Korean airliner KAL 007 that killed hundreds including U.S. Congressman Lawrence McDonald from Georgia. The hijacking of the *Achille Lauro*, an Italian cruise ship that resulted in the murder of an American wheelchair bound victim Leon Klinghoffer, the space shuttle Challenger explosion on January 28, 1986, that snuffed out the lives of seven American explorers seventy-three seconds after liftoff. Thirty-seven sailors were killed on the USS Stark by Iranian fanatics in May 1987. The scourge of terrorism against Americans was consistently making headline news and after the lessons learned the Iranian hostage crisis that crippled Jimmy Carter's administration, Reagan pursued attacks on Americans. When the *Achille Lauro* hijackers surrendered in Egypt and Reagan learned that an Egyptian aircraft was taking them to Tunisia, he ordered the aircraft intercepted by four Navy F-14's who forced the plane down in Sicily, where Italian authorities jailed and tried them. This serious approach to terrorism would be repeated months later when the terrorist headquarters and other selected targets held by the fanatical Libyan leader Muammar Qaddafi in Tripoli were bombed by US aircraft under orders of the president. The action was in retaliation of the death of a US serviceman and others in a West Berlin discotheque on April 5, 1986, of which Qaddafi was behind. Qaddafi had threatened US warships in international waters in northern Africa and members of the Reagan administration with death before the discotheque bombing. Hard US action against him, through the bombing of his headquarters, had silenced the Libyan leader for the remainder of the Reagan's stay in Washington, DC.

The Iran-Contra scandal was fodder for the American press corps and put Reagan in the middle of a presidential scandal. The intent behind the affair was the eagerness of high ranking members of the administration to free American hostages being held by the Islamic group Hezbollah by the illegal selling of military weapons to Iranian interests, funds from the sale were to be rerouted to aid freedom fighting Contras in Nicaragua. In the aftermath of the scandal, the president was found innocent of illegalities but several Cabinet members paid a fine and lost their positions.

Reagan was fond of reviewing the men and women in uniform and was the first president to routinely return the salute of military personnel assigned to protect him on and off Air Force One and Marine One.

His admiration for our protecters of freedom was legendary. One memorable occasion was his strong voice that paid tribute on June 6, 1984, the fortieth anniversary of the D-Day invasion in France to free Europe and end Hitler's regime. Reagan traveled to the shores of Normandy, France and gave a stirring oratory on the courage demonstrated on that fateful day. Reagan spoke directly to the honored veterans who returned to the cliffs. In part he said:

> "These are the boys of Pointe du Hoc.
> These are the men who took the cliffs.
> These are the champions who helped free a continent.
> These are the heroes who helped end a war."

In his presidential farewell speech, the President, summarized his historical two terms in the Oval office in a sincere passionate manner. Anyone that wants to understand Reagan can, by reading his speech, get a sense of what Reagan was all about. What it was like to be 'Reaganesque.' He talked about the honor he had to hold the position, about the "American miracle" that was his economic programs, about the "greatness" of our country and to "Trust, but verify" when dealing with the Communist Soviet Union. He reminded Americans to have "informed patriotism" and to "teach history" to future Americans. His farewell speech was full of visual imagery especially when he spoke of America as "The shining city on a hill." (The term, as Reagan noted, was accredited to John Winthrop, a Puritan minister who came to the New World in 1630 and whose leadership earned him the title of governor of the Massachusetts Bay Colony.)

"...The past few days when I've been at that window upstairs, I've thought a bit of the 'shining city upon a hill.' The phrase comes from John Winthrop, who wrote it to describe the America he imagined. What he imagined was important because he was an early Pilgrim, an early freedom man. He journeyed here on what today we'd call a little wooden boat; and like the other Pilgrims, he was looking for a home that would be free. I've spoken of the shining city all my political life, but I don't know if I ever quite communicated what I saw when I said it. But in my mind it was a tall, proud city built on rocks stronger than oceans, windswept, God-blessed, and teeming with people of all kinds living in harmony and peace; a city with free ports that hummed with commerce and creativity. And if there had to be city walls, the walls had doors and the doors were open to anyone with the will and the heart to get here. That's how I saw it, and see it still. And how stands the city on this winter night? More prosperous, more secure, and happier than it was eight years ago. But more than that: After 200 years, two centuries, she still stands strong and true on the granite ridge, and her glow has held steady no matter what storm. And she's still a beacon, still a magnet for all who must have freedom, for all the pilgrims from all the lost places who are hurtling through the darkness, toward home..."[181]

After leaving the White House, the Reagans returned to California where he gave speeches promoting freedom both at home and abroad. He wrote his memoirs and autobiography entitled *"An American Life: The Autobiography"* and collaborated on other works surrounding his speeches and humor. When he was diagnosed with the debilitating Alzheimer's disease he chose to share the grim news with the world to bring awareness to the disease and to say goodbye. At age eighty-three he wrote this heartfelt letter on November 5, 1994.

"My Fellow Americans,

I have recently been told that I am one of the millions of Americans who will be afflicted with Alzheimer's Disease. Upon learning this news, Nancy and I had to decide whether as private citizens we would keep this a private matter or whether we would make this news known in a public way. In the past Nancy suffered from breast cancer and I had my cancer surgeries. We found through our open disclosures we were able to raise public awareness. We were happy that as a result many more people underwent testing. They were treated in early stages and able to return to normal, healthy lives. So now, we feel it is important to share it with you. In opening our hearts, we hope this might promote greater awareness of this condition. Perhaps it will encourage a clearer understanding of the individuals and families who are affected by it. At the moment I feel just fine. I intend to live the remainder of the years God gives me on this earth doing the things I have always done. I will continue to share life's journey with my beloved Nancy and my family. I plan to enjoy the great outdoors and stay in touch with my friends and supporters. Unfortunately, as Alzheimer's Disease progresses, the family often bears a heavy burden. I only wish there was some way I could spare Nancy from this painful experience. When the time comes I am confident that with your help she will face it with faith and courage. In closing let me thank you, the American people for giving me the great honor of allowing me to serve as your President. When the Lord calls me home, whenever that may be, I will leave with the greatest love for this country of ours and eternal optimism for its future. I now begin the journey that will lead me into the sunset of my life. I know that for America there will always be a bright dawn ahead. Thank you, my friends.

May God always bless you.

Sincerely,
Ronald Reagan"

Almost ten years later on June 5, 2004, a nation mourned when Ronald Wilson Reagan passed away at his home in Bel Air at age ninety-three. Thousands of mourners lined up on both coasts to pay their respects for this beloved man. His flag draped casket was at his presidential library in Simi Valley California and then ceremoniously flown by Air Force One to Washington D.C. carried by horse-drawn caisson to lie in state at the Capital Rotunda. His personal riding boots placed backwards in the stirrups on a riderless horse to symbolize that the rider was gone. A week of eulogies, reverence and honor were finalized on June 11, when his body was returned to the Ronald Reagan Presidential Library to be entombed forever.

"Freedom is never more than one generation
away from extinction.
We didn't pass it on to our children in the bloodstream.
It must be fought for, protected, and handed on for them to do
the same, or one day we will spend our sunset years telling our
children and our children's children what it was once
like in the United States where men were free."
*Ronald Reagan-Remarks at the Annual meeting Phoenix Chamber of
Commerce, March 30, 1961*

"One legislator accused me of having a nineteenth-century
attitude on law and order. That is a totally false charge.
I have an eighteenth-century attitude.
That is when the Founding Fathers made it clear
that the safety of law-abiding citizens should be one
of the government's primary concerns."
*Ronald Reagan-Speech to the Republican State Central Committee,
September 7, 1973*

"God had a divine purpose in placing this land between
two great oceans to be found by those who had
a special love of freedom and the courage
to leave the countries of their birth"
Ronald Reagan- Speech "To Restore America,"
during his Campaign for the Presidency, March 31, 1976:

"At the root of everything that we're trying to accomplish
is the belief that America has a mission.
We are a nation of freedom, living under God, believing all
citizens must have the opportunity to grow, create wealth, and
build a better life for those who follow.
If we live up to those moral values, we can keep the American
dream alive for our children and our grandchildren,
and America will remain mankind's best hope."
Ronald Reagan-Remarks Celebrating Hispanic Heritage
September 15 1982

"The first amendment was not written to protect
people and their laws from religious values,
it was written to protect those values from government tyranny."
Ronald Reagan-Annual Convention of Religious Broadcasters
January 31, 1983

"I've never felt more strongly that America's best days and
democracy's best days lie ahead. We're a powerful force for
good. With faith and courage, we can perform great deeds and
take freedom's next step. And we will. We will carry on the
tradition of a good and worthy people who have brought light
where there was darkness, warmth where there was cold,
medicine where there was disease, food where there was hunger,
and peace where there was only bloodshed. Let us be sure that
those who come after will say of us in our time, that in our time
we did everything that could be done.

We finished the race; we kept them free; we kept the faith."
President Reagan 'State of the Union' speech, Jan 25, 1984
"There is no limit to what a man can do or where he can go
if he doesn't mind who gets the credit"
sign on the Presidential desk of Ronald Reagan

"We in America have learned bitter lessons from two World
Wars: It is better to be here ready to protect the peace,
than to take blind shelter across the sea,
rushing to respond only after freedom is lost.
We've learned that isolationism never was and never will be an
acceptable response to tyrannical governments
with an expansionist intent."
*Ronald Reagan- at the U.S. Ranger Monument at Pointe du Hoc
on the fortieth anniversary of D-Day June 6, 1884*

"With me, abortion is not a problem of religion, it's a problem of
the Constitution. I believe that until and unless someone can
establish that the unborn child is not a living human being, then
that child is already protected by the Constitution, which
guarantees life, liberty, and the pursuit of happiness to all of us."
Ronald Reagan- Debate with Walter Mondale, October 7, 1984

"America will never be whole as long as the right to life
granted by our Creator is denied to the unborn."
Ronald Reagan- State of the Union Address February 4, 1986

"I hope we have once again reminded people that man
is not free unless government is limited. There's a clear cause
and effect here that is as neat and predictable as a law of physics:

as government expands, liberty contracts."
Ronald Reagan-Farewell Address January 12, 1989
"And whatever else history may say about me when I'm gone,
I hope it will record that I appealed to your best hopes,
not your worst fears, to your confidence
rather than your doubts."
Ronald Reagan-speech at the Republican National Convention 1992

"So the president resisted Soviet expansion and pressed down
on Soviet weakness at every point until the day came when
communism began to collapse beneath the combined weight
of those pressures and its own failures.
And when a man of good will did emerge from the ruins,
President Reagan stepped forward to shake his hand and
to offer sincere cooperation.
Nothing was more typical of Ronald Reagan than that large-
hearted magnanimity, and nothing was more American.
Therein lies perhaps the final explanation of his achievements.
Ronald Reagan carried the American people with him
in his great endeavors because there was
perfect sympathy between them.
He and they loved America and what it stands for:
freedom and opportunity for ordinary people."
Eulogy for President Reagan by Margaret Thatcher June 11, 2004

Margaret Thatcher
"The Iron Lady"

Poise and self-assurance go hand-in-hand as the attributes necessary to bring skeptics aboard when tasks that are deemed impossible need to be set right. Margaret Thatcher was a principled leader whose spotlighted accomplishments transformed her country, Great Britain. Her influence transcended the borders of her country and the world took notice. She was born Margaret Roberts on October 13, 1925 in Grantham, England to Alfred and Beatrice Roberts and joined an older sister Muriel born in 1921. Their family income depended on the two grocery stores their hard working parents ran, and living above one of the shops, provided the local customers access to goods beyond the store's set hours. The Roberts girls were involved in the inner workings of the store, including the task of delivering groceries to others. Sundays were spent at Sunday school followed by eleven o'clock service and then back to Sunday school in the afternoon. Her Methodist upbringing promoted deeply held religious values, reinforced in her church, and by her father who was sought after as a lay preacher as well. The church was a major source of her spiritual and social well being. As a teenager she saw the swift rise of Hitler's Third Reich and witnessed first hand the folly of Prime Minister Arthur Neville Chamberlain's appeasement foreign policy in trusting the German dictator. She remembered, after the Battle of Britain, as devastation rained down into the cities of England, killing seventy-eight in her town, that she was comforted by the words of a preacher that stayed with her for a lifetime, "it is always the few, who save the many."[182] Alfred Roberts was involved in the Grantham community by holding town positions as councillor, Chairman of the Borough Finance Committee and in 1945 as mayor. Margaret would recall that he was a staunch Conservative who held to the ethics of individual responsibility and sound finance; a "highly principled man" holding "upright qualities, which entailed a refusal to alter your convictions just because others disagreed or you became unpopular,"[183]

These convictions were implanted into her at a young age.

While the war raged on, she attended Oxford in 1943 to study Chemistry, and during her attendance there joined the Oxford University Conservative Association. The organization held to her way of thinking, sponsoring lively debates, participating in election campaigns and bringing her into the company of many well-known politicians and civic leaders. Her involvement focused her attention to receive lessons in public speaking which served her well when she was later elected president of the group. She admired the fortitude and resilience of Prime Minister Winston Churchill during Britain's nightmarish times of World War II and was an eyewitness to the treachery and hopelessness of Hitler's state controlled dominance. While at Oxford she read accounts of the D-Day invasion, the dropping of the atomic bombs in Hiroshima and Nagasaki, and the surrender of Germany and Japan. Graduating in 1947 with a degree in Chemistry, Margaret Roberts found employment in the research and development field for a company that specialized in plastics, but outside the workplace she joined the Conservative Association and like her father, pursued political office. Her goals were ambitious, striving to be democratically elected to Great Britain's lower house of Parliament otherwise known as the House of Commons. Impressed by her political passion, she was brought to the attention of her party's leadership and set her sights on an industrial stronghold seat of Dartford held by the opposition Labour Party in the 1950 election. The campaign brought the twenty-four year old national attention as the youngest female candidate to speak in front of postwar audiences and listen attentively to their concerns. It was during the Borough of Dartford office run that she met wealthy businessman Denis Thatcher, and discovering that they had much in common, began dating. Despite the rigorous effort, she lost the election but severely cut into the Labour majorities. She married Denis Thatcher on December 13, 1951, moved to London and in 1953 birth to twins, a daughter Carol and a son

Mark. As a new mother she studied taxation law and passed the bar, reentered politics, and in 1959 was elected as a Member of Parliament for the town of Finchley in Middlesex County. Their home was hectic with conflicting demands on their time, but despite the needs of two six year olds, her parliamentary duties and his work oftentimes abroad, Margaret insisted on full family attendance at breakfast. Sundays were spent together for religious services. At the House of Commons, the first bills she was exposed to were trade union rise and abuse of power, she studied the facts and learned well from senior members. Over the years, with budget numbers at the ready, she was not impressed with the management of the economy and out of control government spending. On foreign affairs in 1961, she followed the frosty relationship between the Soviet leader Khrushchev and U.S. President Kennedy as well as the communist construction of the Berlin Wall. Prime Minister Harold Macmillan appointed her as Parliamentary Under Secretary in Ministry of Pensions and National Insurance on October 9, 1961. The Labour Party became dominant in the years 1964 to 1970, however when Conservatives won the general election in 1970, she became the Education and Science Secretary under Prime Minister Edward Heath. Years later, Heath's leadership as head of the Conservative party came into question. Topping the list of problems was the miners' strike and one million unemployed workers, coupled with two back to back election losses which returned political authority back to Labour jurisdiction. Heath had a string of broken promises, reversing his conservative ethics by not standing up to unions and ignoring free market positions. When oil prices rose in 1974 due to punishing Middle East positions, Heath (like President Nixon in America) sought government intervention. Thatcher challenged Heath on the management of the issues at hand. In 1975 she was elected the head of her Conservative party, the first woman to that position, but the Labour Party in control from 1974 to 1979 catapulted England into an economic tailspin. The value of the currency was diminished to the point that bankruptcy was near certain, forcing Britain to pay its bills with borrowed money from the International Monetary Fund, and trade union wage demands resulted in labor strikes that took their toll. Thatcher read the work of Frederick Hayek, *The Road to Serfdom*, which soundly criticized socialism, and documented the point that the socialist state must be avoided. "The mid 70's was also a time of advance by the Left...in many areas and ways. Communist parties seemed to be on the verge of entering governments in Mediterranean Europe"[184] Unwilling to ignore the obvious, Thatcher used the occasion of a speech in Kensington Town Hall on January 19, 1976 that both made a stinging attack on the Soviet Union and accused the Labour Government of 'dismantling our defense at a moment when the strategic threat to Britain and her allies from an expansionist power is graver than at any moment since the end of the last war:

"The Russians are bent on world dominance, and they are rapidly acquiring the means to become the most powerful imperial nation the world has seen. The men in the Soviet Politburo do not have to worry about the ebb and flow of public opinion. They put guns before butter, while we put just about everything before guns." [185] In response, the Soviet propaganda newspaper *Red Star* called Margaret Thatcher the "*Iron Lady.*" A nickname that would become a title she would relish and live up to.

Elected Prime Minister on May 4, 1979, she inherited a country at its worst. Britain was known throughout the world as the "sick man of Europe" following the government's paralyzing 'Winter of Discontent' caused by industrial chaos, heavy snow and floods and the need for trade union reform. The "National Health Service and local authority workers Union turned down a five per cent pay raise and announced their intent to 'strike' in the New Year (1979), the Transport and General Workers' Union called a strike after seeking a twenty-five per cent pay raise, terminally ill hospital patients were denied treatment, Gravediggers went on strike and refuse piled up in Leicester

Square. Britain ground to a halt"[186] The public was desirable of change and the Conservatives were swept into power.

Prime Minister Thatcher was determined to put the 'great' back into Great Britain. On October 10, 1980, "The Lady is Not for Turning" speech at the Conservative Conference outlined her seriousness and unwavering determination:

"If our people feel that they are part of a great nation and they are prepared to will the means to keep it great, a great nation we shall be, and shall remain. So, what can stop us from achieving this? What then stands in our way? The prospect of another winter of discontent? I suppose it might. But I prefer to believe that certain lessons have been learnt from experience, that we are coming, slowly, painfully, to an autumn of understanding. And I hope that it will be followed by a winter of common sense. If it is not, we shall not be—diverted from our course. To those waiting with bated breath for that favourite media catchphrase, the 'U-turn', I have only one thing to say: 'You turn [U-turn] if you want to. The lady's not for turning. I say that not only to you but to our friends overseas and also to those who are not our friends"[187]

As a leader there was no denying she was setting a clear unapologetic conservative agenda of her policies, driven by personal confidence while possessing the talent to explain in clear uncompromising terms the significance of her positions, but most importantly, she was able to organize and garner support to see her plans succeed.

As prime minister she knew the British people deserved much better than the dreary outlook that surrounded and smothered them. Thatcher's main duty was to improve the economy by bravely standing up to the trade unions whose fiscal demands were, in a sense, holding the public hostage, and appeasement to water down her visions was not in her vocabulary. Drastic reforms were necessary and the moral courage to oppose principle weakening compromise had to be vocalized unapologetically loud and clear. She knew her cost cutting agenda would be reported unfairly by the opposition and knew harsh public ridicule by instituting privatization of vital services, would follow. Above all, she valued free markets, entrepreneurship and faith in individual freedoms.

Across the pond, she found the like-minded, newly elected President Ronald Reagan abundantly supportive of her goals. Reagan like Thatcher, held to conservative ideals, and had challenged his own party leader, 'moderate' Republican President Gerald Ford for the nomination of his party in 1976, however, unlike Thatcher, he was unsuccessful, yet undaunted. He launched a victorious campaign four years later. On January 20, 1981 President Ronald Reagan took the oath of office and Thatcher was quick to congratulate him and "was determined to display her devotion to their common perception of how to solve the world's problems by arriving in person to clinch their working relationship."[188] Reagan understood that the prime minister had economic woes that surpassed any rationality. After World War II, the heavy government regulations, universal health care and cradle to grave pensions for everyone, (not just the unemployed and disabled) took their toll and any cut back of government spending would be met with loud public outcries.
Not only did Reagan and Thatcher share fiscal misery in their respective countries, they realized the Soviet build up of nuclear arms spending and the dangerous spread of communism threatened trade and left misery in its wake. Together they, with the blessings of Pope John Paul II and 'Solidarity' leader Lech Walesa both from Poland, they were able to beat back the Soviet Cold War without firing a shot.

On April 2, 1982, Argentina invaded the Falkland Islands, located in the south Atlantic Ocean, the islands were under the jurisdiction of the British crown and lay eight thousand miles from mainland England. The Argentine invasion was motivated by its close location to the islands and the claim that the land belonged to Argentina. Its leadership, headed by General

Galtieri felt strongly that there would be no military response from Great Britain. When warning signs of trouble were witnessed a month earlier, talks to diffuse a conflict went nowhere, despite negotiations to avoid armed battle, even Reagan called Galtieri, but was unable to diffuse the situation. Galtieri informed him that the Falklands "rightfully belonged to Argentina, not a European colonial power, and that Argentina's national honor was at stake in establishing sovereignty over them."[189] The sixty British marines stationed there were overwhelmed and forced to surrender, the Falkland governor was removed to Uruguay and spoke to Thatcher relaying that Argentine military units attacked the capitol by land and sea.

Prime Minister Thatcher fiercely defended her decision to attack the unprovoked aggressors in the Falklands, from a "common dictator." Despite the naval logistics and the nearest support airbase four thousand miles away, she ordered up a task force to retake the Falklands. The Queen's navy and Royal Air Force were dispatched, reaching the islands on May 21 and gunfire was exchanged. When the white flags of Argentine surrender were flown over Port Stanley, Thatcher arrived at the House of Commons to claim victory on June 14, 1982. She spoke to the assembly, "We have ceased to be a nation in retreat. We have instead a new found confidence born in the economic battles at home and tested and found eight thousand miles away..."[190]

The skirmish in the Falklands was not diversionary enough to stop fiscal problem solving back at home. There was much room for improvement by promoting private enterprise and ownership by moving ahead and selling off British state-owned industries to the free market. Privatization lists included British Telecom, British Airways, the airports, Rolls Royce, and others. A year after the Falkland victory, her respect at home was climbing, she, along with her conservative majority won an impressive landslide second general election on June 9, 1983. The momentum for Thatcher's economic revolution was gaining speed, but on March 12, 1984, The National Union of Mineworkers launched a coal strike. This important strike controlled the vast amount of the energy needed to run the country and its tentacles reached into other industries as well. The union leader, Arthur Scargill was a radical socialist who once proposed to "take into common ownership everything in Britain."[191] The thrust of the strike was the government's reported closure of mine pits that were unprofitable due in part with the dangers and high costs of deep shaft mining and the competition of other global energy markets. Reputable sources determined that seventy-five percent of British mines were generating huge losses and surviving "only because the government was spending more than a billion pounds a year to subsidize it..."[192] Thatcher pointed out the bureaucrats that managed the coal industry and the miner's union were perfect examples of socialism: wasteful, irresponsible and unaccountable. The strike made the headlines, mob rule turned violent often with clashes between Scargill's picketers and police. Thatcher was reminded that in August 1981 President Reagan faced a crippling strike with PATCO union air traffic controllers that affected airline safety. He knew their actions violated federal law and when 'return to work' ultimatums were not met, he had the lawbreakers fired. Valid actions that won the respect and approval of the American people. Thatcher knew there was no alternative but to beat Scargill. Having the foresight to see the strike before it fully materialized, she ordered the stockpiling of coal and warned to prepare for alternate fuel sources. Laws were made to make unions liable to civil suits. Month after month dragged on and Scargill was losing the battle, having found to be taking money from terrorist sponsored Libya and Soviet sources, the brutality of the strikers lost public support and members sued their union for striking without a ballot. Thatcher remained firm, determined not to give in to their demands and the miners started to cross the picket lines to return to work. After nearly a year on March 3, 1985, union delegates of the National Union of Mineworkers admitted defeat, shunned Arthur Scargill and the strike was over. The prime minister, like her political confidante and friend Ronald Reagan, survived an assassination   attempt by an Irish

Republican Army terrorist bomb near her hotel room on October 12, 1984. She and Denis were spared, five friends were killed, and the wife of her cabinet minister was paralyzed. She gave her speech as scheduled hours later to the Conservative Party conference upholding her government's economic policies and warning the terrorist that their attempt to destroy democracy has failed.

The Soviet Union leadership turned over four times during Thatcher's reign as Prime Minister. Starting with Leonid Brezhnev, Yuri Andropov, Konstantin Chernenko and finally Mikhail Gorbachev. It was Gorbachev that Thatcher felt she could negotiate with when he emerged on the scene as a prospective future Soviet leader and invited him to Britain in December of 1984 days before she was to meet with Reagan. Throughout their meeting she found Mikhail, confident and likable but she made it well known she detested communism and the weakness of the Soviet system. She diplomatically explained that she and Reagan agreed that regarding arms control, they "had an obligation to try to resolve the differences between East and West."[193] She warned him of the sound allied relationship with America by sharing the same ideas and defending the same principles. Gorbachev was the chosen successor three months later when Chernenko died, Thatcher's opinions paved the way for President Reagan to meet the Soviet leader and discuss matters of mutual importance. In spring 1986, the disastrous meltdown of the Ukrainian Chernobyl nuclear power station and resulting explosion left death and a cancer causing cloud of radiation across Europe. This was further evidence of the trouble with the Soviet government and exposed the logic of reducing nuclear arms. Reagan was unyielding in his support for the U.S. Strategic Defense Initiative in defending against a nuclear attack and the Soviet Union soon collapsed under the weight of self imposed economic burdens. The Soviet choice was simple; either feed your people or feed your missile silos. As a serious player on the world stage, Prime Minister Thatcher's career was a testament to the recklessness of socialism and the world's communist nations could not ignore the strength she demonstrated by defending U.S., Great Britain, and Western Europe unity to stand up to Soviet aggression by supporting the deployment of Pershing II missiles to guard against Soviet missiles. She supported the defeat of a foreign aggressor on British holdings and turned around a failed socialist economy at home by initiating liberty for all through conservatism. Her accomplishments could not be ignored and she won a third general election on June 11, 1987.

Reagan and Gorbachev signed a treaty on December 8, 1987 to eliminate all intermediate-range ballistic and cruise missiles. Later, serious cutbacks of Soviet military presence in Eastern Europe opened up free speech in Hungary and in 1989 the removal of troops in Afghanistan, and free elections in Poland. The leadership role Thatcher played in ending the Cold War is historically noteworthy, she opened up and maintained beneficial communications. The example she set by installing free markets and individual freedom defined the folly of socialism, her grasp on judging personalities and opening dialogue, notably Gorbachev and her trust in Reagan gave way to grand goals and the world took notice. Thatcher wrote years later in her book, *The Downing Street Years*, "The credit for these historic achievements must go principally to the United States and in particular to President Reagan, whose policies of military and economic competition with the Soviet Union forced the Soviet leaders, in particular Mr. Gorbachev, to abandon their ambitions of hegemony and to embark on the process of reform which in the end brought the entire communist system crashing down."[194]

In Britain, a new tax system was put into place for local governments named the Community Charge and the localities took advantage by raising tax rates and pointing the finger at the Thatcher administration. In addition, the reunification of Germany had stepped up discussion of creating a European Union with a single currency, and major members of her cabinet rallied for Britain to enter this arrangement, against the viewpoints of the Prime Minister, who wanted Britain's control of its currency to remain in Britain, not in a European community. She saw a super-state European Union as problematic. Verbal disputes gave way to key staff resignations, resulting in crucial rifts in the party and her tenure was questioned. Thatcher resigned as Prime Minister in 1990 after three terms and was the longest office holding prime minister of the twentieth century. She was honored by President George H.W. Bush with the U.S. Presidential Medal of Freedom on March 7, 1991. The medal is the highest civilian award in the United States that appreciates those individuals who have made "an especially meritorious contribution to the security or national interests of the United States, world peace, cultural or other significant public or private endeavors" and is not limited only to U.S. citizens.

Remaining dominant as a political figure, she became Baroness Thatcher in the House of Lords, devoting her time to lecturing throughout the world, and writing two books on her memoirs, *The Downing Street Years* in 1993 and *The Path to Power* in 1995. In March 2002 after suffering several small strokes she ended her public speaking and Denis, her husband of over fifty-two years died in 2003. When doctor's orders prevented her from traveling abroad when President Reagan died in June 2004, she give a stirring eulogy via a video link, that reflected on his accomplishments and their mutual friendship. It began, "We have lost a great president, a great American, and a great man, and I have lost a dear friend."[195]

Margaret Thatcher passed away on April 8, 2013 of a stroke at the age of 87. Her devotion to high moral standards and the cause of liberty for the individual endeared her to millions, and in the process, made her one of the most respected and influential political leaders of her time. Freedom works and she embraced it and shared it with her countrymen. Her most staunch critics regarded her as uncaring for the state welfare institutions but no one could deny the importance of her transformations in her country and abroad. Her legacy is inspirational.

"...Our opponents like to try and make you believe that
Conservatism is a privilege of the few. But Conservatism
conserves all that is great and best in the national heritage...
We say one nation, not one class against another.
You cannot build a great nation by spreading envy or hatred.
Our policy is not built on envy or hatred, but on liberty
for the individual man or woman.
It is not our policy to suppress success: our policy is to
encourage it and encourage energy and initiative. In 1940 it was
not the cry of nationalism that made this country rise up and
fight totalitarianism. It was the cry for freedom and liberty."
Margaret Thatcher, campaign speech, Lowfield Street Church Hall
1950

"And I will go on criticizing Socialism, and opposing Socialism
because it is bad for Britain and Britain and Socialism are not the
same thing. It's the Labour Government that have brought us
record peace-time taxation. They've got the usual Socialist
disease --they've run out of other people's money."
Margaret Thatcher-Speech to Conservative Party Conference
October 10, 1975

"To me, consensus seems to be the process of abandoning all
beliefs, principles, values and policies.
So it is something in which no one believes
and to which no one objects."
Margaret Thatcher, Speech at Monash University
October 6, 1981

"Mr. Chairman, people want to live in peace, real, lasting peace...
The peace that comes from independence of the state and being
able to run your own life, spend your own money and
make your own choices.
And, above all, the peace of a country which is properly
defended against any potential adversary."
Margaret Thatcher; Speech to Conservative Family Rally at Wembley;
June 7, 1987

"I think we've been through a period where too many people
have been given to understand that if they have a problem,
it's the government's job to cope with it.
'I have a problem, I'll get a grant.' 'I'm homeless, the government
must house me.' They're casting their problem on society.
And, you know, there is no such thing as society.
There are individual men and women, and there are families.
And no government can do anything except through people, and
people must look to themselves first. It's our duty to look after
ourselves and then, also to look after our neighbor.
People have got the entitlements too much in mind, without the
obligations. There's no such thing as entitlement,
unless someone has first met an obligation."
Margaret Thatcher; talking with Women's Own magazine;
October 31, 1987

Jesus Christ

"The Son of God"
"The Prince of Peace"
"Liberator of Mankind from the Penalty and Power of Sin"

The literary piece *"One Solitary Life"* says it best.

Here is a man who was born in an obscure village, the child of a peasant woman. He grew up in another village. He worked in a carpenter shop until He was thirty. Then for three years
He was an itinerant preacher.
He never owned a home. He never wrote a book.
He never held an office. He never had a family.
He never went to college. He never put His foot inside a big city.
He never traveled two hundred miles from the place He was born. He never did one of the things that usually accompany greatness. He had no credentials but Himself...While still a young man, the tide of popular opinion turned against him. His friends ran away. One of them denied Him. He was turned over to His enemies.
He went through the mockery of a trial. He was nailed upon a cross between two thieves. While He was dying His executioners gambled for the only piece of property He had on earth – His coat. When He was dead, He was laid in a borrowed grave through the pity of a friend.
Nineteen long centuries have come and gone, and today
He is a centerpiece of the human race and leader of the column of progress.
I am far within the mark when I say that all the armies that ever marched, all the navies that were ever built; all the parliaments that ever sat and all the kings that ever reigned, put together, have not affected the life of man upon this earth as powerfully as has that one solitary life.

The teachings of Jesus Christ along with the parables and writings of the Bible had an immense influence on the minds, hearts and character of everyone aforementioned. What a person believes is unquestionably revealed in their behavior. Why did all these individuals hold to such passionate views of liberty and freedom? Why were they willing to take such risks to personal safety and loss of possessions? The answer is obvious; it was their faith in the great liberator Himself, Jesus Christ.

The book of Galatians (N.T.) chapter 5, verse 1 "Stand fast therefore in the liberty by which Christ has made us free, and do not be entangled again in a yoke of bondage."

The Spirit of God was guiding all of these men and women in their quest for the liberation of their people and although they do not mention Him by name often, His is an unseen hand at work in their lives, the results of which make evident, his influence.

Acknowledgements

The art of writing is a craft that I respect greatly and it is one I struggle with immensely whenever a project comes to my mind. This undertaking was no exception to that rule, but the effort to put thoughts to the keyboard are dwarfed by my enthusiasm to share this project with others. It was that zeal that propelled me forward. I thank my wife Debbie for the many hours I spent in researching this compilation, and the patience she shown in my pursuits. She is the ultimate life partner and the love of my life. My family has grown in recent years and we welcomed two son-in-laws Ben and Jeff into the clan. Ben and Pamela have given us three beautiful grandchildren, Jane, Alison, and Joshua who are the source of our unbounded love and devotion. In the midsts of this writing, their futures frequently occupied my thoughts. Our daughter Patricia continues to make us proud in all her endeavors, her classroom aptitude in teaching her young students the skills they need to become virtuous members in the community is a 'plus' for everyone whose lives she touches. My mother Evelyn is the bright light in all our lives. Our shared love of God keeps us on an even keel. The unique abilities of my brother William provided me with insights into our country's inception with stories from the pulpit. He helped steer this work into a direction I hardly envisioned at first, but one that needed to be reemphasized. His red pen remarks were essential and his emails welcome. I could not have completed these stories without him. To my brothers and sister, their families and my extended family, you are in my thoughts as well. A special appreciation goes out to my nephew, Dereck for his original artwork of Jesus Christ, and my nephew Robert for his help in graphics layout.

The idea for *The Liberty Leaders, A Family Dinner Table Textbook* was spawned from my frustration with the lack of vital information in both my daughter's public school American history textbooks, my love of our country, (my mom and dad were the driving force) and the Talk Radio medium. The ability of talented hosts behind the microphones, to reach their listeners and teach with passion the political and social events of the day as they relate to what has happened in the past. It is a free and insightful education of the highest order.

Historic names and circumstances breathe new life to our memories and find revived places in everyday discussions. These events must not be forgotten, for they are the very essence of what we should respect and hold dear as a nation of free men and women. No one I know does it consistently better than my friend, talk radio host and author, Mark R. Levin. His devotion for America and its founding principles resound warmly with his vast audience, me included. His exhaustive research in delivering attentive monologues and discussions on radio and in his books have long caught my interest and in so doing, inspired me dig deeper into research myself. I was unfamiliar with John Locke, Charles Secondat Baron de Montesquieu, Adam Smith or Alexis de Tocqueville. I heard of Edmund Burke and Milton Friedman but was not as up to speed as to what their sole contribution to the American way was, but I do know now. Thanks in part to Mark.

I have always held deep praise for those American citizens who still hold dear the values that have made their country so exceptional and do not hide their strong held beliefs. These liberty patriots have a fond affection for the gift to humanity that is the United States Constitution and I hold them all in high esteem. I would be remiss if I failed to acknowledge all those men and women who serve in our armed services to protect the freedoms we have inherited, and lastly and most importantly, to the parents and guardians who have taken it upon themselves to home school their children in the virtues and subjects that when applied and reinforced, make for a better society.

Bibliography

The references and materials listed below that were used in this book are exceptional sources of expanded knowledge with the authors providing a comprehensive grasp on the topics they have chosen.

Abraham Lincoln letter to Jesse W. Fell, Tuesday, December 20, 1859; *Abraham Lincoln Papers at the Library of Congress*

Adler, Bill; *The Wit & Wisdom of Abraham Lincoln*; Carol Publishing Corp; New York; 1993

Berlinski, Claire; *There is No Alternative, Why Margaret Thatcher Matters*; Basic Books Publishers; New York, N.Y.; 2008

Brinkley, Douglas; *Ronald Reagan The Notes Ronald Reagan's Private Collection of Stories and Wisdom*; HarperCollins Publishers Inc., New York, N.Y.; 2011

Bradford Sarah H.; *Harriet Tubman The Moses of Her People*; an exact, unaltered and unabridged, reprint of the expanded second edition of 1886; Corinth Books Inc.; New York; 1961

Brogan, Hugh; *Alexis de Tocqueville; A Life*; New Haven & London: Yale University Press; 2006

Burlingame, Michael; *The Inner World of Abraham Lincoln*; University of Illinois Press; Urbana and Chicago; 1994

Burns, James MacGregor & Dunn, Susan; *George Washington*; Times Books Henry Holt & Comapny, New York; 2004

Calkhoven, Laurie; *Harriet Tubman Leading the Way to Freedom*; Sterling Biographies; New York; 2008

Cayton, Andrew; Elisabeth Israels Perry, Linda Reed, Allan M. Winkler; *America Pathways to the Present*; Prentice Hall, Massachusetts and New Jersey; 2000

Crompton, Samuel Willard; *John Adams, American Patriot*; Chelsea House Publishers; Philadelphia; 2006

Cunningham, Noble E. Jr.; *In Pursuit of Reason, The Life of Thomas Jefferson*; Louisiana State University Press, Baton Rouge and London; 1987

Diggins, John Patrick; *John Adams, The American Presidents Series*; Time Books; New York; 2003

Douglass Autobiographies, *Narrative of the Life of Frederick Douglass an American Slave, My Bondage and My Freedom, Life and Times of Frederick Douglass*; The Library of America; New York, N.Y., Volume compilation; 1994

Dreisbach, Daniel L.; *The Mythical "Wall of Separation": How a Misused Metaphor Changed Church–State Law, Policy, and Discourse*; Heritage Foundation Published on June 23, 2006, by First Principles Series Report #6

Ebenstein, Lanny; *Milton Friedman, A Biography*; Palgrave Macmillan, New York, N.Y. 2007

Ebenstein, William; *Great Political Thinkers, Plato to the Present,* fourth edition; Holt, Rinehart and Winston Inc.; New York, Chicago, San Francisco, Atlanta, Dallas, Montreal, Toronto, London, Sydney; 1969

Evans, Thomas W.; *The Education of Ronald Reagan, The General Electric Years and the Untold Story of His Conversion to Conservatism*; Columbia University Press; New York; 2006

Everitt, Anthony; *Cicero The Life and Times of Rome's Greatest Politician*; Random House Inc.; New York; 2001

Flexner, James Thomas; *George Washington and the New Nation*; Little, Brown and Company; Boston, Toronto; 1969

Franklin, Benjamin; *The Autobiography of Benjamin Franklin*; International Collectors Library, Garden City New York, Houghton Mifflin Company; 1923

Friedman, Milton & Rose; *Free to Choose, A Personal Statement*; Harcourt Brace Jovanovich; New York and London; 1980

Gay, Peter; The Enlightenment: An Interpretation Vol.II: The Science of Freedom; Alfred A. Knopf, New York; 1969;

Gonzalez, Justo L.; *The Story of Christianity volume I, The Early Church to the dawn of Reformation*; Prince Press; Peabody, Massachusetts; 1999

Grayling, A.C; *Toward the Light of Liberty, The Struggles for Freedom and Rights that Made the Modern Western World*; Walker Publishing Company Inc.; New York; 2007

Hill, B.W.; *Edmund Burke on Government, Politics and Society*; International Publications Service; 1976

Hort, Lenny; *George Washington, A Photographic Story of a Life*; DK Publishing; New York; 2005

Kengor, Paul; *God and Ronald Reagan A Spiritual Life*; Reganbooks HarperCollins Publishers Inc., New York, N.Y.; 2004

Kinnaird, Clark; *George Washington, The Pictorial Biograghy*; Hastings House Publishers; New York; 1967

Kowalski, Gary; *Revolutionary Spirits The Enlightened Faith of America's Founding Fathers*; BlueBridge Publishers; New York; 2008

Kramnick, Isaac; *Great Lives Observed, Edmund Burke*; Prentice-Hall, Inc., Englewood Cliffs, NJ; 1974

Larson, Kate; *Bound for the Promised Land, Harriet Tubman Portrait of an American Hero*; A Ballantine Book, Random House Publishing; New York; 2004

Lawrence, George; *Democracy in America by Alexis de Tocqueville A New Translation*; edited by J.P. Mayer & Max Lerner; Harper & Row, Publishers, New York, Evanston, London; 1966

Leidner, Gordon; *Lincoln on God and Country*; White Mane Books; Shippenburg, Pa; 2000

Levin, Mark R.; *Ameritopia The Unmaking of America*; Threshold Editions a Division of Simon & Schuster, New York; 2012

Levin, Mark R.; *Men in Black, How the Supreme Court is Destroying America*; Regnery Publishing, Washington D.C.; 2005

Lind, Michael; *What Lincoln Believed The Values and Convictions of America's Greatest President*; Doubleday; New York; 2005

Lindsay, Lawrence; *The Growth Experiment*; New York Basic Books; 1990

Marsden, George M.; *The Short Life of Jonathan Edwards*; Wm. B. Eerdmans Pub.; Grand Rapids, Michigan; 2008

McCullough David; *John Adams*; Simon & Schuster; New York; 2001

McGowan James A & Kashatus William C.; *Harriet Tubman A Biography*; Greenwood Biographies; ABC-CLIO, LLC; Santa Barbara, Ca; 2011

Meese, Edwin III; *With Reagan: The Inside Story; Regnery Gateway*; Washington D.C.; 1992

Morris, Richard B.; *The Encyclopedia of American History*; Harper & Brothers Publishers; New York; 1953

Mount, Daniel J.; *The Faith of America's Presidents*; Living Ink Books; Chattenooga, Tennessee; 2007

Nelson, Michael, editor; *The Presidency The History of the President of the U.S. from 1789 to the Present*; Smithmark Publishers; New York, N.Y.; 1996

Noonan, Peggy; *When Character Was King A Story of Ronald Reagan*; Penguin Putnam Inc., New York N.Y.; 2001

Pangle, Thomas L; *Confronting the Constitution; Chapter 2 The Philosophic Understandings of Human Nature Informing the Constitution*; The AEI Press, Washington D.C.; 1990

Peterson, Merrill D.; *James Madison, A Biography in His Own Words*; Harper & Row Publishers Inc., New York; 1974

Phillipson, Nicholas; *Adam Smith An Enlightened Life*; Yale University Press,New Haven & London; 2010

Ross, Ian Simpson; *The Life of Adam Smith*; Clerendon Press, Oxford; 1995

Sahakian, Mabel Lewis & William S.; *John Locke*; Twayne Publishers, Boston; 1975

Skousen, Mark Ph.D.; *The Completed Autobiography of Benjamin Franklin*; Regnery Publishing, Inc., Washington D.C.; 2006

Southworth, Gertrude and John Van Duyn; *The Story of Our America*; Iroquois Publishing Company Inc. Syracuse New York; 1951

Sterngass Jon; *Leaders of the Civil War Era Frederick Douglass*; Chelsea House Publishers; New York, N.Y.; 2009

Thatcher, Margaret; *The Downing Street Years*; HarperCollins Publishers; New York N.Y.; 1993

Thatcher, Margaret; *The Path to Power*; HarperCollins Publishers; New York N.Y.; 1995

Wallison, Peter J.; *Ronald Reagan, The Power of Conviction and the Success of His Presidency*; Westview Press, Boulder Colorado; 2003

Wapshott, Nicholas; *Ronald Reagan and Margaret Thatcher A Political Marriage*; Penguin Group Publishers; New York, N.Y.; 2007

Warner, Michael; *American Sermons, The Pilgrims to Martin Luther King Jr.*; Literary Classics of the United States; New York; 1999

Wright, Benjamin F.; *The Federalist, the Famous Papers on the Principles of American Government*; Barnes & Noble, New York; 2004

http://www.biograghy.com/articles/Edmund-Burke-9231699

http://www.margaretthatcher.org

Notes

All pictures and photos used in this book have been obtained via public domain fair use sources.

My 'Introduction' Ronald Reagan quote from his March 30, 1961, speech to the Phoenix Chamber of Commerce. President Ronald Reagan photo courtesy of The Ronald Reagan Presidential Library.

Jefferson quotes source: www.monticello.org

President Abraham Lincoln photo courtesy of the National Archives; Mathew Brady series Photographs of Civil War-Era Personalities and Scenes.

Frederick Douglass photo courtesy of the National Archives, Frank W. Legg Photographic Collection of Portraits of Nineteenth-Century Notables Collection.

The Milton Friedman photo from The Friedman Foundation for Educational Choice.

"A Time for Choosing" speech excerpt from the Ronald Reagan Presidential Library.

The essay 'One Solitary Life' was adapted from a sermon by Dr. James Allan Francis in "The Real Jesus and Other Sermons" ©1926 by the Judson Press of Philadelphia (pp 123-124 titled "Arise Sir Knight!")
Dereck D. Gallerani provided the original artwork of the Jesus Christ illustration.

Book cover photograph and design by Donald R. Gallerani
Book front and back graphic layout by Robert L. Gallerani

Endnotes

[1] Everitt, Anthony; *Cicero The Life and Times of Rome's Greatest Politician*; New York; 2001; page 182

[2] Ibid; page 183

[3] Ibid; Preface vii

[4] William Ebenstein; *Great Political Thinkers, Plato to the Present forth edition*; Holt, Rinehart and Winston Inc.; New York; 1969 page136

[5] Ibid; pages 137-138

[6] William Ebenstein; Great Political Thinkers, Plato to the Present; 4th edition; 1969, page 392

[7] Mabel Lewis & William S. Sahakian; *John Locke*; Twayne Publishers, Boston; 1975; page 48

[8] Roger Woolhouse; *Locke a Biography*; New York; Cambridge University Press; 2007 page 182

[9] Ibid page 183

[10] James A. Donald; *Natural Law and Natural Rights;* http:// jim.com/rights.html; June 29, 2010

[11] William Ebenstein; *Great Political Thinkers, Plato to the Present 4th Edition*; Holt, Rinehart & Winston Inc.; New York; 1969, page 394

[12] Mabel Lewis & William S. Sahakian; *John Locke*; Twayne Publishers, Boston;1975; page 95

[13] Peter Gay; *The Enlightenment: An Interpretation Vol.II: The Science of Freedom*; Alfred A. Knopf, New York 1969; page 506

[14] A.C. Grayling; *Toward the Light of Liberty, The Struggles for Freedom and Rights that made the Modern Western World*; Walker Publishing Company Inc., New York 2007; page 140

[15] William Ebenstein; *Great Political Thinkers, Plato to the Present 4th Edition*; Holt, Rinehart & Winston Inc.; New York; 1969; page 433

[16] A.C. Grayling; *Toward the Light of Liberty, The Struggles for Freedom and Rights that made the Modern Western World*; Walker Publishing Company Inc., New York 2007; page 142

[17] William Ebenstein; *Great Political Thinkers, Plato to the Present 4th Edition*; Holt, Rinehart & Winston Inc.; New York; 1969; page 436

[18] Thomas L. Pangle; *Confronting the Constitution*; *Chapter 2 The Philosophic Understandings of Human Nature Informing the Constitution*; The AEI Press, Washington D.C. 1990; page 17

[19] Mark R. Levin; *Ameritopia The Unmaking of America*; Threshold Editions, New York; 2012; page 158

[20] Mark Skousen, Ph.D.; *The Completed Autobiography of Benjamin Franklin*; Regnery Publishing Inc.,*Washington D.C.; 2006; page 42*

[21] http://www.artdaily.com/index.asp?int_new=41381&int_sec=2#

[22] Mark Skousen, Ph.D.; *The Completed Autobiography of Benjamin Franklin*; Regnery Publishing Inc.,*Washington D.C.; 2006; page* 57

[23] Ibid; page 79

[24] Ibid, page 145

[25] Ibid, page 153

[26] Ian Simpson Ross; *The Life of Adam Smith*; Clarendon Press, Oxford; 1995; page xxiv

[27] Nicholas Phillipson; *Adam Smith An Enlightened Life*; Yale University Press,New Haven & London; 2010; page 217

[28] Ibid; page 237

[29] I Ian Simpson Ross; *The Life of Adam Smith*; Clareendon Press, Oxford; 1995; pages 280-281

[30] Burton Yale; *Reagonomics and Conservatism's Future: Two Lectures in China*; The Heritage Foundation; published March 14, 1987

[31] B.W. Hill; *Edmund Burke on Government, Politics and Society*; International Publications Service, 1976; page 12

[32] www.biography.com/articles/Edmund-Burke-9231699

[33] Ibid

[34] Isaac Kramnick; *Great Lives Observed, Edmund Burke*; Prentice-Hall, Inc., Englewood Cliffs, NJ; 1974, page 22

[35] Ibid page 23

[36] B.W. Hill; *Edmund Burke on Government, Politics and Society*; International Publications Service, U.S.A. 1976; page 48

[37] Ibid, page 34

[38] William Ebenstein; *Great Political Thinkers, Plato to the Present forth edition*; Holt, Rinehart and Winston Inc.; New York; 1969; page 478

[39] Ibid, page 41

[40] Ibid, page 84

[41] Ibid, page 85

[42] Douglas Brinkley; Ronald Reagan The Notes Ronald Reagan's Private Collection of Stories and Wisdom; HarperCollins Publishers; 2011; page 39

43 http://www.richmondhillhistory.org/clergy.html

44 Justo L. Gonzalez; *The Story of Christianity volume I, The Early Church to the dawn of Reformation*; Prince Press, Peabody, Massachusetts; page 230

45 Michael Warner; *American Sermons, the Pilgrims to Martin Luther King Jr.*; Literary Classics of the US; New York; 1999; page 362

46 George M. Marsden; A Short Life of Jonathan Edwards; William B. Eerdmans Publishing Co.; Grand Rapids, Michigan; 2008, page 187

47 *The Autobiography of Benjamin Franklin*; International Collectors Library, Garden City New York, Houghton Mifflin Company 1923. page 149

48 George M. Marsden; *The Short Life of Jonathan Edwards*; Wm B.Eeermans Publisher; Grand Rapids, Michigan; 2008; page 54

49 George Grant; *The Patriot's Handbook Second Edition*; Cumberland House Publishers; Nashville Tn.;2004; page 145

50 Michael Warner; *American Sermons, The Pilgrims to Martin Luther King Jr.*; Literary Classics of the United States; New York; 1999; page 902

51 James MacGregor Burns & Susan Dunn; *George Washington*; Times Books Henry Holt & Comapny, New York; 2004; page 6

52 Richard B. Morris, Editor; *The Encyclopedia of American History*; Harper & Brothers Publishers; New York; 1953; page 67

53 James MacGregor & Susan Dunn; *George Washington*; Henry Holt & Co.; New York; 2004; page 26

54 Clark Kinnaird; *George Washington, The Pictorial Biography*; Hastings House Publishers; New York; 1967; page 77

55 Ibid; page 77

56 Ibid; page 127

[57] Burns, James MacGregor & Dunn, Susan; *George Washington*; Times Books Henry Holt & Co.; 2004; page 36

[58] McCullough David; *John Adams*; Simon & Schuster; New York; 2001, page 403

[59] Flexner, James Thomas; *George Washington and the New Nation (1783-1793)*; Little, Brown & Co.; Boston; 1969; page 183

[60] Clark Kinnaird; *George Washington, The Pictorial Biograghy*; Hastings House Publishers; New York; 1967; page 245

[61] McCullough David; *John Adams*; Simon & Schuster; New York; 2001, page 533

[62] Clark Kinnaird; *George Washington, The Pictorial Biograghy*; Hastings House Publishers; New York; 1967; page 246

[63] McCullough David; *John Adams*; Simon & Schuster; New York; 2001, page 33

[64] Samuel Willard Crompton; *John Adams, American Patriot*; Chelsea House Publishers; Philadelphia; 2006; page 25

[65] David McCullough; *John Adams*; Simon & Schuster; New York; 2001, page 68

[66] John Patrick Diggins; *John Adams, The American Presidents Series;* Time Books; New York; 2003; page 29

[67] David McCullough; *John Adams*; Simon & Schuster; New York; 2001, page 118

[68] Ibid; page 114

[69] Ibid; page 119

[70] John Patrick Diggins; *John Adams, The American Presidents Series;* Time Books; New York; 2003; page 35

[71] David McCullough; *John Adams*; Simon & Schuster; New York; 2001, page 336

[72] John Patrick Diggins; *John Adams, The American Presidents Series;* Time Books; New York; 2003; page 42

[73] Ibid page 73

[74] Ibid; page 44

[75] Ibid; page 98

[76] Ibid; page 111

[77] David McCullough; *John Adams*; Simon & Schuster; New York; 2001, page 537

[78] Ibid; page 552

[79] Ibid; page 622

[80] Gary Kowalski; *Revolutionary Spirits, The Enlightened Faith of America's Founding Fathers*; BlueBridge Publishers; New York; 2008; page 147

[81] David McCullough; *John Adams*; Simon & Schuster; New York; 2001 page 646

[82] Noble E. Cunningham, Jr.; *In Pursuit of Reason, The Life of Thomas Jefferson*; Louisiana State University Press, Baton Rouge and London; 1987; page 13

[83] Ibid; page 28

[84] Ibid; page 50

[85] Ibid; page 47

[86] Ibid; page 55

[87] Ibid; page 72

[88] Andrew Cayton, Elisabeth Israels Perry, Linda Reed, Allan m. Winkler; *America Pathways to the Present;* Prentice Hall, Massachusetts, New Jersey page 176

[89] McCullough David; *John Adams*; Simon & Schuster; New York; 2001, page 535

[90] Noble E. Cunningham Jr.; In Pursuit of Reason, The Life of Thomas Jefferson; Louisiana State University Press, Baton Rouge and London; page 216

[91] http://americasfoundingfathers.com/index.php/wall-of-separation-1801

[92] Mark R. Levin; *Men in Black, How the Supreme Court is Destroying America*; Regnery Publishing, Washington D.C. page 41

[93] Daniel L. Dreisbach; *"The Mythical "Wall of Separation"* How a Misused Metaphor Changed Church–State Law, Policy, and Discourse; Heritage Foundation Published on June 23, 2006, by First Principles Series Report #6

[94] Noble E. Cunningham, Jr.; In Pursuit of Reason, *The Life of Thomas Jefferson*; Louisiana State University Press, Baton Rouge and London; page 332

[95] http://tenthamendmentcenter.com/2012/06/04/thomas-jefferson-on-judicial-tyranny/

[96] Richard B. Morris; *The Encyclopedia of American History*; Harper & Brothers Publishers; New York; 1953; page 117

[97] Joseph L. Gardner, Editor; *James Madison, A Biography in His Own Words*; Harper & Row, Publishers, Inc; New York; page 188

[98] Ibid; page 143

[99] Benjamin F. Wright, Editor; *The Federalist the Famous Papers on the Principles of American Government;* Barnes & Noble, New York; page 133

[100] Ibid, page 134

[101] William Ebenstein; *Great Political Thinkers, Plato to the Present 4th Edition*; Holt, Rinehart & Winston Inc.; New York; 1969; page 536

[102] Ibid, page 356

[103] Joseph L. Gardner, Editor; *James Madison, A Biography in His Own Words*; Harper & Row, Publishers, Inc. New York, page 226

[104] Ibid, page 407

[105] Hugh Brogan; *Alexis de Tocqueville A Life*; New Haven & London: Yale University Press 2006; page 268

[106] George Lawrence; *Democracy in America by Alexis de Tocqueville A New Translation*r; Harper & Row, Publishers; page 667

[107] Ibid; page 240

[108] Ibid; page 240

[109] Hugh Brogan; *Alexis de Tocqueville; A Life*; New Haven & London: Yale University Press 2006; page 163

[110] Ibid; page 274

[111] Michael Burlingame; *The Inner World of Abraham Lincoln*; University of Illinois Press; Urbana and Chicago; 1994; page 37

[112] Tanya Lee Stone; *Abraham Lincoln, A Photographic Story of a Life*; DK Publishing, Inc.; London; 2005; page 17

[113] Ibid, page 31

[114] Gordon Leidner; Lincoln on God and Country; White Mane Books; Shippenburg, Pa. 2000; page 15

[115] http://memory.loc.gov/cgi-bin/query/r?ammem/ mal:@field(DOCID+@lit(d4339100))_Abraham Lincoln letter to Jesse W. Fell, Tuesday, December 20, 1859; *Abraham Lincoln Papers at the Library of Congress*

[116] Richard B. Morris; *The Encyclopedia of American Histor*y; Harper & Brothers Publishers; New York; 1953; page 225

[117] Gordon Leidner; Lincoln on God and Country; White Mane Books; Shippenburg, Pa. 2000; page 122

[118] Michael Nelson, Editor; *The Presidency The History of the President of the U.S. from 1789 to the Present*; Smithmark Publishers; New York, N.Y. 1996; page 101

[119] Bill Adler; *The Wit & Wisdom of Abraham Lincoln*; Carol Publishing Corp; New York; 1993; page 14

[120] Ibid; page 4

[121] Ibid; page 30

[122] Richard B. Morris, Editor; Encyclopedia of American History; Harper & Brothers Publishers; New York; 1953; pages 244-245

[123] Michael Burlingame; *The Inner World of Abraham Lincoln*; University of Illinois Press; 1994; page 33

[124] Tanya Lee Stone; *Abraham Lincoln, A Photographic Story of a Life*; DK Publishing, Inc.; London; 2005; page 109

[125] Douglass Autobiographies, *Narrative of the Life of Frederick Douglass an American Slave*; The Library of America; Volume compilation 1994; page 42

[126] Ibid; page 286

[127] Douglass Autobiographies, *My Bondage and my Freedom*; The Library of America; Volume compilation 1994; page 362

[128] Ibid; *The Life and Times of Frederick Douglass*; page 675

[129] Ibid; page 700

[130] Ibid; page 701

[131] Ibid; page 706

[132] Ibid; page 709

[133] Ibid; page 793

[134] Ibid; page 795

[135] Ibid; page 797

[136] Jon Sterngass; *Leaders of the Civil War Era, Frederick Douglass*; Chelsea House Publishers; New York, N.Y.; 2009; page 109

[137] Douglass Autobiographies, *The Life and Times of Frederick Douglass*; The Library of America; Volume compilation 1994; page 804

[138] Ibid; page 877

[139] Kate Clifford Larson; *Bound for the Promised Land, Harriet Tubman Portrait of an American Hero*; A Ballantine Book, Random House Publishing; New York; 2004; page 36

[140] James A McGowan & William C. Kashatus; *Harriet Tubman A Biography*; Greenwood Biographies; ABC-CLIO, LLC; Santa Barbara, Ca; 2011; page 12

[141] Ibid; page 5

[142] Ibid; page 3

[143] Laurie Calkhoven; *Harriet Tubman Leading the Way to Freedom*; Sterling Biographies; New York; 2008; page 35

[144] James A. McGowan & William C. Kashatus; *Harriet Tubman A Biography*; Greenwood Biographies; ABC-CLIO, LLC; Santa Barbara, Ca; 2011; page 72

[145] Laurie Calkhoven; *Harriet Tubman Leading the Way to Freedom*; Sterling Biographies; New York; 2008; page 48

[146] Sarah H. Bradford; *Harriet Tubman The Moses of Her People; an exact, unaltered and unabridged, reprint of the expanded second edition of 1886;* Corinth Books Inc.; New York; 1961; page 94

[147] Kate Clifford Larson; *Bound for the Promised Land, Harriet Tubman Portrait of an American Hero*; A Ballantine Book, Random House Publishing; New York; 2004; page 205

[148] Sarah H. Bradford; *Harriet Tubman The Moses of Her People;* Corinth Books Inc.; New York; 1961; page 99

[149] Kate Clifford Larson; *Bound for the Promised Land, Harriet Tubman Portrait of an American Hero*; A Ballantine Book, Random House Publishing; New York; 2004; page 232

[150] Sarah H. Bradford; *Harriet Tubman The Moses of Her People;* Corinth Books Inc.; New York; 1961; pages 134-135

[151] James A. McGowan & William C. Kashatus; *Harriet Tubman A Biography*; Greenwood Biographies; ABC-CLIO, LLC; Santa Barbara, Ca; 2011; page 122

[152] Lanny Ebenstein; *Milton Friedman A Biography;* Palgrove Macmillion 2007; page 14

[153] Ibid; pg. 27 and from *Milton and Rose Friedman, Two Lucky People: Memoirs*, Chicago: University of Chicago Press 1998; page 4

[154] Milton & Rose Friedman; *Free To Choose, A Personal Statement*; Harcourt Brace Jovanivich, New York & London 1980; page ix

[155] Ibid; page 1

[156] Free To Choose "The Power of the Market" PBS Television; 1980; http://www.freetochoosemedia.org transcript

[157] I Milton & Rose Friedman; *Free To Choose, A Personal Statement*; Harcourt Brace Jovanivich, New York & London 1980; page 2

[158] Ibid; page 11; *The Freeman* December 1958.

[159] Milton & Rose Friedman; "The Power of the Market" *Free To Choose*; PBS Television; 1980

160 Video: http://www.youtube.com/watch?v=e_Ds_LRROLl

161 Peggy Noonan; *When Character Was King*; Penguin Putnam Inc., New York, NY 2001; page 22

162 Ibid; page 56

163 Ibid; page 57

164 Daniel J. Mount; *The Faith of America's Presidents*; Living Ink Books; Chattenooga, Tennessee; 2007; page 23

165 Thomas W. Evans; E*ducation of Ronald Reagan,The General Electric Years and the Untold Story of His Conversion to Conservatism*; Columbia University Press, New York; 2006; page 40

166 Ibid; page 57

167 Ibid; page 85

168 Edwin Meese III; *With Reagan: The Inside Story*; Regnery Gateway; Washington D.C.; 1992; page 33

169 Ibid; page 33

170 Paul Kengor; *God and Ronald Reagan A Spiritual Life*; Reganbooks, HarperCollins Publishers; 2004; page 155

171 President Reagan First Inaugural Address; January 20, 1981;*The Public Papers of President Ronald W. Reagan*; The Ronald Reagan Presidential Library;

172 Edwin Meese III; *With Reagan: The Inside Story*; Regnery Gateway; Washington D.C.; 1992; page 84

173 Peter J. Wallison; *Ronald Reagan The Power of the Conviction and the Success of His Presidency*;Westview press Books; Bolder Colorado; 2003; page 82

174 Peggy Noonan; *When Character Was King*; Penguin Putnam Inc., New York, NY 2001; page 226

[175] Peter J. Wallison; *Ronald Reagan The Power of the Conviction and the Success of His Presidency*; Westview press Books; Bolder Colorado; 2003; page 59

[176] Ibid; page 51; Lawrence Lindsay; *The Growth Experiment*; New York Basic Books; 1990; page 4

[177] President Reagan Remarks at the Annual Convention of the National Asso. of Evangelicals; March 8, 1983; *The Public Papers of President Ronald W. Reagan*; The Ronald Reagan Presidential Library

[178] Peggy Noonan; *When Character Was King*; Penguin Putnam Inc., New York, NY 2001; page 295

[179] President Reagan Remarks on East West Relations at the Brandenburg Gate in West Berlin; June 12, 1987; *The Public Papers of President Ronald W. Reagan*; The Ronald Reagan Presidential Library

[180] Douglas Brinkley; *The Notes, Ronald Reagan's Private Collection of Stories and Wisdom;* HarperCollins Publishing, New York, N.Y.; 2011; page 223

[181] President Reagan Farewell Address to the Nation; January 11, 1989; *The Public Papers of President Ronald W. Reagan*; The Ronald Reagan Presidential Libraryl

[182] Margaret Thatcher; *The Path to Power*; Harper Collins Publishers; Great Britain; 1995; page 11

[183] Ibid; page 7

[184] Ibid; page 340

[185] Ibid; page 360

[186] Ibid; page 420

[187] http://www.margaretthatcher.org/speeches/ displaydocument.asp?docid=104431

[188] Nicholas Wapshott; *Ronald Reagan and Margaret Thatcher A Political Marriage*; Penguin Group Publishers; New York, N.Y.; 2007; page 126

[189] Ibid; page 165

[190] Ibid; page185

[191] Claire Berlinski; *There is No Alternative, Why Margaret Thatcher Matters*; Basic Books Publishers; New York, N.Y.;2008; page 192

[192] Ibid; page 203

[193] Nicholas Wapshott; *Ronald Reagan and Margaret Thatcher, A Political Marriage*; Penguin Group Publishers; New York, N.Y.; 2007; page 233

[194] Margaret Thatcher; *The Downing Street Years*; HarperCollins Publishers; New York N.Y.; 1993; page 813

[195] The Margaret Thatcher Foundation; *Eulogy for President Reagan speech June 11 2004*; http://www.margaretthatcher.org/document/110360

Index

Also Available by Donald R. Gallerani

Everything Worth Knowing I Heard on Talk Radio